access to history

D1137212

Henry VIII to Mary I: Government and Religion 1509–58

9112000160306

access to history

Henry VIII to Mary I: Government and Religion 1509–58

Roger Turvey and Keith Randell

 **HODDER**
EDUCATION
AN HACHETTE UK COMPANY

BRENT LIBRARIES	
91120000160306	
Askews & Holts	13-Nov-2013
942.052	£13.99

Study guides revised and updated, 2008, by Sally Waller (AQA), Angela Leonard (Edexcel) and Geoff Woodward (OCR).

The Publishers would like to thank the following for permission to reproduce copyright illustrations: © Birmingham Museums and Art Gallery/The Bridgeman Art Library, page 92; Chateau de Versailles, France, Lauros/Giraudon/ The Bridgeman Art Library, page 76; Getty Images, pages 177, 183; National Portrait Gallery, pages 20, 33; Mary Evans Picture Library, pages 135, 163, 175, 222; National Portrait Gallery, London, UK/The Bridgeman Art Library, pages 38, 221; Private Collection, Ken Welsh/The Bridgeman Art Library, pages 83, 143, 191, 206; Private Collection, The Stapleton Collection/The Bridgeman Art Library, pages 131, 132; The Royal Collection © 2008 Her Majesty Queen Elizabeth II, page 99.
The Publishers would like to acknowledge use of the following extracts: Edexcel Limited for extracts used on page 169.

Every effort has been made to trace and acknowledge ownership of copyright. The publishers will be glad to make suitable arrangements with any copyright holders whom it has not been possible to contact.

Orders: please contact Bookpoint Ltd, 130 Milton Park, Abingdon, Oxon OX14 4SB. Telephone: (44) 01235 827720. Fax: (44) 01235 400454. Lines are open 9.00–5.00, Monday to Saturday, with a 24-hour message answering service. Visit our website at www.hoddereducation.co.uk

© Roger Turvey and Keith Randell 2008
First published in 2008 by
Hodder Education,
an Hachette UK company
338 Euston Road
London NW1 3BH

Impression number   5 4 3
Year   2012

All rights reserved. Apart from any use permitted under UK copyright law, no part of this publication may be reproduced or transmitted in any form or by any means, electronic or mechanical, including photocopying and recording, or held within any information storage and retrieval system, without permission in writing from the publisher or under licence from the Copyright Licensing Agency Limited. Further details of such licences (for reprographic reproduction) may be obtained from the Copyright Licensing Agency Limited, Saffron House, 6–10 Kirby Street, London EC1N 8TS.

Cover image of Henry VIII, c.1600, courtesy of Bridgeman Art Library
Typeset in Baskerville 10/12pt and produced by Gray Publishing, Tunbridge Wells.
Printed and bound by CPI Group (UK) Ltd, Croydon, CR0 4YY

A catalogue record for this title is available from the British Library

ISBN: 978 0340 965924

Contents

Dedication

Keith Randell (1943–2002)

The *Access to History* series was conceived and developed by Keith, who created a series to 'cater for students as they are, not as we might wish them to be'. He leaves a living legacy of a series that for over 20 years has provided a trusted, stimulating and well-loved accompaniment to post-16 study. Our aim with these new editions is to continue to offer students the best possible support for their studies.

1 Introduction: Reformation in Religion and Revolution in Government

POINTS TO CONSIDER

This chapter is intended to help you to understand what is meant by the terms 'Reformation in religion' and the 'Revolution in government'. It explains why historians continue to debate the causes, course and consequences of the Reformation and the Revolution. The chapter will also introduce you to Tudor England, its monarchs and the kingdom's place in European politics. These issues are examined as four themes:

- Introduction
- Debating the English Reformation
- Assessing the changes in government
- The kingdom of England and its continental neighbours

1 | Introduction

Key question
What are the two key areas of study for Tudor historians?

By the beginning of the twentieth century it was commonplace for the importance of the reigns of Henry VIII, Edward VI and Mary I to be debated in academic circles. As a result, during the last century or so a bewildering range of issues from the years 1509 to 1558 has been identified as being worthy of historical debate. There are so many of them that they could not all be adequately aired in books the size of the current volume. However, two general strands of inquiry are discernible, although they are a long way from being either self-contained or all-embracing. The first strand concerns the 'revolution in religion' and the second 'the revolution in government'.

The first has three foci: a discussion of the role of the monarchy and its government in carrying through religious change; an explanation on how the relationship between Church and State altered; and an assessment of how the State and people were affected by the political and religious developments of the period.

The latter has two foci: a long-running debate on the personality and character of the monarch, including a consideration of the part he or she played in the politics and government of their time; and an assessment of the significance of the monarchy, and its chief ministers, in the long-term political development of the country which may, for the sake of convenience, be described as England.

The key themes that run through both strands concern the personality, power and influence of the monarch. Thus to properly appreciate the way in which religion and government changed in this period it is important to gain an understanding of the nature of and the authority wielded by the monarchy. Equally important is an understanding of how personal, political, diplomatic, religious and financial factors affected both the growth and the practical limits of royal power in early sixteenth-century England.

The powerful element in Tudor monarchy

English monarchs claimed to rule *dei gratia* or by the will of God. This belief in divine right, that, as a person apart, the monarch was regarded as God's instrument on earth, was supported by the Church and regularly upheld in the pulpit. Parish priests would regularly remind their parishioners of the terrible torments of hell that awaited those who dared rebel against the Crown. In practical terms this meant that any rebellion against the monarch was regarded as being the same as a rebellion against God.

> **Key term**
>
> *Dei gratia*
> By the will of God.

This is why the charge of treason, to betray one's king (or queen) and country, was regarded as a serious crime. The only armed rebellion to succeed in the sixteenth century was that involving Mary Tudor who claimed that her rightful place as monarch in legitimate succession to her brother Edward VI had been usurped by traitors. Her success in seizing the throne in 1553 was due not only to the legality of her position, as she was the legal heir to the throne according to the Act of Succession of 1544, but also to her actions being represented as a triumph of the divine will.

For a monarch who had once been declared illegitimate in 1533 (she was later legitimised in 1537) this was indeed a triumph. This shows the importance of the law and the legal structure that had evolved in tandem with the development of the monarchy. The monarch was expected to act as the protector and enforcer of the laws of the kingdom. The old Latin maxim *Rex is Lex* and *Lex is Rex* (the king is the law and the law is the king) demonstrates the extent to which English monarchs had come to identify with the processes of lawmaking. Although they came to hold a highly privileged position within the legal structure of the kingdom, they could not ignore or break the law but were expected to set a good example by acting within the accepted structure. This partly explains why Charles I, who some thought was behaving as if he was above the law, was executed in 1649.

This does not mean that English monarchs were weak or had little power, on the contrary, their powers were extensive, but there were limits to their authority. For example, the monarch alone could raise troops, wage war and conclude peace, conduct foreign affairs, summon and dissolve parliament, pardon offenders, manage the coinage and arrange the marriages of

Key terms

Royal prerogative
Certain rights and privileges enjoyed by the monarch such as making war, negotiating peace treaties, calling and closing parliament.

Schism
Literally meaning break, but used by historians to describe England's break with the Pope in Rome.

members of the royal family. These political, military and economic powers constituted what became known as the **royal prerogative**.

On the other hand, the monarch could not levy taxes or make laws at will, set aside the rights of the subject or behave as a tyrant especially as the Church had long taught that it was lawful to kill a tyrant. In short, the monarch had a duty to respect the notion that all who lived within the kingdom, from the lowliest peasant to the mightiest king, were bound by the common 'weal' or good.

Even a king as powerful as Henry VIII recognised the need to give legal basis to his break from Rome by seeking the consent of his people, via parliament, and by framing the **schism** in English statute law. The fact that he may have bullied and harried his subjects into consenting to the break with Rome does not alter the fact that he had to be seen to be seeking their support. This balance of rights and duties between monarch and subject allowed for co-operation, compromise and even partnership.

The personal element in Tudor monarchy

The Tudor monarchy was one in which the ruler was directly responsible for policy and closely involved in the business of government. An agenda for the monarch's attention might be such as to require his or her signature on state papers several times a day. Because monarchy was personal everything depended on the monarch's willingness to devote himself or herself to business.

Henry VII had been a model in this respect, but not his son. Henry VIII frequently behaved as though he wanted government to take care of itself. Henry did almost all his work by word of mouth so that state papers had to be either read to him or summarised for him. Nor was Henry willing to delegate his authority on a consistent basis. He always reserved for himself the freedom to intervene as and when he wanted.

In contrast, his daughter Mary found the business of government a burden she had not desired and a task for which she had had little training or preparation. Nevertheless, from the beginning of her reign she indicated she would take an active part in governance. This she did throughout her short reign working long hours in trying to solve problems that would have tested the limits of her father's abilities. Since Mary was the first woman to rule England in her own right, issues of gender complicated the early days of her reign.

The need by contemporaries to accommodate Henry VIII and Mary's particular brand of personal monarchy explains why the dispute over their respective personalities has been running since the early seventeenth century and why it shows no sign of ending. For most of this time writers have tended to take up extreme positions.

Henry VIII

They have either seen Henry as a wicked tyrant, possibly with a few redeeming features, or portrayed him as the 'Bluff King Hal' who was a cross between Father Christmas and John Bull, although he was sometimes forced to take actions that 'were not quite nice'. For example, Sir Walter Raleigh, one of the earliest authors to pass general comment in print, was in no doubt where he stood:

> Now for King Henry the eight: if all the pictures and patterns of a merciless prince were lost in the world, they might be again painted to the life out of the story of this king.

Mary

'Bloody' Mary too has suffered her fair share of criticism. John Strype in the seventeenth century and James Froude in the nineteenth perpetuated the 'black legend' of persecution, corruption, mismanagement and national betrayal ascribed to Mary by propagandists writing in the reign of Elizabeth. For example, John Foxe, one of the earliest of the Elizabethan propagandists to criticise Mary in print, states that:

> we shall never find in any reign of any Prince in this land or any other, which did ever show in it so many great arguments of God's wrath and displeasure, … whether we behold the shortness of her time, or the unfortunate event of all her purposes.

Edward VI

Edward VI alone has escaped the kind of critical analysis reserved for his father and half-sister mainly on account of his youth and lack of involvement in policy-making. Consequently, it is not Edward who concerns historians so much as the men who governed in his stead, namely, Edward Seymour, the Duke of Somerset and John Dudley, the Duke of Northumberland. Traditionally Somerset has been viewed as the 'good Duke', an idealist, friend of the common man and an opponent of religious persecution. However, this opinion has been challenged by revisionist historians who see him as arrogant, self-seeking and prone to making mistakes when under pressure. Similarly, Northumberland's image has been transformed from that of a cynical schemer devoid of principle to that of a talented minister who led, in Professor Sir Geoffrey Elton's opinion, ' a genuine reform administration'.

2 | Debating the Reformation

For centuries the overwhelming majority of historians accepted uncritically that their task was to recount the doings of the rich and famous. This meant that political history dominated and that women (unless the absence of male heirs forced them into the spotlight) were rarely mentioned. 'Ordinary' people provided the backcloth, especially in times of war or civil disturbance, but were

> **Key question**
> What are the key features of the debate regarding the Reformation?

treated much like the extras in a Hollywood film – they were seen but not heard. It is therefore not surprising that most histories of the English Reformation have concentrated on the actions of kings and queens and of those close to them.

The 'top-down' approach

This 'top-down' approach to the study of history generally and of the Reformation in particular, rapidly became established as the norm during the early decades of History's existence as a respectable academic discipline. One of the most prominent English historians of the nineteenth century, J.A. Froude, completed his 12-volume history of the mid-Tudor period in 1870. The analysis he developed provided a framework of study for several generations to come. The terms 'official Reformation' and 'political Reformation' were used to describe what was thought to be of real importance in England's change from Catholicism to Protestantism. The story was thought of as having a prologue and four main chapters.

The prologue

The prologue was Henry VIII's struggle to persuade the Pope to grant him a divorce from his first wife, Catherine of Aragon. This took place between 1527 and 1533. Each of the 'chapters' covered the events of one monarch's reign.

The first 'chapter' – the Henrician Reformation 1533–47

In the first 'chapter' (1533–47), Henry VIII took over the Pope's powers and much of the Church's property, while generally succeeding in preventing change in the Church's teachings or practices. He established an independent Church of England that was Catholic in doctrine.

The second 'chapter' – the Edwardian Reformation 1547–53

His son, Edward VI, was an ardent Protestant and, although he was only a child during his six-year reign, he actively supported those who ruled in his name – the dukes of Somerset and Northumberland – when they introduced radical religious beliefs and practices. By the time he died in 1553 England had become a Protestant country.

The third 'chapter' – the Marian Reformation 1553–8

Henry VIII's elder daughter, Mary, was queen from 1553 to 1558. She was a devout Catholic who tried to reverse what her father and brother had done.

The fourth 'chapter' – the Elizabethan Settlement 1558–1603

She was succeeded by her younger sister, Elizabeth I, who was a Protestant. Because she reigned for 45 years (1558–1603), she was able to ensure that the Church of England moved permanently away from Catholicism.

In all four parts of the story the doings and beliefs of the population at large were mentioned only in passing. However, from the time of Froude onwards, the 'top-down' school of historians explicitly recognised that there was a second strand –

the 'popular Reformation' – to the story, but they were certain that it was of less importance than the 'official Reformation'. This view was effectively challenged for the first time by A.G. Dickens, who published his masterly *The English Reformation* in 1964. This book did much to establish a new orthodoxy.

The 'bottom-up' approach

Dickens' book was based on the contention that a 'bottom-up' approach, concentrating on the activities and enthusiasms of ordinary people, would provide a more meaningful explanation of how England became Protestant than would an account of the 'official' or 'political' Reformation. But Dickens did not suggest that the actions of government were unimportant. He merely argued for a shift of emphasis in favour of the 'popular' Reformation. He wrote his book according to the new balance he advocated. In order to do this he had had to carry out an enormous amount of original research into topics (such as the spread of Protestant and the demise of Catholic beliefs and practices among the general population) that had previously been largely ignored by historians. In the process, he had uncovered numerous new sources of evidence and had developed new techniques for evaluating them. At the same time others were arguing that the English Reformation ought to be thought of in different conceptual terms.

The English Reformation as an 'event'

The Reformation in England had traditionally been portrayed as a long, drawn-out event, lasting for up to 70 years (1533–1603), although with the major actions all falling within the first half of the period. The problem was that it had been assumed the individual happenings that comprised it were all linked together in a chain of cause and effect, giving unity and coherence to England's change from being a Catholic to being a Protestant country. As a result, the readers of narratives of this 'event' could hardly avoid reaching the conclusion that the outcome of the story had been inevitable from the beginning. This was especially so as the majority of both authors and their readers regarded the Reformation story as an account of the triumph of 'good' over 'evil' and therefore as 'progress' and something to be welcomed.

Unease about these assumptions grew in the decades after 1920 when **objectivity** (as opposed, in Reformation studies, to a commitment to either a Catholic or a Protestant point of view) became the hallmark of academic respectability and when historians became more aware of the dangers of hindsight. Some of them recognised that the accepted ways of looking at the English Reformation were good examples of flawed thinking – of knowing what occurred in the end, and of viewing previous happenings primarily as steps towards that final position. It seemed to them that the end-point had been reached as much by chance as by design and that the direction of events could have been altered by random factors at almost any time.

Objectivity
Focusing on an issue without bias.

Key term

They, therefore, came to the conclusion that the coherence given to the 'event' by most historians only existed in the minds of later observers and certainly had not been apparent at the time. In the light of this fact, they judged that it might be more accurate to think of the English Reformation as a 'process' (a sequence of related rather than closely linked happenings), and not as an 'event'.

The English Reformation as a 'process'

This change in perception made particular sense when adopting a 'bottom-up' approach to what happened. Dickens' way of looking at things especially lent itself to this concept, and his book was effectively a charting of the 'process' by which Protestantism replaced Catholicism in England between 1529 and 1559. For some time historians acted as if the concepts of 'event' and 'process' were incompatible, and that one must be 'right' and the other 'wrong'. However, it is now accepted that, as long as the dangers of assuming cause and effect and of using hindsight are kept in mind, both concepts are helpful in gaining an understanding of what the Reformation was, what were its causes and what were its effects.

Revisionism and the revisionist interpretation

Key question
How have revisionist historians contributed to the debate on the Reformation?

Key term

'Revisionist'
Historians who revise earlier historical opinions or interpretations.

Although Dickens has remained the standard text on the English Reformation, and is likely to be so for some time to come as a result of a substantially re-written second edition of the book being published in 1989, the central conclusion he reached (rather than the approach he adopted) has been disputed by a numerous band of **'revisionist'** historians. Dickens argued that Henry VIII was able to carry out his political Reformation – breaking with Rome, establishing himself as the Supreme Head of the Church in England, and dissolving the monasteries – largely because his actions coincided with both the advanced stages of a decline in popular support for the Catholic Church and a rapid spread of Protestant beliefs. His contention was that the Reformation from below happened early and speedily.

The 'revisionists' have generally maintained the exact opposite inasmuch as they firmly believe that the Reformation brought Protestantism, not Protestantism the Reformation. Basing their conclusions mainly on a sequence of detailed local studies, they have advanced the view that Protestantism was adopted by most of the people of England and Wales towards the end of the Reformation period (if at all) – 'late and slowly' as opposed to 'early and rapidly'. They have produced telling evidence to support the argument that Catholicism stubbornly remained the majority belief in some parts of the country throughout the Tudor period despite all the efforts of central government and the missionary activities of Protestant preachers.

It is a telling point that despite six years of Protestantism under Edward VI, Mary did not encounter significant resistance when she returned England to the authority of Rome and restored Catholic worship in the Church. But the 'revisionists' have not yet been able to win for their interpretation the status of being the new orthodoxy. Much of the evidence they have used to support their views is too partial and too open to differing interpretations to allow them to establish a totally convincing case.

However, the balance of opinion is certainly tipping in their favour. This is because many historians have been convinced by the interpretations put forward by Christopher Haigh, the best known of the 'revisionists'. In particular, there has been considerable support for his contention that there was not just one English Reformation. He argues that there were several 'political' Reformations between 1533 and 1559. He claims that they should be treated as distinct happenings and that it is unhelpful to think of them as chapters in a single event. His view is that the English Reformations were separate but linked.

'Top-down' or 'bottom-up' – the debate continues

It has been suggested that at a **macro-political level** (the actions of the monarch and of parliament) nothing was done before 1540 that was both important to the Reformation and difficult to reverse. The significance of the break with Rome and of the royal supremacy were unchallenged, but attention was drawn to the fact that it was an accepted part of the constitution that whatever one Parliament passed a later one could repeal. This was proved by the way in which the Parliaments of Mary's reign restored the link with Rome, revoked the royal supremacy, and reversed the Protestant doctrinal changes that had occurred while Edward VI had been king. It was accepted that the dissolution of the monasteries was effectively irreversible once most of their former lands had been sold to the aristocracy and the gentry, but it was argued that the closure of the religious houses had been peripheral to the real Reformation – that the dissolution could have taken place without there being a Reformation and that there could have been a Reformation without the monasteries being dissolved.

On the **micro-religious level** (the beliefs and practices of ordinary people) enough examples of change being minimal or non-existent were uncovered to allow it to be argued that the evidence presented by Dickens was a typical and that the majority of people were untouched by Protestantism before the second half of the century. The cumulative effect of these 'revisionist' historians' findings was to open a new debate – a debate that has, as yet, not been concluded.

In the process those historians who are more interested in the monarch – Henry VIII, Edward VI and Mary I – than in the Reformation have been reinforced in their belief that, when studying the whole of the period 1509 to 1558, it makes more sense to think of religion as an aspect of politics rather than as a topic in its own right, forming the first act of a four-part saga of England's change from Catholicism to Protestantism. Thus, for them the 'top-down' approach continues not only to be acceptable but also to be necessary if a meaningful account of what happened is to be constructed.

Key terms

Macro-political level
Term used to explain the bigger picture such as in this instance the actions of the monarch and of parliament.

Micro-religious level
Used to explain the smaller picture such as in this instance the beliefs and practices of ordinary people.

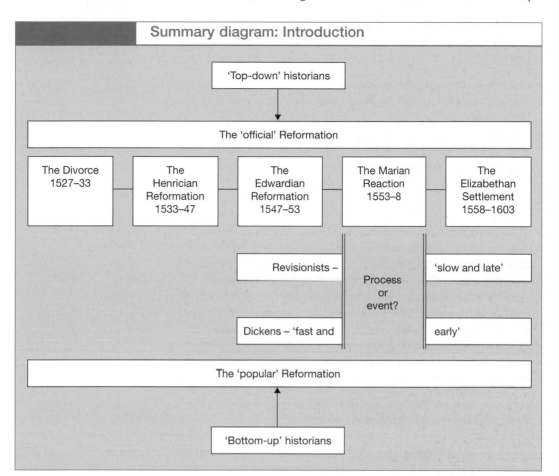

Summary diagram: Introduction

'Top-down' historians

The 'official' Reformation

| The Divorce 1527–33 | The Henrician Reformation 1533–47 | The Edwardian Reformation 1547–53 | The Marian Reaction 1553–8 | The Elizabethan Settlement 1558–1603 |

Revisionists –   Process or event?   'slow and late'

Dickens – 'fast and   early'

The 'popular' Reformation

'Bottom-up' historians

Key question
What is the key focus of the debate regarding the changes in government?

3 | Assessing the Changes in Government

Arguably, the most important debate on Tudor history was started by Professor Sir Geoffrey (then G.R.) Elton in the early 1950s. Since its publication in 1953 Elton's *Tudor Revolution in Government* has been the focus of many debates about Tudor government. He identified the reign of Henry VIII, and more specifically the 1530s under the influence of Thomas Cromwell, as the time when revolutionary changes took place in the way England was governed. His claim was that the period marked the transition from 'medieval' to 'modern' forms of government, which was only paralleled in importance in British history by the changes that took place in the middle of the nineteenth century. Such was the brilliance and freshness of Elton's work (which he continued to build on for more than 30 years) that few historians of the period have subsequently been able to distance themselves from the storm of controversy that has swirled around the issue ever since.

The Elton Thesis

Essentially Elton's 'revolution' thesis concentrated on highlighting significant change in the following key areas:

Key question
What are the key features of Elton's revolution in government theory?

- the structure and organisation of central government
- the role of parliament together with the scope and authority of **statute law**
- the relationship between Church and State
- extension of royal authority in the regions – regional councils in Wales, the North and the West.

Statute law
Acts or laws passed by parliament.

Key term

Elton summarised his argument and placed it in a wider historical context by claiming:

> When an administration relying on the household was replaced by one based exclusively on bureaucratic departments and officers of state, a revolution took place in government. The principle then adopted was not in turn discarded until the much greater administrative revolution of the nineteenth century, which not only destroyed survivals of the medieval system allowed to continue a meaningless existence for some 300 years, but also created an administration based on departments responsible to parliament – an administration in which the crown for the first time ceased to hold the ultimate control.

In Elton's opinion the fact that Henry VII had ascended the throne of a 'medievally governed kingdom', while Elizabeth I was able to hand to her successor, James I, a country 'administered on modern lines' was indicative of radical change in the structure, machinery and operation of government.

This transition from 'medieval' household government, whose efficiency and effectiveness depended on the personal energy and ability of the monarch, to a more 'professional' and 'modern' national bureaucracy which could function efficiently without the close supervision of the monarch, was, in Elton's view, done in accordance with Cromwell's blueprint in the eight years between 1532 and 1540. For Elton, these developments amounted to no less a revolution than the Reformation that accompanied them.

Few historians would deny that the middle decades of the sixteenth century witnessed remarkable changes in royal authority and in the government of the kingdom but they are reluctant to go as far as Elton in claiming that a 'revolution' took place. Indeed, the problem lies in the use of the term 'revolution' for some historians, notably David Starkey, who totally reject the idea that anything approaching a 'revolution' took place, while others prefer to see the changes in terms of an 'evolutionary' process spanning a longer period and involving more people than simply Cromwell and his tight-knit group of servants. Norman Stone sums up the problem of assessing the changes in government very well:

> Evolution or revolution, English government in Elizabeth's day was something very different from government in her grandfather's (Henry VII) day.

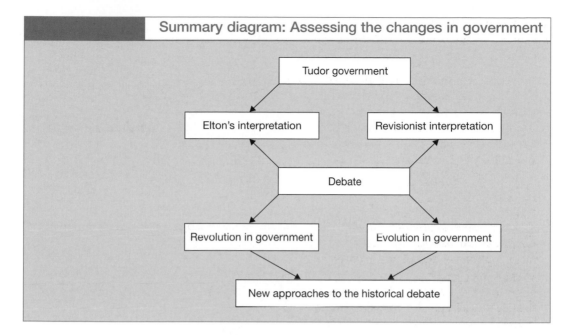

Summary diagram: Assessing the changes in government

Key question
What did contemporaries mean by the terms 'home' and 'abroad'?

4 | The Kingdom of England and its Continental Neighbours

Introduction

It might be expected that the phrases 'foreign policy' or 'foreign affairs' would appear in the title of this sub-chapter. After all, this is what it is all about. However, there are some preconceptions that need to be cleared away before such terms can safely be used. Most modern-day thinking about international relations takes place within a framework of assumptions that is not really relevant to the situation in the Europe of the first half of the sixteenth century. To make sense of Henry VIII's dealings with his neighbours it is necessary to make a conscious effort to lay aside the patterns of thought that are used to organise an understanding of modern-day foreign affairs.

Some might argue, but not very convincingly, that it may even be necessary to dispense with the very concept of foreign policy when studying events during Henry VIII's reign. This is because the idea of 'foreign policy' depends on there being a clear distinction between 'home' and 'abroad'.

'Home'

Where such a distinction was made by the vast majority of Henry VIII's subjects, 'home' was the local area of a few square miles and 'abroad' was everywhere else. There was no identification of 'home' with the territories ruled over by the king, or of 'abroad' with other states. This is hardly surprising. Henry VIII's territories in no sense comprised a unitary state. Even the heartland of England, which is the somewhat misleading name with which we label the conglomeration, was not a single entity. Only the south, the east and the midlands were clearly and regularly part of a country centred on London.

England and its near neighbours in the reign of Henry VIII.

The inhabitants of the north regarded themselves, and were regarded by southerners, as being largely separate, with different customs, interests and methods of conducting public affairs. The people of the south-west, especially Cornwall with its linguistic and cultural differences, regarded themselves as being virtually independent of England, which, in part, explains why they rebelled against the authority of Edward VI's government in 1549.

Most of those living in modern-day Wales, where the language and culture were quite different to those in England, thought of the king as a foreign ruler who occasionally interfered in their affairs. This was despite the fact that Wales had been technically incorporated into England by means of the late-thirteenth-century Statute of Rhuddlan. Royal influence was particularly weak in the 60 or so virtually independent lordships, collectively known as the Marches, which made up most of east and south-eastern Wales and the western fringes of the English midlands.

The territories divided from the mainland by varying amounts of water tended to identify even less with the Henrician state. The largest and richest of these was Ireland, of which Henry was rarely more than nominal lord, even after he assumed the title of King of Ireland in 1541. Beyond the city of Dublin, with its surrounding '**pale**' of English territory, the nobles of the island were left to run the country much as they wished. Indeed, as long as they did not make too much display of their independence, the Tudors were happy to leave Ireland alone. Very much smaller, and of insignificance except when invasion threatened, was the Isle of Wight and the Scilly Isles. The Channel Islands could not be used as a route into England and therefore they did not assume even temporary significance.

This was not the case with Calais, the only other part of the original Norman state that remained in England's possession. The port, with its surrounding 'pale' of English territory, was the front line for most of the king's attempts to interfere militarily in the affairs of Europe. It was strategically very well placed and could act as a secure base for offensive action against either France or the Netherlands, and as such was regarded by the Tudor monarchs as a valuable asset to be defended at almost any cost. Granted representation in the English Parliament in 1536, Calais's civilian population of 5000, a third of whom were English settlers, was supplemented by a virtually permanent army of around 1000 men. Although it played a key economic role as the staple through which all exported wool was directed, Calais proved a constant drain on English resources. Its loss to France in 1558 was keenly felt by Mary Tudor.

'Abroad'

If 'home' was not a unitary concept to most of Henry's subjects, then 'abroad' was even less coherent. There were a few well-known states. Scotland and France were the most obvious of these because they were generally perceived as being 'the enemy'. Northerners were particularly aware of Scotland as a hostile

Key term

Pale
Irish territory (including Dublin) settled by the English. It was the centre of English power in Ireland.

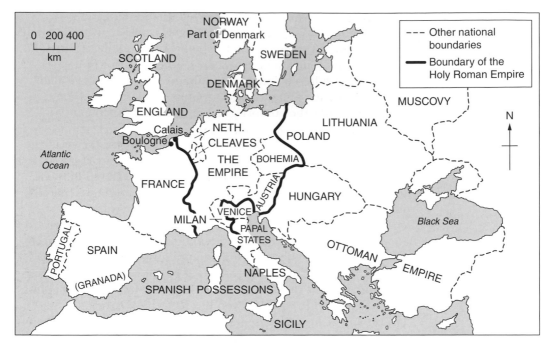

Map of Europe c.1550.

power and as the source of perennially threatened raids, while southerners looked upon France as the country with which their rulers had been at war (with frequent breaks) for several centuries. Conflict with these neighbours was therefore generally regarded as being a 'normal' state of affairs.

The Netherlands (or Low Countries) were widely thought of as an area of vital importance, being the supplier of most imports and the recipient of most exports, especially wool and cloth. But there was little awareness of them as a state with a single ruler as opposed to a geographical area with a specific trading function. This was despite the fact that most of the provinces of the Netherlands had long been an integral part of the Burgundian state, which had been inherited by the Austrian Habsburgs, and which, during most of Henry's reign, was one of the cores of Charles V's extensive personal empire.

Outside this 'inner ring' of territories were some of the other states of western Europe. The Holy Roman Empire was ill-defined to those who lived in it, let alone to those who viewed it from afar. It was to be found in 'Germany' (a much less meaningful label even than England) and was loosely ruled over by the Emperor who, although elected, was traditionally a member of the Habsburg family.

Spain was newly emerging in the popular perception as a state as well as a geographical area, following the destruction of the Moorish states in the south of the Iberian Peninsula, and the inheritance of two of the major Christian kingdoms (Aragon and Castile) by Charles of Habsburg (Charles I of Spain and Charles V as Holy Roman Emperor). Only Portugal remained as an alternative independent state in the peninsula.

Italy was correctly perceived as being a geographical expression rather than a state. It was variously regarded as the distant centre of wealth and civilisation, as the home of the Pope whose territories covered much of the central portion of the peninsula, and as the arena in which the King of France, the King of Spain and the Emperor carried out their struggle for dominance over each other. It was also thought of as the home of some of Europe's major trading states (Venice and Genoa), although these impinged less on the public consciousness in England than did the other major European trading force, the Hanseatic League (the Hanse) of north German ports.

Further 'abroad' were the barely recognised non-Christian empires which were generally shrouded in mystery. Foremost among these was the empire of the Turk (the Ottoman Empire), thought of as the great threat to Christendom which was likely at any time to break out and overrun most of southern Europe. Little was known about it other than that it was believed to be peopled by brutal savages who were obviously in league with the devil. Other empires were known to exist further into Asia, but greater distance reduced the sense of their threat. It was also generally understood that the Spanish explorers had established the existence of a new continent to the west of Europe, but, apart from offering an indeterminate future possibility of plunder, little importance was attached to this.

Key question
What issues need to be kept in mind when making judgements about Henry VIII's foreign policy?

National interests

For writers of modern political history a key concern when making judgements about a government or a ruler's performance in foreign affairs has been the extent to which the country benefited from the policies being followed. Criteria such as 'the strengthening of the country politically or economically' or 'the enhancement of national reputation' have been the ones normally applied. These were what the early academic historians studying the reigns of Henry VIII, Edward VI and Mary in the second half of the nineteenth century had in mind when they formed their judgements of English foreign policy in the period 1509–58. It is not surprising that they found Henry VIII, Edward VI (more specifically his leading ministers Somerset and Northumberland) and Mary to be wanting, for they were judging them by criteria that bore little relation to their own, or their contemporaries', perception of the activity in which they were engaged.

The Tudors were typical of most early-sixteenth-century monarchs in being unaware of the concept of foreign policy as a furtherance of national interests. It was not that they chose to reject the idea in preference for the pursuit of their own selfish ambitions: it was just that it never really occurred to them that there was any real alternative to the assumptions with which they had grown up. Henry, Edward and Mary believed that their territories were their 'property' in a not dissimilar way to that in which a large landowner possessed his estates. It was therefore their duty to utilise their possessions so as to maximise their family's prestige, power and wealth in both the short and the long terms. Any benefits or harm they did to their subjects in the process were largely coincidental, and only to be taken as a serious matter if they were likely to impinge on them directly, by, for example, causing civil disturbances or affecting tax yields.

It follows that writers (whether research historians, students or history educators) must be particularly careful to recognise the criteria they are using when they make judgements about Tudor foreign policy before 1558. It is widely accepted, although certainly not by everybody, that judgements ought to be made using the criteria that were current at the time of the actions being assessed, and that any judgements made using 'modern standards' should be clearly labelled and carefully considered. Perhaps this is why it is important, in advanced historical study, to make a determined effort to understand the context (especially of values and assumptions) in which decisions were made, rather than just finding out 'what happened'.

Henry VIII's foreign policy

It is traditional to divide the study of Henry VIII's foreign policy into two parts: 1509–29 and 1529–47. The break-point is the fall of Cardinal Wolsey, who has often been seen as being the real framer of England's foreign policy in the first half of Henry's reign. It is even common usage to talk about 'Wolsey's foreign policy'. This framework for study has advantages, especially in terms of its coherence as an organising idea, but it should be remembered that it is no more than a general approximation to reality. The most obvious shortcoming of this schema is that Wolsey did not become even the foremost of the king's advisers – let alone the framer of policy – until 1514, thus leaving the first five years of the reign 'unaccounted for'. A potentially more serious problem is that historians have hotly disputed the extent to which Wolsey ever replaced Henry as the policy maker. All agree that there was effectively a partnership between the two: the dispute is over the relative importance of the partners in setting goals and devising long-term strategies. The evidence does not allow there to be a decisive resolution of the dispute.

Edward VI's foreign policy

Edward's foreign policy too has traditionally been divided into two parts: 1547–9 and 1550–3. The division follows the periods of power enjoyed by Somerset and Northumberland. Few historians today would agree with the opinion of R.B. Wernham, as expressed in his book *Before the Armada: The Growth of English Foreign Policy 1485–1588* published in 1966, that Somerset had 'the idealism of the visionary'. Somerset's foreign policy was largely based on that inherited from Henry VIII; he did not initiate policy decisions nor did he plan a coherent strategy. Indeed, neither he, much less his successor Northumberland, were idealists or visionaries, they were essentially pragmatists being reactive rather than proactive in their approach to foreign policy. For them the stability and safety of the kingdom, and the protection of their own positions of power, were what guided their decisions in foreign policy – to control the Irish, to pacify the Scots, to seek an accommodation with the French, and to stay on good terms with Charles V of Spain and the Empire.

Mary's foreign policy

Traditional accounts of Mary's foreign policy have suggested that it was a disaster. This tradition is especially vivid in relating Mary's involvement in the war with France when a reluctant queen, so the story goes, was forced, by her ally Spain, into a disastrous conflict that resulted in the loss of Calais. In addition, Mary's marriage to Philip of Spain, her reliance on her Spanish advisers and her determination to return England to the Catholic Church conspired to cause a swift and lasting loss of popularity. To the Elizabethan Protestant publicist John Foxe, Mary's disastrous conduct in foreign affairs was divinely inspired punishment for her pro-Spanish and pro-Catholic policies. Some modern historians like R.B. Wernham believed that Mary's 'foreign policy was in truth only a manifestation and a consequence of her religious purposes. It hardly existed apart from them'. How does this traditional view hold up?

Today historians are less judgemental and more forgiving in their assessment of Mary's foreign policy. Historians like David Loades no longer believe that the loss of Calais was a 'national disaster' or that England was forced against its will to enter the war against the French. France, in alliance with Scotland, was still regarded as the true enemy of England and although Philip brought great pressure to bear on Mary to declare war, she did not enter the conflict until she and her English advisers were convinced that it was in her kingdom's interests to do so. On the other hand, Mary is:

> criticised for dragging England into the epicentre of the conflict between the Valois rulers of France and Habsburg rulers of Spain, the Netherlands and the Empire.

Summary diagram: Foreign policy 1540–53

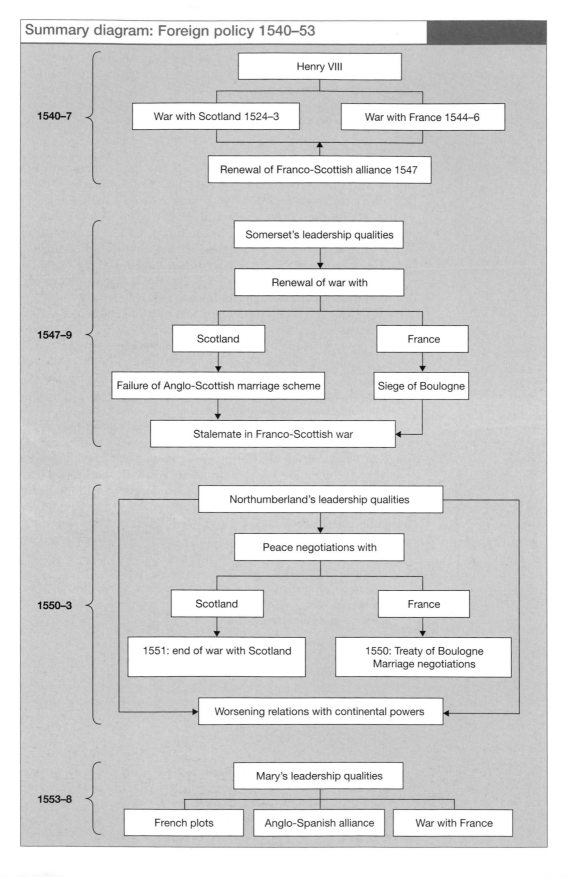

2 Personality and Power

POINTS TO CONSIDER
This chapter is designed to help you to understand why historians find Henry VIII so fascinating. It explains how the views of historians about the king and his power have changed and why there have been so many disagreements about his personality and character. By examining the problems created by his six marriages you should be able to determine how far his private life affected his political role as ruler of England. These issues are examined as two key themes:

• Personality of the king
• Henry VIII and his six wives

Key dates
1491	Birth of Henry VIII, the second son of Henry VII
1502	Henry became heir to the throne on the death of his elder brother, Arthur
1509	Accession of Henry VIII
	Henry married Catherine of Aragon
1516	Daughter Mary born
1533	Henry divorced Catherine and married Anne Boleyn. Daughter Elizabeth born
1536	Execution of Anne Boleyn. Henry married Jane Seymour
1537	Son Edward born. Jane Seymour died
1540	Married Anne of Cleves. Marriage soon dissolved. Married Catherine Howard
1542	Execution of Catherine Howard
1543	Married Catherine Parr
1547	Death of Henry VIII

1 | Introduction

The new king

On 21 April 1509 Henry VIII became King of England at the age of 17 years and 10 months. Most of those who have left a written record of their opinion at the time saw the change of monarch as a dawning of a new age. The contrast between the dead king and his successor could hardly have been more pronounced (see the

Key question
How did contemporaries interpret the new king's actions?

Henry VIII (left) and Henry VII (right) – Hans Holbein's working drawing for a painting of c.1536.

photograph of a working drawing by Holbein). In his final years Henry VII had looked and lived like a mean old man. He had rarely appeared in public and had been best known for the way he extracted money from the wealthier of his subjects by dubious means. He had been feared because of the financial penalties he could exact, but he had not been widely respected.

Henry VII's son, in clear contrast, was young, energetic and accessible, and with a very obvious joy in living and in being king. He spent money with an abandon and a lack of forethought that matched popular expectations of how the mighty should conduct themselves. As if to stress that all had changed, he almost immediately took two very public decisions which announced that it was 'out with the old and in with the new'.

- First, Edmund Dudley and Sir Richard Empson, the two men who had been most responsible for implementing Henry VII's policy of the financial intimidation of his leading subjects, were arrested and imprisoned in the Tower, later to be executed.
- Second, it was made known that Catherine of Aragon was to become the new queen.

The latter decision was generally seen to be a chivalrous action towards an obviously virtuous young woman who, through no fault of her own, had for seven years been used by the old king as a pawn in his complex diplomatic manoeuvrings. During this time (since she had been widowed by the death of Arthur, Henry VII's eldest son) her ex-father-in-law had refused either to return her to her parents, along with her dowry, as should have been done, or to marry her to his second son as he had periodically promised to do. As a result, Catherine had become a virtual prisoner in a foreign land, and had won widespread admiration by the dignified way in which she had conducted herself throughout her adversity.

Contemporary propaganda

The new king's decisions were interpreted as a conscious attempt to put right the wrongs of the past. But, startling as the change of monarch was, it would be sensible to exercise caution in accepting the statements of contemporaries at their face value. Not only is it likely that some of them were lured into exaggeration by their enthusiasm about what they imagined would be the consequences of the accession of a promising young king, but it was also customary for monarchs to be written about in glowing terms, whether or not the facts justified the statements. To do so was a literary convention of the age, even in writings that were intended to be only for private consumption. This is made very clear by what was written about other rulers who are known to have been very 'ordinary', and by the accounts of Henry in later life when other evidence proves that he was anything but the stately and dignified figure he was often claimed to be. However, this is not to suggest that the flattering descriptions of the young Henry should be totally discounted, but rather that they should be regarded as possibilities for which corroborative evidence needs to be sought.

Henry the man

Henry VIII was king for more than 37 years. During this time he both matured and aged. Certainly, he did not remain the same. In some things he changed as a result of his experiences or of the passage of years: in others he became more entrenched as his confidence grew and as some of the uncertainties and flexibilities of youth disappeared with the progression through middle age to, what was for the period, old age. Thus, over the course of his entire reign he was that mixture of constancy and change, consistency and contradiction that should realistically be expected of most people.

It is normal to contrast the young Henry with the ageing king of the final years and to assume that his life saw a steady progression from one state to the other. The stages by which the change took place are not well documented, but what is not in doubt is that the 17-year-old who became king was a young man with considerable physical attributes and that the 55-year-old who died repulsed most of those who saw him.

Judgement of looks, of course, is a matter of taste which varies from society to society and from time to time. The visual impact Henry made for much of his reign was largely the result of his fine physique. He was tall, large-framed, well proportioned and very muscular. In fact, he well deserved the modern description of being 'a bull of a man'. And he knew how to make the best of his physical attributes. He carried himself well and he paid great attention to the clothes he wore. A foreign observer described him as 'the best dressed sovereign in the world'. His most famous portrait (reproduced on page 20) illustrates well both his physique and the use he made of it. It also hints strongly at the enormous pride he took in his appearance.

Henry the king

It is certain that Henry made no distinction between himself as a person and himself as a king. To him they were one and the same thing. He was a 24-hour-a-day monarch, for he had no private life that existed outside his official capacity. Yet, for him, being king was not a vocation, to be worked at, as it had so obviously been for his father. He regarded it as being a natural state of affairs – as one that required no special effort and no particular training. This was possibly the result of a combination of two factors. He knew from a relatively early age (he was ten when his elder brother, Arthur, died in 1502) that he was destined to succeed to the throne, and it seems that his father made absolutely no effort to prepare him directly for the responsibilities that were to be his as king. Therefore, Henry assumed that to be king he merely had to be himself. Hence the importance that historians have attached to their attempts to establish what sort of man Henry was.

Key question
Why is it so difficult to separate Henry the man from Henry VIII the king?

2 | Personality of the King

The debate

Key question
What was Henry VIII like and why is the issue so hotly debated?

Historians have disagreed radically about what sort of man Henry was. The controversy has been over whether he was fundamentally strong or basically weak; whether he was the puppet or the puppeteer. No lasting consensus has emerged and the issue is likely to be argued over into the foreseeable future. The problem is that there is sufficient evidence to allow a persuasive case to be made for both points of view, but not enough to prove one or the other conclusively. While each writer can rationalise the position he or she takes up, the decision on which 'side' to support is usually made according to that indefinable attribute we call 'feel'.

Fundamentally strong

It would be fair to say that the majority of the current generation of leading researchers have concluded that Henry was essentially strong. Their view has been that he possessed sufficient determination, self-assurance, intellectual ability and political shrewdness to ensure that the conduct of public life in his kingdom and its dealings with other states followed the lines that he determined (in as far as any individual can meaningfully control the course of events). They accept that he frequently allowed his leading servants, especially Wolsey, considerable scope for independent action, but that he always retained control of the direction of policy and was fully able to assume the detailed direction of events whenever he wished. They also admit that he was periodically weak and indecisive, especially in the latter part of his reign when severe pain sometimes sapped his resolve, but they maintain that such occasions were the exceptions rather than the rule. Their overall contention is that Henry did not only appear to be the colossus who dominated affairs in his domains, but that was essentially the reality of the situation. Thus they maintain that the king made use of his two great ministers (Cardinal Wolsey and Thomas Cromwell) rather than being manipulated by them, and that he exploited the factions during the final years of his reign rather than being 'captured' by each of them in turn.

Basically weak

However, the 'weak' school remains very active. Its members have judged Henry to have been essentially lacking in confidence, from which they have seen most of his other characteristics stemming. Thus, in their view, he was a ditherer, uncertain of which policy to pursue; suggestible, having no direction of his own to follow; a bully, having enormous power but little except whim to guide him in its use; and cruel, needing to convince himself of his own importance by degrading others. Those who have accepted the essentials of this interpretation have seen Wolsey as a real *alter rex* (alternative king), deciding on policies that he was able to persuade the king to accept almost at will, and only having to change course on those rare occasions when his nominal master intervened briefly but forcefully. Equally, Thomas Cromwell has been viewed as the king's puppet-master (although he took a lower profile), persuading Henry to break with Rome in order to secure the end of his marriage to Catherine of Aragon, to dispense with Anne Boleyn when her strong views became tiresome, to plunder the monasteries in order to solve his financial problems, and to institute a reign of terror by which anybody who voiced the least opposition to the royal policy could be charged with treason and executed if need be. Followers of this school have judged the 1540s to have been a time of relative political chaos, with a king who made disastrous decisions as he was buffeted by rival political factions that were led by mediocrities when compared to the ministers of previous decades. Here, it has been thought, lay the origins of the 'mid-Tudor crisis'. (See Chapters 7 and 8 on the reigns of Edward VI and Mary for a fuller discussion of this idea.)

The evidence
Interests

Considering Henry's physical form it is perhaps to be expected that his chief interest lay in sport. His greatest love was competitive physical activity: he regularly jousted, played an early version of tennis and hunted on horseback.

Key question
What evidence do historians turn to in order to help them explore Henry VIII's personality and character?

Undoubtedly the most publicly visible of Henry's sporting activities was jousting. This was thought to be the true sport of kings. There was an immense amount of play-acting and ceremony involved. However, the act of charging on heavily armoured horses in an attempt to unseat an opponent with a lance was highly dangerous for the participants. This was despite the fact that they were theoretically well protected by full suits of armour, the survival of which has allowed historians to chart the king's steadily increasing girth! Henry began his jousting career soon after he ascended the throne and he continued it for 25 years. In the process, he established and maintained a reputation as a fine athlete – besides being very nearly killed on one occasion. It has even been argued that the accident that finally persuaded him to hang up his spurs in 1536 left him permanently brain damaged.

It was a brave (or foolhardy) man who allowed himself to emerge victorious in any sporting contest with his monarch, and it is therefore impossible to reach any conclusions about the extent to which Henry really excelled as an athlete. But it seems likely that he would (in his prime) have been able to hold his own on equal terms with all but the best sportsman in the land. Otherwise, some of his less intelligent companions would surely have failed to lose to him as regularly as they did!

His love of food and drink was huge and abiding. He ate and drank enormous quantities on a regular basis and was fortunate to survive the effects for so long. But it should be remembered that his gluttony was typical of his class at the time (and for centuries to come), for the concept of excessive eating did not then exist. It was assumed that those who were rich enough to be able to afford huge quantities of food – especially meat – would have been silly to deny themselves such obvious and seemingly harmless pleasures. The age of 'sensible eating' was yet to dawn, and those who survived into their forties and fifties, if well-to-do, were expected to be of a size that announced to the world that they were rich enough to afford what they liked. Henry was not unique in ending up with a body too heavy for his legs to support.

Intellectual abilities

Those who wished to ingratiate themselves with Henry were almost certain of success if they told him that he was very clever. This was because the king liked to think of himself as a true **Renaissance man**, adept at all the pastimes (loosely termed 'cultural') that were known to have flourished in ancient Greece and Rome. He was prepared to make the effort required to become a competent musician and a passable scholar. Although Henry made no secret of the fact that he found both reading and writing (even the signing of his name) to be laborious and to be avoided if possible, he prided himself on the quality of his mind. And he was right to do so, because he appeared to have the ability to think his way around complicated issues almost as well as the most able of his subjects. It has even been suggested that the favour he extended to men of outstanding ability (at least until he believed that they, with one exception, had betrayed him) such as the four Thomases – Wolsey, More, Cromwell and Cranmer – was probably based on the fact that they could function at his intellectual level.

Contemporary writings contain many references to his intellectual powers. Even when the exaggeration is stripped away from verdicts such as those that describe him as having 'exceptional and almost more than human talents', and the judgement of **Erasmus**, the arch-flatterer of the early sixteenth century, that, as a child, he had possessed 'a vivid and active mind, above measure able to execute whatever tasks he undertook … You would say he was a universal genius', there is reason to believe that he should be numbered among the gifted.

But, of course, it is the way he performed during the 37 years of his reign that offers the most reliable evidence of his relative intellectual ability. And the picture is clear. He could, and regularly did, out-think all members of the English aristocracy. He was also personally more than a match for the other leading rulers of western Europe, although, of course, not necessarily for their advisers. His mind may not have been as well trained as those of some of his most able subjects, but this was hardly surprising given his lack of formal educational training. Nevertheless, he could both appreciate the strengths and spot the weaknesses of any argument that was laid before him, however skilful the presentation. As a result, it was almost impossible for 'the wool to be pulled over his eyes' – at least, for long.

Key term

Renaissance man
Someone open to new ideas in politics, culture and education.

Key figure

Erasmus (1466?–1536)
A key figure in religious and educational thinking in Europe who played a pivotal role in the establishment of humanism in universities. Erasmus's influence on the English episcopal and aristocratic patrons that came of age under Henry VIII was immense, especially in education.

On the few occasions when he was hoodwinked by those who advised him – as over the supposed treacheries of Cardinal Wolsey, Anne Boleyn and Thomas Cromwell – it was his emotions rather than his intellect that were persuaded, and then only after concerted campaigns of suppressing evidence and perverting the facts. Even the best minds reach incorrect conclusions if they are persistently fed with false information! Although there is no scientifically valid evidence available to support the contention, it is probable that Henry VIII was the most academically able monarch in English history.

Values and attitudes

Views on gender

Henry was a **conformist**. It is, therefore, not surprising that he adopted and retained most of the values and attitudes of his sex, his class and his age. His assumption that women were inferior to men was deeply ingrained and was only temporarily suspended for brief periods during his relationship with Anne Boleyn. Anne was a remarkable person in many respects, but especially in her refusal to be treated as a second-class citizen because of her gender. However, for most of his life Henry treated women like **chattels** (possessions) and was swift to remind any female who did not 'know her place' that subservience was expected of her.

His anger at Catherine of Aragon for refusing to accept being 'put aside' with a good grace was never assuaged and largely explains why he celebrated her death with public relish in 1536. He was equally affronted when his daughter Mary refused to accept the bastardy that resulted from the annulment of her parents' marriage, and was only prepared to return her to his favour when she promised to accept his authority in all matters unreservedly in future. It can even be maintained that Anne Boleyn's final undoing, resulting in her execution, was made possible only because the king's dislike of her stubbornness eventually became stronger than the fascination she exercised over him.

Certainly a large part of the lasting affection that Henry felt for Jane Seymour, which long survived her death following the birth of their son (later Edward VI) in 1537, resulted from the fact that she fully accepted her husband's views about the inferiority of women. Equally, Anne of Cleves not only survived but also flourished following the rapid dissolution of her marriage with Henry because she was prepared to accept the king's will without demur. Even the more personable Catherine Parr was able to survive a concerted effort to remove her (see page 32) by throwing herself unreservedly on her husband's mercy and by declaring that she wished to follow his instructions in every detail.

Views on social structures

Just as Henry unthinkingly accepted the prevailing attitudes about the hierarchical relationship between the sexes, so he was also unquestioning about the validity of the existing social hierarchy. He accepted that God had ordered society as it then

Key terms

Conformist
Someone who follows the rules of the State.

Chattels
Possessions.

was and that it was a sin for anyone to challenge the place he or she had been assigned within it. As did almost all of those around him, he assumed that not only morality, but also the preservation of civilisation as he understood it, depended on the maintenance of existing social distinctions. He, therefore, behaved ruthlessly towards any groups or individuals who dared to endanger the prevailing order of things.

The value that Henry attached to human life and human suffering was similarly in line with the prevailing orthodoxy. This was that the time spent on earth was merely a brief interlude in the soul's eternal life. Whether it was lengthened or shortened by a few years, or made more or less painful by the use of, for example, judicial torture was therefore of minimal importance in the wider scheme of things. Given this scale of values, it would have indeed been surprising had he felt any sustained guilt or sorrow about the thousands of premature deaths for which he was probably directly responsible. Many would argue that this did not make him an ogre, as he was merely acting according to the accepted standards of his time.

Henry differed from his father in his attitude towards self-discipline and endeavour. But Henry VII, with his insistence on working on the detail of governing his kingdom, had been atypical and had been despised (if feared) by most of his leading subjects for failing to live up to popular expectations of how a ruler should conduct himself. There was no danger that Henry VIII would fall into the same trap. He happily accepted that work was generally something that was done by servants, while masters devoted their time to activities that better befitted their status.

In the case of kings this was performing grand deeds, whether in court, sport or battle. It was acceptable to strive mightily in such endeavours, but other affairs were to be taken lightly and with studied casualness. If servants were well chosen, their supervision should require a minimum of effort. They would undertake whatever smacked of 'business' once the direction in which affairs should move had been made clear to them. In early sixteenth-century western Europe the distinctions were not nearly so hard and fast. As a result, Henry was able to apply himself diligently from time to time to the minutiae of kingship without endangering his regal reputation.

Beliefs
Religion

Henry was a man with strong beliefs that remained largely unchanged throughout his adult life. He seemingly never doubted either the existence or the nature of the Christian God, nor the detail of what this deity expected of him. There seems to have been little that could be described as spiritual in his beliefs. It appears that Henry thought of God as a sort of super-man, sitting on a throne somewhere in the sky, from where he could observe all that was happening on earth and be ready to reward or punish those who followed or broke his commandments. It also seems that Henry believed that his position as a king empowered him to make special deals with God whenever the need arose.

Code of chivalry

As a child Henry had been brought up to believe that his role in life was to be a 'true knight', according to the code of chivalry which had been developed at the Burgundian court in the Netherlands during the previous century and which had been given a particularly English flavour by the widespread retelling of the legends about **King Arthur and the Knights of the Round Table**. One important aspect of this code was the need for men to perform 'valiant deeds'. These could be in ceremonial form – by partaking in jousting or in the elaborate mock battles that were sometimes staged as grand court spectacles – but in their highest form they could only be undertaken in real-life warfare, where the risks and the rewards were genuine.

It seems that he had also been repeatedly told the story of his namesake-predecessor, Henry V, who, less than a hundred years previously, had earned eternal glory by winning a great victory at Agincourt against the French and by securing the crown of France for the English royal family. It is therefore hardly surprising that Henry entered manhood believing that his destiny was to perform similar deeds of valour on the far side of the Channel.

'Courtly love'

Closely associated with the martial aspect of chivalry was the concept of 'courtly love'. A 'true knight' was not expected to perform valiantly on the field of battle in order to win wealth or worldly power (although these might naturally follow a victory), but so that he would have worthwhile trophies to lay at the feet of his 'fair lady'. The woman he thus served might be his own wife, might be unattached or might even be the wife of another. In any case, no impropriety would be involved and (hopefully) no offence given, because there need be no physical contact, beyond the possible kissing of a hand, between a knight and the recipient of his 'love'. The relationship was one that was meant to represent romance in its purest form – a knight carrying out disinterested service for a lady.

Evidence of Henry's attachment to this code as a young man abounds, not only in the way he treated Catherine of Aragon at jousts and court festivities, but in the way he hurried back to her to present her with the symbols of his victorious campaign in France in 1513. Although the king seems to have become less enamoured with such conventions when he passed out of his twenties (the Field of Cloth of Gold in 1520 was the last of Henry's great chivalric extravaganzas), they certainly continued to flourish among the younger members of his court. Even as late as 1536 Anne Boleyn acted as the 'fair lady' for several young men, a willingness that was made the basis of the charges of adultery that were fatally levelled against her.

Key term

King Arthur and the Knights of the Round Table
The Arthurian legends would have been very popular at the time.

Concept of honour

However much Henry cooled towards the romance of chivalry, there was one aspect of the code that remained central to his beliefs throughout his life. This was the concept of honour. His initial approach to most issues was shaped by his understanding of this concept – that kings should always be obeyed and that they should never be under the influence of others. It would hardly be an exaggeration to claim that all his public actions and all his reactions to the doings of others were initially planned by Henry in terms of their effect upon his honour. The documents he left behind him and the reports that survive of his explanations of his actions strongly support this contention. 'What was the honourable way in which a king should act?', and 'Was the action reported to him an affront to his honour?', were the questions that he most frequently asked himself when considering what he should do.

Key question
Why did Henry VIII marry six times?

3 | Henry and his Six Wives

Almost everybody knows about Henry VIII and his six wives. It is an integral part of British folklore:

> Divorced, beheaded, died,
> divorced, beheaded, survived

is a jingle that tens of thousands of students have memorised in preparation for a test on the key facts of Henry's reign. It has been very useful for this purpose, but it seems to have had the unintended side-effect of suggesting that there was a particular pattern to Henry's marital history, when there was not.

It has sometimes been assumed that a man who was sport-mad and who married six times must also have been blessed (or punished) with a strong sex-drive. However, it seems that this was not so in Henry's case. In fact, he was probably more interested in the romantic side of lovemaking than in its physical aspects. He had fewer mistresses and fewer illegitimate children (probably only two) than most male rulers of his time, and he was prepared to wait six years for Anne Boleyn, the major passion of his life, to surrender to his sexual advances. However, this is not to suggest, as some writers have done, that his virility was questionable. It is merely to argue that Henry was in no sense the sexual predator that he has sometimes popularly been made out to be. But this was not because he had any moral objection to promiscuity, or any belief that he should be faithful to his wife of the moment. He was just not very interested in women. In fact, some historians have claimed that he viewed them as little more than child-bearing machines.

Catherine of Aragon

For most of his adult life (from 1509 to 1533) Henry was married to the same person – Catherine of Aragon, a daughter of Ferdinand and Isabella whose own marriage had united all of the **Iberian kingdoms**, except Portugal, to form the new country of Spain. Catherine (so spelt by a mysterious modern convention, despite the fact that contemporaries almost universally began it with a 'K') was in almost all respects a model wife judged by the standards of the time. She was dignified yet dutiful, rejoiced in her husband's attentiveness but was uncomplaining about his indiscretions, and played the part of the seemly consort to perfection in both public and private. She created a positive impression on all who met her, in the process acquiring many friends and admirers but no real enemies. She even obliged her husband with a steady stream of pregnancies. It is true that some of these miscarried, but at least five of them resulted in live births.

However, only one of these (Mary) survived for long. The others, including three sons, died within hours or days, and this was her undoing. By the early 1520s it was established beyond reasonable doubt that she would bear no more children. Henry thus became painfully aware that while the marriage continued he was certain to be denied one of his most fervent desires – male heirs to continue the Tudor dynasty. Although he already had one illegitimate son, whom he created the Duke of Richmond and whom he seemed to be grooming to succeed him, he knew in his heart of hearts that his subjects would be unlikely to accept such an arrangement once he was dead and no longer able to enforce it.

Anne Boleyn

As the years passed Henry's concern about his lack of legitimate sons became an obsession. Added to this, he became captivated by Anne Boleyn, a woman who refused to have sex with him until he was in a position to marry her. He therefore became determined that his marriage ties with Catherine must be broken – and an ideal excuse appeared to be available. Catherine had first been married to Henry's elder brother (Arthur), and a plausible argument could be advanced that the Bible forbade remarriages of a man with his brother's widow. However, it took seven years and the beginnings of a revolution (issues discussed in detail in *Henry VIII and the Reformation in England* in this series) for Henry and Catherine's marriage to be annulled in a way that most Englishmen were prepared to accept as being legal.

At last (in 1533) the king was free to marry a woman young enough to offer him the prospect of bearing many children. But Anne Boleyn was a disappointment in this respect. Although she was already pregnant at the time of her marriage, the resulting offspring (a daughter, Elizabeth) was to be her only successful experience of child-bearing. In 1536 'Anne of a Thousand Days' was found guilty on spurious charges of adultery with, among others, her brother, and was executed. Her husband was thereby freed to enter a third partnership in his increasingly desperate attempt to sire a son who would survive into adulthood.

Key term

Iberian kingdoms Portugal and Spain, which occupy the Iberian peninsula.

Key dates

Henry married Catherine of Aragon: 1509

Henry's daughter Mary born: 1516

Henry divorced Catherine and married Anne Boleyn; daughter Elizabeth born: 1533

Anne Boleyn executed: 1536

Key dates

Henry married Jane Seymour: 1536

Henry's son Edward born; Jane Seymour died: 1537

Henry married Anne of Cleves; marriage dissolved: 1540

Jane Seymour

Jane Seymour was not only able to face the world as the undisputed Queen of England – Catherine of Aragon having died of natural causes shortly before Anne Boleyn met her less peaceful end – but she was also successful at her first attempt in the 'maternal stakes'. In 1537 she gave birth to the future Edward VI. But she paid for her triumph with her life, dying of the effects of childbirth a few days later. Thereafter, Henry's matrimonial affairs assumed a large element of farce. Although Edward's survival beyond the dangerous early weeks removed most of the panic from the situation, both the king and his leading minister (Thomas Cromwell) believed that there were diplomatic and dynastic advantages to be gained from a well-chosen fourth marriage. The fact that Henry insisted on seeing portraits of all the potential brides (once the King of France had declined to arrange 'a parade' of the leading contenders at Calais on the grounds that to do so would be unseemly) strongly suggests that he still thought of his own marriages in terms of personal satisfaction, which he had singularly failed to do when arranging the marriages of others.

Anne of Cleves

For some now-unfathomable reason Henry took an immediate dislike to Cromwell's preferred (on diplomatic grounds) candidate – Anne, the 34-year-old daughter of the ruler of the strategically placed dukedom of Cleves (see the map on page 14). Dishonestly flattering reports and a less than accurate portrait were used by Cromwell to win his master's agreement to the match, but the prospective bridegroom's doubts remained. These became certainties once he set eyes on his bride-to-be and found that (seemingly without good reason) her looks repelled him. It took all Cromwell's skill as a persuader to convince Henry that it was not practical for him to withdraw from his commitment to Anne of Cleves at such a late stage. He was assisted in this task by Henry's recognition of the dire diplomatic consequences that might have resulted had he given offence to England's potential Protestant allies at a time when it looked as if a coalition of Catholic states might be about to invade the country to restore the Pope's authority. So the wedding went ahead (in January 1540), but the king had already determined that he would never consummate his marriage with the 'Flander's mare'. Nor did he. Instead, Cromwell was disgraced and executed – partly because of the matrimonial embarrassment his policy had caused – while later that year Anne contentedly accepted the annulment of a marriage she had not welcomed, together with a sizeable financial settlement which allowed her to live the quiet life she sought, free from the danger of being used as a pawn in the international game of politics and dynastic marriage-making.

Catherine Howard

Henry's fifth marriage, to Catherine Howard in 1540, was a clear case of 'old man's folly'. His passion was enflamed by a flighty young protégée of one of the court factions and he allowed himself to be manoeuvred into marrying her. Unfortunately the new queen had little common sense and less discretion. She soon provided her political enemies with the evidence that she had at least seriously contemplated adultery, which was sufficient grounds for a charge of treason to be levelled against her. She was executed in 1542.

Catherine Parr

By now Henry had given up hope of fathering further sons, and all his hopes rested on the frail health of Edward. However, in the year following Catherine Howard's execution he married yet again. This time his choice fell upon the twice-widowed Catherine Parr, who provided him with just the quality of level-headed care and concern that was needed in the king's ailing years. Whether or not her qualities of good housewifery were recognised before she became queen is not known. But whether by luck or by judgement, Henry's last foray into matrimony was a success and his need for quiet companionship and devout solace was well met.

Key dates

Henry married Catherine Howard: 1540

Catherine Howard executed: 1542

Henry married Catherine Parr: 1543

Henry VIII died: 1547

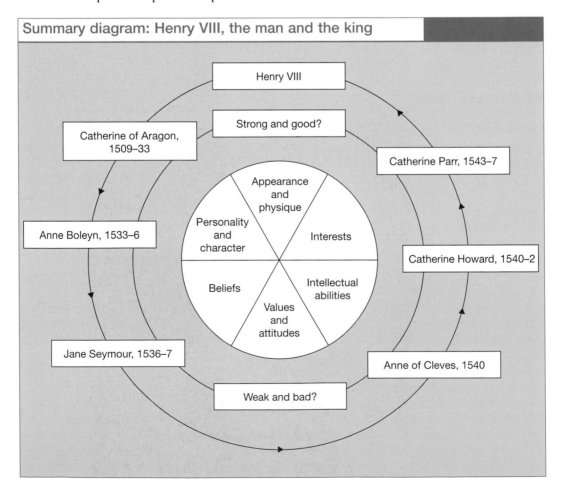

Summary diagram: Henry VIII, the man and the king

Henry VIII

Strong and good?

Catherine of Aragon, 1509–33

Catherine Parr, 1543–7

Appearance and physique

Personality and character

Interests

Anne Boleyn, 1533–6

Beliefs

Intellectual abilities

Catherine Howard, 1540–2

Values and attitudes

Jane Seymour, 1536–7

Anne of Cleves, 1540

Weak and bad?

Study Guide: AS Questions

In the style of Edexcel
Study Sources 1, 2 and 3.
How far do the sources suggest that the young Henry VIII was an impressive figure as king? Explain your answer, using the evidence of Sources 1, 2 and 3.   (20 marks)

Source 1

From a diary written by John Taylor in 1513. Taylor was a royal official and also the King's chaplain. This extract is from the record of Henry's expedition to France in 1513.

8 July
The King was practising archery in a garden with the archers of the guard. He hit the mark in the middle, and surpassed them all, as he surpasses them in stature and personal graces.

Source 2

From a report by the Venetian Ambassador, Pasqualigo, in 1515.

His Majesty [Henry VIII] addressing me in French, said 'The King of France, is he as tall as I am?' I told him there was but little difference. He asked 'Is he as stout?' I said he was not; and he then enquired 'What sort of legs has he?' I replied 'Thin'. Whereupon, placing his hand on his thigh, he said 'Look here and I also have a good calf to my leg.'

Source 3

A portrait of Henry VIII c.1520. The artist is unknown.

Exam tips

This is an example of your first-part question, question (a), which is compulsory. It is a short answer question, and you should not write more than three or four paragraphs. Note that you are only required to reach a judgement on the evidence of these sources. The question does not ask you to write what you know about Henry VIII. However, you will apply your own contextual knowledge to the sources when you use them. For example, you should know about Henry VIII's rivalry with the King of France at the time Source 2 was written. The details in the source caption enable you to see Source 1's author as knowledgeable and authoritative, given his position close to the king, but your own understanding of this period will enable you to consider whether he would have put in writing a comment unfavourable to his royal master.

When you deal with (a) questions you are weighing up the evidence. You will first have to analyse the image of Henry given in all three sources, but bear in mind that the evidence of the sources you are given in the examination will point in different directions. So in this case, you will know immediately that there is some evidence suggesting that Henry was an impressive figure and some evidence which will lead you to question this. You will be placing evidence on both sides.

It is not advisable to deal with the sources one by one. Develop a short plan under two headings 'impressive' and 'not impressive', entering the evidence from Sources 1, 2 and 3 underneath, and then come to your own conclusion.

You could explore the following issues:

- Henry's physical size: Sources 1 and 2, but note that the King of France appears to be the same height, but less well built (what is the evidence for this?). This helps both to confirm the evidence of Source 1 and to encourage you to treat Source 1 with caution. Remember, too, that the Venetian Ambassador was reporting the replies he gave Henry. Why is that important?
- Henry's skill as an archer: Source 1 – your own knowledge of context will enable you to note that sporting or fighting prowess would have been seen as an important attribute in a king at the time.
- Henry's impressive appearance: Source 1 refers to 'personal graces' and you will need to analyse the impression the artist aimed to create in Source 3.

Before you come to an overall judgement, you will need to explore any elements of the nature or purpose of the source which add weight to it, or cause you to treat it with caution. For example, when analysing the portrait, Source 3, keep in mind that every element of it has been deliberately produced to create a certain impression – and that a contemporary artist would be unlikely to attempt to portray the king in an unfavourable light.

In the style of OCR

Assess how far Henry VIII's personality influenced his aims as king between 1509 and 1529. (50 marks)

> ### Exam tips
>
> *The cross-references are intended to take you straight to the material that will help you to answer the question.*
>
> Two main approaches are likely to be taken when answering this question. The first is that Henry's personality had a direct impact on his aims and policies, and that, in an age of personal monarchy, his character was 'larger than life'. The second approach is to argue that factors other than Henry's personality were as much if not more influential. Evidence that supports the premise might include:
>
> - Henry's athleticism, love of sport and physical activities (page 24)
> - Henry's materialism and love of court spectacles (pages 24 and 28)
> - Henry's intellectual and theological interests (pages 25, 27–8)
> - Henry's lack of interest in governmental business (page 3)
> - Henry's love of chivalry, honour and women (pages 28–9)
> - Henry's desire to be popular with his nobles and courtiers
> - Henry's interest in war and in particular emulating Henry V.
>
> You need to link these features to particular aims such as the king's desire to be his own man, his delegation of administration to councillors (e.g. Wolsey), his need for a male heir, his rivalry with Francis I and Charles V, and his wish to gain lands on the continent through war.
>
> A counter-argument can also be made that other factors were important influences. These might include:
>
> - the legacy of Henry VII that shaped royal policies in the first years of the new reign, e.g. the limited finances in the Treasury, the influence of Warham
> - the role of Wolsey in Church, State and foreign affairs between 1514 and 1529
> - the resurgent power of France after 1515 that threatened England's security
> - the growing French influence in Scotland after the death of James V
> - the emergence of Lutheranism and Henry VIII's attachment to the Catholic faith.
>
> Answers need to be balanced whereby key personality traits are identified and linked to specific aims in both domestic and foreign affairs.

3 Wolsey: Government, Diplomacy and the King's 'Great Matter' 1514–29

POINTS TO CONSIDER

In order to understand the political and religious issues taking shape during the reign of Henry VIII it is important to know something about the man on whom the king relied for advice and support. Therefore, this chapter is intended to explore in depth the life, career and influence of one of the most powerful men in Henrician England after the king. The political, religious and foreign affairs that involved Wolsey are examined as six themes:

- Rise to pre-eminence
- Wolsey in control
- Wolsey the politician: government
- Wolsey the diplomat: foreign policy
- The King's great matter
- Fall from power

Key dates

1514	Wolsey became the king's chief minister
1515	Wolsey appointed lord chancellor and made a cardinal
1518	Wolsey appointed papal legate
	The Treaty of London (also known as the treaty of Universal Peace)
1520	The Field of Cloth of Gold
1521	Wolsey met Charles V in Bruges
	Pope awarded Henry VIII the title of 'Defender of the Faith'
1522	The general proscription
1524	Wolsey appointed papal legate for life
1526	Eltham Ordinances
1527	Henry instructed Wolsey to explore with the Pope the possibility of obtaining a divorce
1528–9	Failed attempt to obtain a divorce using Cardinal Campeggio
1529	Wolsey removed from power
1530	Wolsey died at Leicester while being taken under arrest to London

1 | Rise to Pre-eminence

Introduction

Key question
What factors promoted Wolsey's rise to power?

The career of Cardinal Wolsey was one of the most amazing episodes in an amazing reign. Thomas Wolsey was born the son of a butcher in Ipswich in 1470 or 1471. From these lowly origins he defied all the rules of social mobility by becoming the richest and most powerful man in England besides the king. It has often been claimed that he acted as the effective ruler of the country (as an *alter rex*) for the 15 years up to his fall in 1529. At the height of his influence, in the mid-1520s, his word was almost law and it was widely understood both at home and abroad that there was little point in attempting to secure any royal favour except through him. His court rivalled the king's in size and splendour and often outstripped it in day-to-day political importance. His palaces, especially Hampton Court and York House (later known as the Palace of Westminster), were developed to be fit for a king, as Henry VIII discovered long before he acquired them for himself. No other commoner was to rival his career for several centuries, and the extent to which he achieved personal political success was unique in Tudor England.

Character and personality

Key question
What kind of man was Wolsey?

How was it that the low-born butcher's son was able to become the 'better' of the entire English aristocracy? It would be surprising if it were not because of a mixture of merit and good fortune. Wolsey was outstandingly able. He possessed a very fine mind. This was apparent from very early in his life. He took considerable pleasure in recounting in later years how he had been sent to Oxford as a relatively young boy, and had been awarded the unofficial title of boy-bachelor because he had gained his first degree at the age of 15. But it was his character and personality that marked him out as much more than a young man of high intellectual ability.

He possessed the drive and confidence necessary to seize the opportunities that came his way. He was seemingly afraid of nothing (certainly not of failure) and he was prepared to take calculated risks whenever the need arose. One contemporary reported (although some historians doubt the reliability of the account) that when he was put in charge of his college funds he made the unilateral decision to initiate some ambitious building works, assuming that his colleagues would be too timid to challenge his authority. He was wrong, and had rapidly to seek preferment elsewhere. But it was in winning the patronage of important people that he showed the essential attributes of the up-and-coming man. He could flatter outrageously while at the same time making himself welcome as an interesting and attractive companion. And most important of all, he could be relied upon to carry out whatever task was entrusted to him with exemplary skill and application. He thrived on hard and intensive work in an age when most people sought and found a gentle pace of life.

A painting of Cardinal Wolsey in his cardinal's robes. In your opinion, is the artist who painted this portrait sympathetic or hostile to Wolsey?

This marked him out from most of his potential competitors, as did his single-minded and totally unscrupulous pursuit of his objectives. If anybody got in his way they were elbowed aside with whatever force was necessary. Many tales exist about his nefarious activities as a young man. It does not matter that many of them are probably apocryphal. What is significant is that Wolsey liked to pretend that they were true, presumably because they showed him as the type of person (an unprincipled and selfish go-getter) he was pleased to be.

Rise to prominence

He first came to major notice during the final years of Henry VII's reign as the man of business for Bishop Fox. Fox was one of the king's more trusted counsellors, and Wolsey was able to shine as a most efficient and flamboyant conductor of the king's business.

Key question
What steps did Wolsey take to aid his rise to prominence?

Royal counsellor

His major break came in the situation that prevailed in the early years of the new king's reign. Henry VIII was initially surrounded by most of his father's old counsellors. This is not to be wondered at because he came to the throne at the age of 17, having lived a life virtually devoid of public business, and having no followers of his own to promote to senior positions. However, what angered Henry and gave Wolsey his chance was that the old counsellors seemed very reluctant to become the new king's men. They not only tried to browbeat him into continuing his father's policies (especially in foreign affairs) when what he wanted was to follow a 'forward' policy of his own, but also constantly criticised him for not taking his kingly 'work' duties seriously enough, and for spending too much time in leisure pursuits, such as hunting and feasting.

King's adviser

Wolsey later claimed that he took advantage of the situation by giving the king the advice he wanted to hear, thus winning his approval. At the same time, he claimed to have encouraged the king to continue with his life of gaiety while leaving the boring work of government to people such as him, who could be relied on to carry out the king's wishes, which the senior counsellors could not be trusted to do. Although it has rightly been pointed out that Wolsey oversimplified matters in his reported account of events, it is highly likely that his version accurately reflected the spirit of what happened. It is just that it foreshortened events, making it seem that what took several years was achieved in one shrewd move.

Wolsey was also assisted by the fact that many of the leading figures from the previous reign either were removed from the scene, such as Empson and Dudley, or were pleased to seek a quieter life in political retirement, such as Archbishop Warham and Bishop Fox. This left Wolsey a relatively uncontested route in his rise to the top. But he still had to prove himself worthy of the king's confidence.

Expedition to France

His opportunity to do this in a resounding manner came in 1512–13. Somebody was needed to organise the **expeditionary force** to invade France under Henry's leadership in the summer of 1513. Wolsey was prepared to take on this responsibility, despite the fact that more senior and experienced officials shrank from a challenge that was likely to bring nothing but problems and aggravation, followed by criticism over what was almost certain to be a disaster.

But Wolsey defied all the pundits by achieving the seemingly impossible. He ensured that all the right people and supplies were in the right places at the right times. In the process he antagonised most of those in authority by riding roughshod over their rights and sensibilities in order to achieve results in the necessary timescales, arguing at every turn that the king's wishes

Key term

Expeditionary force
An army sent to fight in another country.

must take precedence over all other considerations. However, the more people complained to Henry about Wolsey's ruthlessness in getting done what was necessary, the more the king warmed to the servant who seemed able to overcome all obstacles in implementing his wishes. By the middle of 1514 Henry was referring almost all matters of business to Wolsey, in the certainty that they would be dealt with efficiently, and generally along the lines that he desired.

Wolsey and the Church

In the circumstances Henry was not well placed to resist whatever requests Wolsey might make of him for his own advancement, given that his informal position as the king's chief minister was not reflected in any official appointments. Wolsey was not slow to utilise the argument that the king's honour and dignity demanded that his leading counsellor should both hold positions of the greatest possible status and receive an income that allowed him to adopt a lifestyle befitting his standing as Henry's most favoured servant. The cheapest way for Henry to reward Wolsey was by securing his appointment to posts that were not paid for from the royal finances. The Church was traditionally the source of such preferments.

Key question
Why was Wolsey able to obtain so much power in the Church?

From Dean to Archbishop

Before his emergence as a leading counsellor, Wolsey had already benefited from appointment to posts of secondary importance within the Church. For example, he was made Dean of Lincoln. Once the success of 1513 was behind him, he was in line for major appointments. In rapid succession he was made Bishop of Tournai (particularly fitting for the man who had made its capture by Henry possible, although he was never able to make good his claim to this position), Bishop of Lincoln, and Archbishop of York. The Archbishopric was particularly significant because it made Wolsey the second most senior person within the Church in England.

Cardinal

However, Wolsey was rarely satisfied with second best. He wished to be seen to be number one. Although the leading position within the English Church (the Archbishopric of Canterbury) was held by Archbishop Warham, a man who made it very clear that he had no intention of resigning in order to make way for the king's favourite, there was another way of securing clerical pre-eminence for Wolsey. Pope Leo X could appoint him to a position that outranked Canterbury. A campaign to exert pressure on the Pope to do so was orchestrated by Wolsey and was fully supported by Henry. In 1515 Leo X succumbed to the pressure and made Wolsey a cardinal, a position that outranked all churchmen except the Pope. But this did not satisfy the new 'prince of the Church' because, although it gave him precedence over Archbishop Warham of Canterbury on ceremonial occasions, it did not give him control over the English Church as a whole. This remained in Warham's hands, and to reverse the situation a further honour would be necessary.

Legatus a latere

Wolsey would have to be appointed the highest category of papal representative – a **legatus a latere** – a position normally awarded for a specific purpose so that a representative with full papal powers could be present at a decision-making occasion far distant from Rome. Wolsey, with Henry's assistance, campaigned vigorously to receive such an appointment. In 1518 he engineered a situation whereby he was accorded the honour, along with a fellow cardinal sent from Rome, to act on the Pope's behalf in negotiations for what was hoped to become a general truce between the major European states. This was to be done so that a crusade against the Turks could take place. By exploiting every diplomatic advantage he could, Wolsey at first secured the extension of his **legatine powers** for a number of years, and then in 1524 contrived to win what for him was the major prize – the confirmation of his powers for life. This was a remarkable achievement and was for Wolsey the most cherished of his positions.

There was much less need for Wolsey to be appointed to official positions within the State than there was for formal grants of power within the Church. After all, he enjoyed the full support of the head of State (Henry VIII), whereas he was never in a similar position with the Pope in Rome. As long as the king was prepared to back him up in his decisions, Wolsey had nothing to fear from his fellow countrymen.

Wolsey and the State

In the early sixteenth century the government was still the king's government in practice as well as in theory, and it was generally accepted that the monarch could change the rules (but not the laws) as and when he wanted. If the king wished to entrust sweeping powers to Wolsey, that was his decision and few would contest it, even though existing areas of responsibility were invaded in the process. The way the system worked in practice had been well illustrated at the time when Wolsey was organising the expedition to France in 1513. Although he had held none of the major offices of state he had been able to mobilise the whole machinery of government to carry out his commands. This had been possible because the king had willed it. But Wolsey was very concerned about issues of status and precedence.

Lord Chancellor

He was not satisfied with the reality of power: he also wished to be seen to be wielding it. He was therefore insistent that Henry should appoint him to the senior office of state, the lord chancellorship. But as was normal in most public affairs at the time when Wolsey was not the decision maker, it took a long time for the intention to become the deed. Although Wolsey was the **de facto** chief minister by the middle of 1514, it was not until the

Key terms

Legatus a latere
A position normally awarded for a specific purpose so that a representative with full papal powers could be present at a decision-making occasion far distant from Rome.

Legatine powers
Having the powers of the Pope.

De facto
Existing in fact, whether legal or not.

Key dates

Wolsey appointed papal legate: 1518

Wolsey appointed papal legate for life: 1524

Wolsey became the king's chief minister: 1514

Wolsey appointed lord chancellor and made a cardinal: 1515

next year that Henry was prepared to request the resignation of Archbishop Warham, the current lord chancellor, and to appoint Wolsey in his place. But the wait had been worthwhile for the cardinal. It would now be very difficult for anybody to challenge his decisions successfully, because Wolsey now had direct control of the legal system of the State.

Contemporary and modern assessments

The papal collector and author of *Anglica Historia*, Polydore Vergil, loathed Wolsey, and represented him as 'singing, laughing, dancing and playing with the young courtiers'. Vergil further asserted that 'Wolsey, with his arrogance and ambition … claimed he could undertake himself almost all public duties'. Wolsey's biographer and gentleman usher, George Cavendish, agrees that his master recognised the young Henry's dislike of routine work, and describes him as 'putting the king in comfort that he shall not need to spare any time of his pleasure for any business that should necessary happen in the Council as long as he being there'. But there was more to Wolsey's assessment of Henry than that, and Cavendish also records, in an illuminating passage, how 'all his endeavour was only to satisfy the king's mind knowing rightwell that it was the very vain and right course to bring him to high promotion'.

Yet professional historians have generally shunned Wolsey. Only one major biography in English has been published by A.F. Pollard, and that appeared in 1929. Peter Gwyn's huge volume which was published in 1990 was essentially a long-term 'labour of love' rather than an academic study. Why has Wolsey been so ignored? It is certainly not because there is a lack of available documentary evidence about his activities. If anything, there is almost too much. This is despite the fact that on any one issue there is rarely enough detail for an uncontestable conclusion to be drawn. Because he operated in the arena of international political and church affairs, as well as within all aspects of English public life, there is a mass of relevant research material scattered throughout the archives of Europe.

It would take a lifetime of study to become familiar with it all. But it is probably not the daunting nature of the task that explains historians' reluctance systematically to update Pollard's pioneering biography, which was researched so long ago, in the years immediately before and after the First World War. It is more that Wolsey is widely viewed as being a historical dead-end; the last of a long line of powerful medieval royal servants who was almost an anachronism in his own time, and therefore not a very worthwhile subject of study. He is seen as being the end of something rather than being the beginning; as someone who had little long-term effect on anything, and therefore as being of little historical significance. In these circumstances there has seemed little justification for devoting a professional career to studying his activities. To do so might almost seem to be self-indulgent antiquarianism.

> **Key question**
> How has Wolsey been portrayed by contemporary and by modern commentators?

Key question
What did Wolsey do to maintain his power once he had established himself as the king's chief minister?

Key term

Dictator
Non-democratic rule of a country by a single person or party.

2 | Wolsey in Control

Power and authority

It has often been claimed that Wolsey was in practice a **dictator**. There are powerful arguments to support this contention, although it must be remembered that in secular matters he could always be overruled by the king. This sometimes happened when Henry decided to grant the wishes of his friends. But such royal interventions were certain to be few and far between once it was well known that those who 'went behind the cardinal's back' and successfully secured the direct support of the king would be made to pay for their effrontery in the long run. For Wolsey was extremely vindictive in such circumstances and was relentless in his subsequent pursuit of those who had gained even a slight temporary advantage over him. And the 'punishment' was always considerably in excess of the 'crime'. Financial ruin could be brought to a family when one of its members was reported to have said something unflattering about Wolsey in the hearing of the king.

Wolsey the dictator: secular dictatorship

What was the nature of this normally effective dictatorship in secular matters? As with most dictatorships, it struck randomly and depended on fear for its success. But it was certainly not a totalitarian dictatorship of the twentieth-century type. The vast majority of the population were completely untouched by it, for Wolsey was not concerned about what they thought, said or did, as long as they did not cross him. The ones who suffered from the cardinal's activities were those who found themselves at odds with Wolsey's purpose. Often they would be innocent bystanders who happened to be in the wrong place at the wrong time, and who were required to make some sacrifice in order to further one of the minister's projects. It might be a matter of selling a piece of property that Wolsey needed for some purpose, or making an interest-free loan with no agreed date for repayment, or withdrawing from a legal case that Wolsey would find inconvenient.

Those who were unwise enough to raise some objection to what was required of them would find themselves in considerable difficulties. If they were 'unimportant' people they might find themselves imprisoned on trumped-up charges, with nobody prepared to listen to their side of the story. If they were more influential they might find a complicated and expensive law suit started against them, which was guaranteed to drain their resources of both time and money. They might even find the verdict in a law suit that they had already won reversed on Wolsey's personal authority in order to punish them for some lack of co-operation.

Not even the most powerful in the land were safe from the cardinal's vengeance – at least in the long term. Nobody who had offended him could sleep peacefully in their beds at night, because they did not know when they might be called to account for some seemingly innocent action they had taken. It was widely believed at the time that the disgrace and execution of the Duke of Buckingham, one of the leading nobles in the land, in 1521 (see page 51), happened because Wolsey wished to seek revenge on him for the scornful way he had been treated in the past. Although it is now clear that Buckingham had left himself open to treason charges by the careless things he had said, the suspicion remains that he would have remained safe had Wolsey not engineered the king's displeasure against him.

By the early 1520s an established fact of political life in England was that you did not incur the cardinal's displeasure if you held any aspirations for the future. For, whereas he was known to be kind and generous to those who acknowledged his social and political superiority, he was equally renowned for the vigour with which he sought redress for even an imagined slight. The fact that retribution was often slow in coming, and appeared to be totally unconnected with any original incident, made it all the more to be feared. Even those who had never suffered at his hands were fearful that one day they might.

Wolsey the dictator: ecclesiastical dictatorship

Wolsey's dictatorship in ecclesiastical matters came to be even more complete than it was in secular affairs. Once he had acquired the title *legatus a latere* for life there was nothing, in practice, that anybody could do to limit his powers over the Church in England. Although it was technically possible to appeal over his head to Rome, such were the difficulties in doing so that it was not a realistically available option for his opponents. So Wolsey was effectively free to do what he liked in spiritual affairs. However, his interventions were on a surprisingly narrow front, almost exclusively having to do with appointments to clerical posts and the levying of fees for the provision of services. He made very little use of his sweeping powers either to reform abuses (perhaps because he was the principal culprit himself) or to prevent the spread of **heresy** (possibly because he attached so little importance to what people actually believed).

He successfully claimed the right to nominate whomever he wished to any clerical vacancy when it arose. He even managed to 'create' additional vacancies by forcing incumbents to resign where it could be shown that there had been some technical flaw in their original appointments. It is almost certain that he was acting illegally in many cases but nobody could successfully challenge his actions. Those who tried found that they lost more than they had bargained for.

Sometimes a preferment was used to reward one of his followers or the client of one of his supporters, but more often it was simply a matter of extracting the largest possible bribe from the person or institution that had the normal legal right to nominate to the post so that the appointment could be made as was desired. It was the Church courts' power to confer legality on wills by 'proving' them and to settle disputes over inheritances that provided Wolsey with his most profitable type of interference.

Heresy
Refusal to conform to the State religion.

Key term

He claimed that as *legatus a latere* he had the right to make all legal decisions relating to wills and inheritances, and he used all his other powers to make good his claim. Once he had overcome all opposition to his pretensions, he instituted what was in effect a ten per cent inheritance tax for his personal profit.

Wolsey's reputation for greed

Wolsey rapidly gained a well-deserved reputation as a rapacious enforcer of all his rights. He worked long hours and with a close attention to detail in order to maintain an encyclopaedic knowledge of what was happening throughout the country, and especially in the affairs of the nation's leading families. But he would have been unable to carry out his activities without a large band of informers and agents to provide him with evidence and to carry out his instructions. Although it is not possible to piece together a complete picture of his operations, enough information has survived for historians to be able to capture the flavour of what was happening. It is known, for instance, that rewards were paid to those who gave news of the impending death of any clerical postholder. This was vital information for Wolsey to have because his right to nominate to a position was only valid if it were implemented before the normal nominator had done so. He, therefore, needed to be the first to hear of any vacancy arising.

In the circumstances it is not surprising that a few informants exercised an imagination that was far too lively, and that some churchmen heard of their own deaths when they were still in what they considered to be the peak of health! But in all the collection of money and the extraction of favours, physical violence was never employed. It was not necessary. Wolsey controlled both of the country's legal systems and thus could always act within the law, as he interpreted it, whenever he wanted to exert pressure on those who were reluctant to act as he wished. And he was completely unscrupulous in his manipulation of the law, transferring cases from one court system to another as best suited his purposes, in complete defiance of past practices and existing conventions. In the process he generated huge amounts of impotent rage among those who suffered from his actions. Rarely has a public servant created so many enemies.

The maintenance of power

Key question
What was the nature of Wolsey's relationship with Henry VIII and the Pope?

Wolsey was a man who could not relax. He was incessantly active with seemingly no interests other than his work and the keeping up of appearances. All of his effort was concentrated on these two activities. Much of his time (several hours on most days) was devoted to building up and maintaining his power base, without which he would 'have been nothing'.

Wolsey and the king

Although he was rarely in the same place as the king, who spent a significant part of most years 'progressing' around the southern part of his kingdom, Henry featured, almost, in Wolsey's every thought. 'What should he be told and what should be hidden from him?' 'How could he best be persuaded to follow a particular line of policy?' 'What interpretation could be placed on his instructions so that they would not be in conflict with Wolsey's own wishes?' 'How could the influence of those who had close personal contact with him on a day-to-day basis be minimised?' 'How much could he get away with?'

Wolsey and the Pope

Similarly, concentrated thought needed to be given to his dealings with Rome at the times he was attempting to win a new concession for himself. But there the situation was more difficult. Not only was he attempting to influence people he did not know and whose individual quirks he could only guess at, but there was often a considerable time lag between one move in his campaign and a reaction to it. Several months could pass between the writing of a dispatch to Rome and the receipt of a reply upon which he could base decisions about his next move. It is no wonder that it sometimes took several years for even minimal progress to be made. But the need to consider Rome so carefully disappeared once the title of *legatus a latere* had been granted for life in 1524. Thereafter Wolsey normally treated his ecclesiastical superior with ill-disguised contempt, ignoring letters altogether, or dealing with them in a dilatory and partial manner – that is, until he once again needed papal support, this time to facilitate the annulment of Henry's marriage to Catherine of Aragon (see Chapter 4).

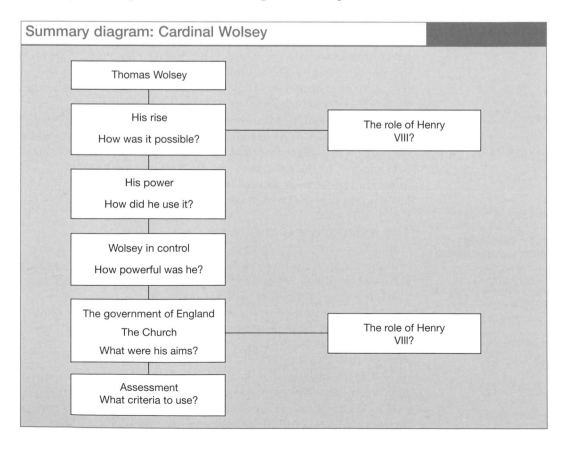

Summary diagram: Cardinal Wolsey

Thomas Wolsey

His rise
How was it possible?

The role of Henry VIII?

His power
How did he use it?

Wolsey in control
How powerful was he?

The government of England
The Church
What were his aims?

The role of Henry VIII?

Assessment
What criteria to use?

Key question
What kind of politician was Wolsey and how did he manage the government?

3 | Wolsey the Politician: Government

Introduction

Wolsey was Henry VIII's chief minister for 15 years and historians have been generally disappointed by how little he achieved in domestic affairs. The orthodox interpretation has been that he devoted most of his attention to foreign affairs, to establishing and maintaining his personal power and to increasing his income. The implication has been that he should have been reforming and modernising the way the realm was governed, as Thomas Cromwell was to do (see pages 154–60). But perhaps this expectation reveals an anachronistic attitude towards the purposes of government in early sixteenth-century England. Although leading **humanists** throughout western Europe were arguing the case for radical changes in both the aims and the methods of government, the vast majority of leading figures in public life expected very little of the royal government. They wished it to keep things much as they were (a widespread belief in 'progress' was still several centuries in the future), and to maintain law and order if it were threatened by major public disorders. But they did not wish it to interfere in the normal course of events more than was absolutely necessary. There was little contemporary disappointment that Wolsey did not do more.

Key question
What reforms of the legal system did Wolsey undertake?

Legal reforms

Yet, minimal as was Wolsey's input into improving the state of England, it would be incorrect to suggest that he contributed nothing. A case could be made that he seriously attempted to bring greater justice to the English legal system. The issue was the balance of influence between two systems of law.

Common law

The common law was the system that had enjoyed a dominant position in England since before the **Norman Conquest**. Civil (or equity) law was the system derived from the practices of the Roman Empire. It was in vogue in most of southern Europe, and was used in the courts in England that were based on the king's person (especially the king's council when it acted as a court of law).

Civil law

Civil law was much favoured by the forward-looking elements in English society because it placed an emphasis on natural justice in decision making, rather than on precedent (what had been done before), which was the basic approach of the common law. It was felt in advanced circles that, although the common law protected **litigants** from partiality on the part of the judges by forcing them to reveal the reasoning, based on past practice, for their judgements, it did lead to some unjust verdicts where the party in the wrong could win a case on a technicality.

Key terms

Humanists
Scholars who question the belief systems of the Church and who embrace free-thinking, culture and education.

Norman Conquest
Conquest of England after 1066 by Duke William of Normandy.

Litigants
People who take their disputes to court.

Head of the secular legal system

As lord chancellor, Wolsey was the head of the country's secular legal system and was directly responsible both for the legal work of the king's council and for the courts that had originated from it, such as **Star Chamber and Chancery**. He devoted a considerable amount of time and attention to this aspect of his responsibilities, hearing many cases himself and often taking care to make public the reasons for his decisions. However, it is clear that he was unscrupulous in using the system to further his own interests, especially by overturning common law decisions that adversely affected him and by using the law to harry those against whom he had a grudge.

The most frequently quoted example of this, although doubt has been cast on its authenticity, is his treatment of Sir Amyas Paulet. Sir Amyas had incurred his passionate hatred by treating him with contempt (including having him put in the stocks) when he entered his first benefice as an arrogant and overbearing young man who many thought deserved to be cut down to size. When, more than a decade later, Wolsey became lord chancellor, he was swift to exact a spiteful revenge. He summoned his enemy to appear before him, and kept him waiting in daily attendance for more than five years under threat of the confiscation of all his property for contempt of court if he left London without permission. Wolsey used him as a very public reminder of what would happen to those who caused him offence, and as living proof that his memory was as long as it needed to be.

Yet personal satisfaction was certainly not his only motive in his legal work. He seems genuinely to have desired to see justice better served in the land, both by advancing civil law at the expense of common law and by ensuring that the courts for which he was directly responsible were accessible to the poor and the weak. This group stood little chance of maintaining their rights against the rich and the strong in the common law courts, where the ability to pay large legal fees was normally an essential component of success. Thus he took pleasure in calling cases into one of his own courts when he learnt that a common law verdict had gone against what he considered to be natural justice, and he ensured that, especially in Star Chamber, cases in which restitution was being sought from the strong (except himself) were given an early hearing. He took most opportunities to try to convince the legal profession of the advantages of civil over common law. John Stow later commented that 'It was a strange matter to see, a man not trained up in the laws, to sit in the seat of judgement, to pronounce the law'. Given his lack of training in canon and civil law, it is perhaps significant that many historians believe that Wolsey's impact on the legal system constituted, in many ways, his most enduring achievement.

Self-interest

However, it must be admitted that Wolsey was much less determined in the pursuit of justice for all than he was in furthering his own interests and that his interventions in cases

Key term

Star Chamber and Chancery
Royal courts.

probably caused more chaos than they did good. He attempted no institutional changes that would have ensured that his approach was continued once he was no longer available to champion them, and he was quick to abandon his support of the weak whenever matters that affected him personally demanded his attention. Wolsey's modern biographer Peter Gwyn laid great stress on the action he took against those who enclosed common land for personal profit, but, on balance, the evidence suggests that his approach was piecemeal and that he showed no determination to tackle the issue as a whole.

The case in favour of Wolsey is also weakened by the alternative interpretations that can be put on many of his actions in this area. It can quite reasonably be maintained that his championing of the poor against the rich was merely a part of the vendetta against the nobility and gentry which he conducted against them as classes because he had so frequently been treated with contempt as a common and lowborn person by members of the social élites. It is perhaps significant that the one aspect of legal affairs that he conducted with consistent determination was the prosecution of members of the nobility for breaches of the laws against maintenance and affrays. Although this was a vital part of any policy of upholding law and order, it also smacked of a strong desire to get even with those who thought of themselves as being his social superiors.

Financial management

It has sometimes been suggested that Wolsey's attempts to reform the king's privy chamber show that he sought to make permanent improvements in the system of government he inherited. However, to suggest that Wolsey's interest in finance was confined to the king's household is unfair. In the opinion of John Guy, 'in the mainstream of finance Wolsey made a permanent contribution to government'. Guy believes that Wolsey invented a more efficient system: 'the Tudor Subsidy'.

Eltham Ordinances and the reform of the king's privy chamber

Key date

Elthan Ordinances: 1526

Particular attention has been paid to the Eltham Ordinances of 1526 which were aimed at regularising the chaotic finances of the privy chamber and which attempted to ensure more effective administration in the king's household. But a close examination of the circumstances leading up to the formulation of the ordinances, and of the way in which they were quickly allowed to lapse in all important respects, suggests that Wolsey's motives had little to do with more efficient administration and greater financial accountability.

His prime concern was to reduce the scope that others had for influencing the king, and to increase the control that he could exercise over all aspects of government. The drive for greater efficiency was seen by all concerned to be no more than a ruse designed to make it appear that another piece of power seeking was an initiative designed to further the public interest. Once

Wolsey had gained as much control as he could over the selection of the gentlemen who were to wait upon the king, the plans for an overhaul of the administrative procedures of the Privy Council were conveniently forgotten. Some historians argue that Wolsey had shown that his domestic policies went little further than attempting to extend or consolidate his own position. Arguably it has been suggested that any idea of public service was largely foreign to him.

The 'general proscription' and subsidy

In 1522 Wolsey organised a national survey, the so-called 'general proscription', to assess the population's taxable wealth. Armed with the information provided he was able to levy some £200,000 by two forced loans in 1522–3. But still more was needed, and it became apparent that adequate finance required a parliament. In April 1523 Wolsey sought a much larger grant from the Commons than ever before – a subsidy to be levied at the rate of 4s. in the pound on property as it had been reassessed a year earlier, to bring in perhaps £800,000. In reality it brought in around £300,000 so Wolsey sought to make up the shortfall by taxing the Church, which brought in nearly £250,000. It is to Wolsey's credit that for the first time since 1334 the Crown was raising more realistic taxation.

Key date

The general proscription: 1522

Relations with parliament

Wolsey has often been criticised for his attitude towards parliament. In particular he has been accused of attempting to dispense with its services altogether. This is an essentially accurate diagnosis of the situation, as during his period in power only two parliaments were summoned. This was in stark contrast to the situation in the generations to either side of him, when parliament met for at least a short session in many years. But Wolsey made no secret of his dislike of an institution which almost seemed to be designed to stir up trouble for the government, and whose members appeared never to understand that their prime function was to carry out the king's wishes.

After a bad experience in 1515, he only acted against his better judgement and allowed a parliament to be summoned in 1523 because it was obvious to him that there was no other way of raising the large sum of money that Henry needed to implement his forward policy in Europe. If he could have found some way of avoiding the necessity he would have done so, but his subsequent experience with the Amicable Grant (see page 59) confirmed that a vote from parliament was the only practical way of securing the additional funds required to pay for a large army.

Key question
How well did Wolsey manage parliament?

Relations with the nobility

Wolsey knew that control of the nobility was essential for efficient and effective government. The Crown depended on the authority they possessed and Wolsey made it his duty to ensure that noble power, particularly in the localities, was used in the service of the king. Under Henry VII the nobility had been strictly controlled,

Key question
How well did Wolsey get on with the nobility?

but this had been relaxed in the period following his death. Wolsey's first use of his authority as chancellor was therefore to announce a stricter monitoring of noble behaviour.

In 1516 Wolsey attended a meeting of Star Chamber in which he took the opportunity to announce what he termed the new law of Star Chamber. This stated that those responsible for administering justice and governing the localities, be they nobleman or gentleman, should not see themselves as being above the law. And as if to emphasise the point, on that same day the Earl of Northumberland was summoned into court for contempt of the council's jurisdiction and was subsequently committed to **Fleet Prison**. Wolsey was making plain his intention to develop a system of centralised royal authority.

This led some to question Wolsey's motives while others accused him of being a tyrant protected only by the trust and influence of the king. There is some truth in these charges, for example, when Thomas Lucas, formerly Henry VII's solicitor-general, slandered the chancellor he was sent to the Tower without trial. The chancellor incurred the wrath of the Dukes of Norfolk and Suffolk by bypassing the former after he became treasurer in 1522 and in criticising the latter's command of the French expedition of 1523. Indeed, there is evidence to show that Wolsey also attempted to interfere in the marriage arrangements of the aristocracy, something they bitterly resented. Amid simmering noble discontent shadowy rumours of a plot against Wolsey circulated. The most spectacular clash between Wolsey and a nobleman was that involving the Duke of Buckingham. According to Sybil M. Jack, Buckingham was no friend to Wolsey and:

> The duke's royal blood, touchy personality, and penchant for wild talk were all likely to bring him under suspicion, even before it emerged that he had been speculating about what might happen should the king die.

The duke was warned to conduct himself more discreetly, but he failed to do so. Buckingham was summoned to London in April 1521, charged and convicted of treason, and executed the following month. Foreign ambassadors reported that Buckingham lost his head because he 'murmured against the chancellor's doings'.

On the other hand, there is no clear evidence that Wolsey, any more than the king, was hostile to the nobility. In fact, the Earl of Worcester considered the chancellor to be a good friend. In general terms Wolsey's policy towards the powerful can be described as one of offering carrots as well as sticks. By holding out the prospect of desirable appointments he hoped to encourage them to become his clients. In the final analysis, the fact remains that as long as Wolsey had the king's backing most nobles worked well enough with him, and some of them accepted his authority.

Key term

Fleet Prison
A prison in London used by the Crown to imprison criminal gentry and nobles.

4 | Wolsey the Diplomat: Foreign Policy

Introduction

For much of the last century and a half during which researchers have been studying the history of early Tudor England, it has been assumed that the foreign policy of the 15 years following 1514 was Wolsey's. Accounts have been written almost as if, during these years, Henry VIII only existed to rubber stamp the decisions made by his minister.

However, this view has been challenged in recent decades as the interplay between the two men has been more clearly revealed by further research. But no definitive picture has so far emerged. While it is apparent that Wolsey made most decisions on a day-to-day basis and occasionally took major initiatives without the prior agreement, or even knowledge, of his master, it is equally certain that Henry intervened decisively at times to redirect events as he wished them to go.

Additional complications are presented by the fact that, in order to maintain the confidence of the king, Wolsey had at least to appear to be implementing Henry's policies, even if he was in practice pursuing objectives of his own. Very little evidence of the contacts between the king and his minister survives. This is because many of the important exchanges between Henry and Wolsey were by word of mouth, either direct or via a trusted third party.

To make the situation even more difficult for historians, much of the surviving documentary evidence is in the form of letters that were originally written to deceive, and are therefore unreliable as pointers to aims or motives. Therefore it is not surprising that it cannot be established beyond reasonable doubt whether Wolsey was manipulating Henry, or whether he was essentially carrying out the king's wishes. The most that can safely be maintained is that Henry played a more significant role in the formulation and conduct of 'Wolsey's foreign policy' than has traditionally been suggested.

Interpreting Wolsey's foreign policy

Orthodox interpretation: maintaining the balance of power

It has been customary for writers on Wolsey's foreign policy to present an analysis that revolves around the consistent pursuit of a coherent aim or strategy. Up to the time of the First World War the orthodox interpretation was that Wolsey sought to 'maintain the balance of power', which, surprisingly enough, was the way in which contemporary British foreign policy was viewed at the time! It was argued that this aim was pursued in order to preserve some influence for England in foreign affairs, by ensuring that no one person (Charles, Holy Roman Emperor and King of Spain or Francis, King of France) attained such dominance that he could arrange matters without taking into account the interests of other states, such as England. The claim was that Wolsey followed this policy by threatening to give his support to whichever side seemed likely to be worsted by the other. It was maintained that

Key question
How effective was Wolsey's foreign policy?

Key question
How and why have historians disagreed over Wolsey's aims and methods in foreign policy?

this policy was generally successful in ensuring that England's international status remained high.

New orthodoxy: slavish follower of papal policy

This interpretation became discredited when Pollard, writing in the 1920s, established a new orthodoxy that was to survive for 40 years. His contention was that Wolsey was a slavish follower of papal policy, changing England's stance whenever he was asked to do so by the Pope. His motives were said to be a mixture of principle and self-interest. It was claimed that, as the Pope's representative in England, Wolsey believed that it was his duty to do as his spiritual master directed, even at the expense of frustrating the wishes of his king, and that he had a vested interest in doing so because he aspired to be elected Pope at some stage.

Revisionist interpretation: the main aim and preferred method

In the 1960s J.J. Scarisbrick demolished this interpretation by showing that Wolsey ignored papal instructions as frequently as he followed them, and by casting serious doubt on the genuineness of Wolsey's ambition to become Pope. He argued that Wolsey's support of papal diplomatic initiatives was largely coincidental and happened merely because England and the Papacy shared common interests from time to time. Scarisbrick went on to establish a new 'revisionist' interpretation based on the existence of a main aim and a preferred method:

- The aim was the establishment and maintenance of peace.
- The method was a variant of the old 'balance of power' interpretation.

This he established by turning the old argument on its head and claiming that Wolsey sought to achieve an 'unbalance of power' – that he tried always to join the stronger side so that it would create a sufficient imbalance for the other side to realise that fighting was pointless. He claimed that this policy has not been more apparent to observers because Wolsey was not very good at implementing it and frequently made mistakes, which he attempted to justify by pretending that his aims and methods were other than they had been.

Current thinking

In many ways it is a healthy sign that the Scarisbrick interpretation has not been replaced by an alternative straightforward explanation. This is perhaps because it has become more and more apparent that no coherent pattern ever existed in Wolsey's approach to diplomacy. It is now widely accepted that, although there were threads that ran through numbers of incidents, there was no single guiding principle that directed his actions throughout his 15 years in power. At differing times he was motivated by selfish considerations, especially a desire to obtain more extensive or longer-lasting delegated powers from the Pope, by the need to satisfy the expectations of Henry VIII, by a wish to further what he considered to be national or papal interests, and by an altruistic inclination to benefit mankind by inaugurating an era of peace. It is possible to detect many or all of these motives in each of the decisions he made. However, the evidence is not full enough for it to be possible to make judgements about the relative importance of these motives in any but highly speculative terms.

Diplomatic apprenticeship

Wolsey's first and arguably most important role in Henry's service lay in diplomacy. However, before he could reach the dizzy heights of becoming the king's leading diplomatic adviser Wolsey had first to serve his apprenticeship. When England, in alliance with Spain, Venice and the Pope, Julius II, went to war with France in 1512 Wolsey gained his first experience of the duties and pitfalls involved in organising, financing, transporting and feeding an army. Although a junior member of the royal council, Wolsey was blamed by many for the shambles that developed after the army landed in France, forcing the abandonment of the enterprise. Fortunately for Wolsey the king did not made him a scapegoat for England's military failure, in fact, the manner in which he had conducted himself in correspondence with Ferdinand of Aragon (Henry VIII's father-in-law) greatly impressed Henry.

In 1513, following a shuffling of alliances, England sent another large army to France with Henry himself in command. Wolsey, taking on the role of a **quartermaster-general** rather than as a war minister, was called on to manage the preparations. The success of the expedition, a French force was defeated near Thérouanne followed by the capture of that town and Tournai, enhanced Henry's reputation as a warrior and Wolsey's as a master organiser. By putting himself at the heart of royal affairs, Wolsey was given the opportunity to participate in the conduct of the king's business. His success was such that the queen and others in England were now routinely writing to him. The king's growing trust in Wolsey enabled the latter to shape English diplomacy, the guiding principle of which was to ensure that England, the least important of the three great western monarchies, was not left isolated against a **Valois–Habsburg** alliance.

When, in 1514, Louis XII of France became a widower, Wolsey seized the opportunity to propose a Valois–Tudor alliance to be sealed by the offer in marriage of Mary, sister of Henry VIII. With Henry's willing consent, the marriage went ahead and the ensuing treaty gave Wolsey's grateful master an annuity of 100,000 crowns and confirmed English possession of Tournai. Although the treaty was short-lived (the death of Louis early in 1515 put Francis I on the French throne), the success of the negotiations had enabled Wolsey to cement his place as the king's chief diplomat.

Key question
How and where did Wolsey learn the art of diplomacy?

Key terms

Quartermaster-general
The person responsible for feeding, arming and generally supplying the army.

Valois–Habsburg
Names of the French (Valois) and Austrian (Habsburg) royal families.

Key question
Does Wolsey deserve to be regarded as a peacemaker?

Key dates

Treaty of London: 1518

Field of Cloth of Gold: 1520

Wolsey the peacemaker

In October 1518 the Treaty of London (also known as the treaty of Universal Peace) was inaugurated, with England and France as the first signatories. Within a few months it had been adhered to by many other states, including Spain and the Papacy. At the time it was thought to be a triumph for Wolsey and to have reflected considerable glory on Henry VIII. It was truly a 'grandiose scheme', intended to bind the 20 leading states of Europe to perpetual peace with one another. The plan was for all those states with an active foreign policy not only to commit themselves to non-aggression but to promise to make war on any ruler who contravened the treaty, thus making it impossible for any state to benefit from attacking another. The publicly quoted aspiration was for the treaty to bring an end to warfare between the Christian states of Europe. Wolsey delivered an oration in praise of peace that was much acclaimed.

Historians have generally viewed this initiative as yet another example of Wolsey's cynical self-interest. There is much evidence to support this interpretation. Although there is incontrovertible documentary evidence that he had been working on his grand design before the Pope took a similar initiative – the papal plan was for a five-year truce between the powers during which a crusade against the Turks would take place – the public perception was that Wolsey was working to implement the Pope's wishes. It was important to Wolsey that this should be so because he was using the fact that he was acting as the Pope's representative to win for himself the status of *legatus a latere* (see page 41) that he so much desired.

It has even been claimed that this was his primary motivation in the affair. Others have maintained that he was merely seeking to satisfy his sense of his own importance by being seen to be the peacemaker of Europe, and to be treated as such during the extensive public celebrations that accompanied the unveiling of the treaty. Few have been prepared to admit that there may have been a serious intention behind Wolsey's actions. But if there was not, he was guilty of sacrificing national interests for personal gain, for the price paid for French adherence to the treaty was:

- the return of Tournai (admittedly at a very fair price, some 600,000 gold crowns)
- the promise (easily revoked) that Mary, at the time Henry's only surviving child, would be married to the King of France's eldest son in due course
- the inclusion of Scotland in the peace on condition that she abstain from hostilities (easily ignored).

The Field of Cloth of Gold

Over the next two years Wolsey worked to build on the foundations that had been laid by the Treaty of London. His efforts were generously rewarded in 1520 when Henry and Francis met at the Field of Cloth of Gold, near to the border between the two monarchs' possessions outside Calais. The meeting was one of the most spectacular events in modern European history. It lasted for a fortnight and was participated in by a large portion of the senior ruling élites of the two countries. In fact, the representation was so complete (about 3000 from each side) that very few people of national importance were left behind in England to manage affairs during their colleagues' absence.

The two kings vied strenuously with each other in order to create as splendid an impression as possible. No expense was spared in providing the most sumptuous of feasts ('a gastronomic marathon') and entertainments (with daily jousting meticulously carried out according to the medieval rules of chivalry still accepted in both countries at the time), the most richly decorated costumes for the participants, and the most elaborate of settings.

The French prepared a village of richly decorated tents and pavilions to accommodate their party. Its cost was enormous – roughly equivalent to one year of Henry VIII's normal income – and its preparation was a triumph of planning and organisation. Western Europe had to be scoured to locate the huge quantities of luxury materials required. For example, the accounts showed that 72,544 *fleurs de lis* of gold thread mounted on blue velvet were purchased to decorate the walls of the royal pavilions. Unfortunately, much of the effort was wasted as high winds and heavy rain meant that most of the erections had to be dismantled within a few days of their completion. The English effort was much more successful. Its centrepiece was a temporary palace to accommodate the king and a handful of his leading courtiers – the rest of the party lodged in discomfort in a 'settlement' of about 800 tents. The palace was considered to be one of the wonders of the age, such was the splendour of its design and decoration (see the illustration on page 76), and it drew sightseers from far and wide. This was partly, no doubt, because of the two fountains at its entrance which constantly dispensed free wine to all and sundry. The total edifice had taken many hundreds of workmen several months to construct.

Significance of the Field of Cloth of Gold

However, it seems that the meeting achieved nothing of lasting significance. If it was intended to cement Anglo-French amity it patently failed. The members of the English party whose views are known all seem to have been confirmed in their anti-French prejudices rather than having had them removed or weakened. And no agreements of any importance were reached during the fortnight's celebrations. In fact, it seems that Henry and Francis viewed the occasion as no more than an opportunity to impress others of their wealth and international standing. Certainly the Field of Cloth of Gold did nothing to advance the cause of general peace. If anything, it created problems for Wolsey in convincing the rest of Europe that England was not taking sides in the already developing struggle for supremacy between Francis I and Charles V.

Meetings between Henry and Charles were arranged to take place both before and after the Field of Cloth of Gold so that the clear message could be given that there was no English partiality towards France. The fact that these meetings were necessary substantiates the view that the extravaganza in France was essentially a public relations exercise, rather than being a contribution to the cause of general European peace. It is significant that Henry was most grateful to Wolsey for making it appear to the world that he was the equal of the two 'super power' rulers of Europe (no mention of peace making), and that the events of 1520 further confirmed Wolsey in the favour of his monarch. It is impossible to establish the extent to which this factor loomed large in Wolsey's thinking.

The Habsburg–Valois conflict

Key question
What part did Wolsey play in the Habsburg–Valois conflict?

When Charles was elected Holy Roman Emperor in 1519 he added the Emperor's quarrel with the Kings of France over Milan (in north-western Italy) to his existing inheritance of Franco-Burgundian and Franco-Spanish rivalries. Therefore, especially given the aggressive personality of Francis I, it is not surprising that a simmering Habsburg–Valois conflict provided the backcloth to western European international relations for the following decades (in fact until 1559). This situation presented Henry VIII and Wolsey with both continuous opportunities and frequent challenges. Given the strategic position that England enjoyed, being able either to disrupt Charles's communications between Spain and the Netherlands or to open a new front in any attack on France, her favours were certain to be in great demand from the two major powers.

Tudor–Habsburg alliance

It was not long before Wolsey was called on to pay some of the price for his triumph of the Treaty of London. Francis I had been happy enough to receive his reward for agreeing to join the Cardinal's 'grand design' but he had no intention of being constrained by its terms or conditions. He was determined to strengthen his position in northern Italy by military action against Charles and his supporters, and he did not expect the arrangements made in the Treaty of London to be invoked against him. After all, it would be in none of the non-belligerents' interests to do so.

Key date
Wolsey met Charles V in Bruges: 1521

As expected, however, Charles called upon England and others to come to his assistance to halt the aggressor. In August 1521 Wolsey travelled in great pomp to Bruges in the Netherlands in order to meet with Charles on the action to be taken. Once again, promises of future support were easily made, especially as it was hoped that a change in the situation would make it unnecessary to fulfil any obligations. The agreement made with Charles was that an English army would invade France unless Francis agreed to make peace. It has frequently been claimed that Wolsey's expectation was that the mere threat of English action would be sufficient to persuade France to make terms. However, it is unlikely that Wolsey was so naïve. He had so much experience of

Francis's stubbornness that he must have realised that a threat was likely to be insufficient. It is much more probable that he gambled on the war being resolved one way or the other before he ran out of delaying tactics for English action. In the meantime, he was more than satisfied with the kudos that his meeting with Charles had brought him.

War with France

In the event, Wolsey was unable to prevent the Emperor's friends from persuading Henry VIII that England must take some military action once Francis chose to ignore the warnings he had been given. But he was not as unhappy with the situation as he might have been, because it seemed that a dramatic defeat of the French was in prospect. Charles had managed to secure the support of the Duke of Bourbon, one of the foremost French magnates, who was so discontented with the way in which he had been treated by Francis that he was prepared to risk all in an act of open treachery. It was thought that he would be able to carry a significant portion of the French nobility into rebellion with him. So, although half of the campaigning season was already over, an English army was sent to France at short notice in August 1523.

But as so often happened in the sixteenth century, military action proved to be much less decisive than its authors had expected. Bourbon turned out to be a complete disappointment. He only managed to generate minimal support for his cause within France and he soon became, in effect, an armed exile who, despite English money and imperial patronage, was unable to establish himself as a significant factor in the conflict. Thus, even if the English prong of the triple thrust on Paris had not become bogged down in the mud of winter, the allied plan to co-ordinate their forces in a knockout blow on the French capital would have been hamstrung by the failure of Bourbon's army to play its part. As a result, Wolsey's and Henry's passing enthusiasm for armed intervention evaporated, and Wolsey was allowed to implement his original strategy of stalling Charles's demands for action while he secretly attempted to negotiate a general peace with the French.

Pavia and the defeat of France

But luck did not favour Wolsey. In February 1525 Charles secured the decisive victory that Wolsey had estimated to be so unlikely. In a battle that took place outside the walls of Pavia, in northern Italy, the unthinkable happened. Not only was the French army totally destroyed as an effective fighting force, but Francis I and most of his leading supporters were captured. This placed Charles in an overwhelmingly dominant position. Henry VIII was not slow to seek advantage of the situation. He realised that here was a rare opportunity to fulfil his intermittently held dream of securing the French crown for himself. A proposal was rapidly prepared for submission to the Emperor whereby France would be dismembered, with Charles and Bourbon receiving the parts to which they could reasonably lay claim, and Henry taking the remainder along with the title of King of France.

But little except wishful thinking could have been behind this plan. Although Henry promised to fight alongside him in future as his faithful ally, there was little to commend the proposal to Charles. There was nothing that Henry could really do to hurt him, so there was no need to buy his support by allowing him any of his demands. Certainly there was no point in exchanging one powerful and ambitious King of France for another, and one who controlled extensive territories on both sides of the Channel. Charles judged that the greatest advantage was to be gained by leaving France chastened but not too aggrieved, and therefore not feeling compelled to seek a swift revenge. But sound as this strategy was, it was impossible to implement. Although Francis was forced to swear the most binding of oaths concerning his future conduct, and had to provide his own sons as hostages against his further misbehaviour, he was prepared to launch fresh attacks on Charles within a year of his release. In the meantime he had been freed from his oaths by the Pope on the grounds that they had been extorted under duress, and he had correctly guessed that Charles would not be prepared to risk international odium by harming his hostages.

The 'Amicable Grant' and the League of Cognac

At first Henry and Wolsey could do little but rage impotently. Henry did have hopes of launching an attack on France while she was leaderless, but he was forced to abandon these when he was unable to raise the necessary finance. It has been suggested that Wolsey was less than enthusiastic about this venture, as shown by his lack of determination in making a success of the nationwide 'Amicable Grant' of 1525 which was to have provided the money for it. But the evidence is by no means conclusive.

However, Wolsey was certainly diligent in encouraging the formation of an anti-imperial alliance (the League of Cognac) in northern Italy in 1526, with which France could associate in her efforts to reverse the verdict of Pavia. He was also prepared to sign an alliance with France the next year, threatening Charles with English intervention if he did not make a satisfactory peace with his opponents. This resulted in an English declaration of war on Charles in 1528, but it was little more than a gesture. No English army was put into the field and a separate agreement was made to ensure that London's trade with the Netherlands was not interrupted.

It was therefore not surprising that England was only included at the last minute in the Treaty of Cambrai, negotiated between Francis and Charles in 1529 to bring the fighting to an end. If Wolsey had not engineered an English presence in the final stages of the negotiations, it would have been even clearer than it already was that Henry VIII was no longer being treated as an equal by the King of France and the Holy Roman Emperor. Thus Wolsey's final piece of major diplomacy before his fall in October 1529 was no more than a face-saving exercise for an increasingly unappreciative master.

Wolsey and the papal tiara

Key question
Was Wolsey seriously
interested in securing
the Papacy?

Pollard's contention that Wolsey seriously aspired to be elected to the papal throne was based on considerable evidence. It is certain that at times during the electoral processes following the deaths of Leo X in 1521 and of his successor, Adrian VI, in 1523, Wolsey confidently expected to be the successful candidate. He had good reason for his optimism. Not only had Charles V promised to lend his weight to Wolsey's cause, but the news from Rome was of a large amount of positive support among the electoral body of cardinals. But, in the event, it transpired that Wolsey had been misled. In the first election Charles pressed for an alternative candidate (his ex-tutor, who was actually elected), and in the second election he purposely failed to make his wishes known in time. What is more, the cardinals who had appeared to be so strongly in Wolsey's support, turned out to have been doing no more than angling for financial inducements. Thus there was never any realistic possibility that Wolsey would be chosen as Pope.

It now appears that Wolsey generally accepted that this was the case, and only made genuine attempts to secure his own election during the moments when the evidence available to him suggested that he was wrong and that his prospects really were good. For the rest of the time he was probably only humouring those who wished to advance his cause. Evidence that was unknown to Pollard suggests that the initial proposal for Wolsey's candidature came from Charles V, who was probably attempting to create in Henry VIII a 'want' that he would then be able to help satisfy in return for some other favour. Certainly he was not slow to point out to Henry that his international reputation would be greatly enhanced if his chief minister were to be elected Pope, and Henry seems to have taken the bait because it was often only to satisfy him that Wolsey went through the motions of advancing his own candidature.

Although it can never be known for certain, it seems very likely that Wolsey rarely made serious attempts to forward his own papal cause. The major evidence to support this view is provided by a consideration of his long-term dealings with the Papacy. If his aim was to persuade cardinals to vote for him in a future election, he went about it in an atypically ineffectual manner. On numerous occasions he gratuitously insulted the Pope and his advisers, either by failing to answer urgent communications from them, or by constructing replies that were intended to 'score points' rather than to win friends. Wolsey was a skilled politician who would not have made such basic mistakes had his aim been as Pollard claimed.

One strand of Pollard's argument was the evidence of Wolsey's attempts to win support during the electoral periods. He backed this up with a general contention that the thread running through Wolsey's actions in foreign affairs was his desire to curry favour in Rome. This interpretation has long been discredited by later research. This has shown that some of Pollard's conclusions were inaccurate even based on the evidence he used. In addition, other evidence proves that Wolsey acted in opposition to papal policy almost as often as he supported it. It can now be safely concluded that Wolsey had no long-term aim of becoming Pope, and that his short-term enthusiasms for wearing the 'papal tiara' were flights of fancy based on inaccurate information. These were rapidly jettisoned once the reality of the situation became known to him.

Assessment

Most historians have been highly critical of Henry VIII's and Wolsey's foreign policies in the period 1509 to 1529. But there has been little consistency in the nature of these criticisms. England's dealings with her neighbours during these years have been variously described as misdirected, muddled, costly failures, naïve, and shameful. Although some of these judgements tell us more about the values and assumptions of those who made them than they do about the issue under consideration, there is no escaping the fact that whatever criteria for assessment have been chosen the resulting conclusions have rarely been complimentary to either the king or his leading minister.

The least controversial sets of criteria for judgement used by historians tend to be those which concentrate on the extent to which a person managed to achieve his or her aims and objectives. However, it is rare for any writer carrying out an assessment to be satisfied with such a limited range of criteria. It is very normal for the aims and objectives themselves to be held up for scrutiny, and for comment to be made on their appropriateness as well as on their practicality. It is, of course, the issue of appropriateness that gives rise to most subjectivity on the part of commentators. As objectivity has been at the centre of the code of professionalism aspired to by British historians in the twentieth century, this has generally been frowned upon by most of those who have researched English history during the last 100 years. But it must be remembered that in many societies the writing of objective history is not acceptable, and that any account of the past that does not reflect the prevailing value system is highly suspect. However, all students of history in a 'free' society are likely to be encouraged to construct their own set of criteria for making judgements about the past, and should be suspicious of those handed down to them by others.

Thus the first task in making an assessment of England's foreign relations during the first half of Henry VIII's reign is to identify the criteria to be used. It seems safe to assume that most people will wish to include 'degree of success' in their assessment, and that this will be measured against Henry's and Wolsey's aspirations. If this is the case, there is probably room for a less critical conclusion to be reached than has often been drawn in the past. Although there were some obvious large-scale failures, especially between 1525 and 1529, there were many occasions on which both Henry and Wolsey had good reason to think that they had been very successful. After the campaign of 1513 Henry knew that he was internationally regarded as a figure of splendid chivalric kingship and his certainty was increased by events such as those at the Field of Cloth of Gold in 1520. Wolsey was equally successful in creating an outstanding reputation and status for himself (especially in being made *legatus a latere* for life in 1524) which meant that he was treated as being virtually on a par with the leading rulers of Europe. These were no mean achievements to set against the periodic frustrations that beset both men's diplomatic ventures and which became increasingly frequent in the latter stages of their partnership.

5 | The King's Great Matter

Introduction

During the first three-quarters of the twentieth century generations of British school children were taught that the Reformation in England took place largely because Henry VIII wished to obtain a divorce from his first wife (Catherine of Aragon) so that he could marry his second (Anne Boleyn). The 'historical truth' that students learnt was that Henry fell uncontrollably in love with Anne Boleyn soon after he learnt that Catherine of Aragon would no longer be able to bear him children, and would therefore not be able to provide him with the son he so fervently desired. Because Anne Boleyn refused to accept the king's sexual advances until they were married, which drove him almost to distraction, and because Henry was astute enough to recognise that, in any case, a son born to Anne out of wedlock would at best have a contested claim to succeed him, divorce became an urgent necessity.

However, only the Pope could dissolve marriages and he remained stubbornly unwilling to do so in Henry and Catherine's case, despite years of threats and browbeating from England. In the end the only way in which Henry could get what he wanted was to take over the Pope's powers within his own kingdom and arrange the divorce for himself. This he did and the Reformation took place (in essence the establishment of an independent Church of England) as an unintended side effect of political and personal necessity. Thus historians used to be in no doubt that the years 1533–47 were a vital part of the English Reformation.

The majority of the 'top-down' school of historians (notably Professor Scarisbrick) have reached somewhat similar conclusions after carrying out exhaustive research of the type that was beyond the scope of their nineteenth-century predecessors who had established the schoolbook orthodoxy. Naturally there have been significant refinements and changes of emphasis made to the old orthodoxy, but in its essentials it has remained intact. In particular, the central idea continues to be that the engine driving England towards its Reformation was political rather than religious.

The marriage question

Despite the efforts of many researchers, it has proved impossible to locate reliable evidence about the timing of Henry's decision to attempt to bring his marriage to Catherine of Aragon to an end.

> **Key question**
> What was the king's great matter and what part did Wolsey play in it?

> **Key question**
> Why did Henry want a divorce?

It must now be accepted that the best historians can aspire to is to identify the period (rather than the exact date) that is the most likely one, given the circumstantial evidence that exists. It is probable that the king made up his mind later than has often been suggested.

Rumours of divorce

Rumours that Henry intended to divorce his wife circulated from time to time in the years before 1520, but no serious historian has treated them as more than diplomatic gossip that probably arose from comments made in moments of passing anger or disappointment at the failure of a pregnancy or the death of a baby. However, a number of writers have chosen to speculate that the firm intention to divorce was formed in 1524 or 1525, once Henry's medical advisers had informed him that the queen was unlikely to conceive again. This is not a totally implausible theory – certainly there is evidence that Henry was contemplating the possibility of divorce and remarriage as one of the options open to him in his quest for a male heir – but it is not the most likely scenario. The circumstantial evidence that weakens it most is that during this period Henry was seemingly grooming his illegitimate son (born in 1519), whom he had created the Duke of Richmond and made the premier peer of the realm, to fill the role of heir-apparent. In these circumstances it is likely that the need to find a new wife would have been low on his list of priorities.

Desire for Anne Boleyn and doubts over his marriage to Catherine

Most convincing – but by no means certain – is the suggestion that the king made up his mind at some time during 1527. It was then that it seems ('seems' because the evidence is by no means conclusive) he became besotted with Anne Boleyn, one of the young ladies at court and about 15 years his junior. Anne let him know that the attraction was mutual but that she would not become his sexual partner until she was also his wife. It took Henry some time to become convinced that this stance was more than courtly coyness and that the object of his desire intended to maintain her 'virtue' in the face of all the pressure that an English king could bring to bear on any female subject. It is probable that once the reality of the situation became clear to him and he also became aware that his infatuation was growing rather than diminishing, his mind turned increasingly to the doubts he had felt for some time about the validity of his marriage to Catherine.

These doubts revolved around a text from the Old Testament of the Bible (Leviticus chapter 20 verse 16) which read:

> If a man shall take his brother's wife, it is an impurity: he hath uncovered his brother's nakedness; they shall be childless.

Henry was a quite accomplished amateur biblical scholar. This is apparent from the work he did on the book attacking the early teachings of Martin Luther which had been published in his name in 1521, and for which the Pope had awarded him the title of 'Defender of the Faith'. Therefore he would have been well able to recognise the force of the argument presented to him by one of his advisers (we do not know which or when, although Catherine was sure that it was Wolsey) that his lack of surviving legitimate male children was God's punishment for marrying in defiance of divine law. This was because Catherine had previously been married to Henry's elder brother Arthur, whose early death had made her a widow after five months of adolescent married life.

It seems reasonable to surmise from what we know of Henry that his desire for Anne Boleyn led him speedily to convince himself that his marriage was against God's explicit commandment. Certainly, throughout his life he was regularly able to make himself genuinely believe that whatever he wanted to do was morally defensible. Thus the most plausible explanation of his decision to free himself of Catherine of Aragon, probably in 1527, appears to be lust justified by the moral certainty that he was currently living in sin and was therefore in danger of eternal damnation.

Pope awarded Henry VIII the title of 'Defender of the Faith': 1521

Henry instructed Wolsey to explore with the Pope the possibility of obtaining a divorce: 1527

Key dates

Settling his conscience: Henry's moral stance

Although most people, at the time and subsequently, have found it difficult to take Henry's moral stance seriously, those with a deep understanding of the king's personality have generally concluded that his scruples were genuine. This view is substantiated by the lengths to which he went to convince others that he meant what he said and that he was not merely making a propaganda point. Edward Hall recorded that in November 1528 the king:

> assembled at his palace of Bridewell [in London] his nobility, judges and counsellors, with various other persons, to whom he declared the great worthiness of his wife, both for her nobility and virtue and all princely qualities, to be such that if he were to marry again he would marry her of all women, if the marriage were found to be good and lawful.

But, despite her worthiness and the fact that he had a 'fair daughter by her', he said that he was 'wonderfully tormented in his conscience', for he 'understood from many great clerks whom he had consulted, that he had lived all this time in detestable and abominable adultery'. Therefore to settle his 'conscience, and the sure and firm succession of the realm … he said that if by the law of God she should be judged to be his lawful wife, nothing would be more pleasant and acceptable to him in his whole life'.

Decision to divorce

Once the decision had been made to seek a divorce, Henry must have thought that the action to be taken was straightforward and that success was guaranteed. It is probable that he shared his determination to separate himself from his queen in conversation with Wolsey at an early stage, and that his leading minister assured him that there would be no difficulty in meeting his requirements. What was needed was for the Pope to declare that the original papal dispensation allowing the marriage to take place was invalid, thus ruling that Henry and Catherine had never legally been man and wife and that the supposed marriage was annulled.

Wolsey was confident that such an outcome would be speedily achieved. After all, such annulments were relatively commonplace (the Duke of Suffolk had required one to legalise his marriage to Henry's sister, Mary), and the Pope had every reason to please the ruler of a country whose support he often sought in his diplomatic manoeuvrings. In addition, Wolsey was one of the most influential men in the Church and was owed favours by many of those who advised the Pope on matters of policy.

Key question
What steps did Henry VIII take to obtain a divorce?

Persuading Rome: the campaign to obtain an annulment

However, things did not go at all as planned. The attempt to persuade Rome to grant the annulment 'on the nod' was met by obvious stalling tactics, particularly the reference of key issues to groups of advisers who were clearly expected to take their time in formulating any recommendations. As the months passed by and nothing seemed to be happening, Henry's frustration, fanned by Anne Boleyn and her political allies, showed itself in heated outbursts to Wolsey and in demands for more forceful action to be taken. And so, what had been expected to be a matter of a little behind-the-scenes 'fixing' was turned into a very public confrontation between Henry and the Papacy.

In these circumstances Wolsey attempted to work on three fronts at once, expecting that one of them at least would be successful. He could hardly have done more. Two of the approaches required Rome to make the decision Henry wanted.

The first approach

The first involved persuading the Pope, both by reason and by exerting diplomatic pressure, that the original dispensation carried no force because popes had no right to set aside divine law, as the prohibition contained in Leviticus was claimed to be. Logical as this strategy might have seemed, it was politically very inept. No pope was ever likely to admit publicly that one of his recent predecessors had exceeded his powers. To make matters worse, theologians were very divided over many of the issues raised by the case. Not only were there divisions of opinion over whether the law laid down in Leviticus was open to papal dispensation, but there was even widespread disagreement over what the biblical instruction actually meant. There were many who argued that the intention was that a man should not marry his brother's wife while his brother was still living, but that once he was dead the prohibition lapsed. This line of argument appeared to be supported by an Old Testament text from the book of Deuteronomy which instructed that a man should marry his brother's widow if she was childless and should have children by her on his brother's behalf.

The sensible approach might have been to abandon this line of attack once it had ceased to be clearcut. But Henry dug in his heels. He was certain that his theological interpretation was correct and he was determined that the world should see that it was so. In order to achieve this, numbers of leading theologians were paid large sums of money to write treatises supporting the 'English' view. But this did not suffice. An equally powerful sequence of books supporting the opposite point of view soon appeared. And it is generally judged that those who opposed Henry's interpretation – including Bishop Fisher of Rochester who made himself Catherine's leading defender and who published seven books arguing his case – came off best in the dispute. This first approach, supported by a number of fairly clumsy diplomatic initiatives, yielded at best inconclusive results. What was worse, it ensured that the case gained such a high international profile that it became almost impossible for the Papacy to give way without a huge loss of face.

The second approach

The second approach initially appeared more promising because it involved no challenge to the powers of the Papacy. It was to object to the dispensation on technical grounds, by arguing that it was invalid – and that thus the marriage also was – because it was incorrectly worded. This line of argument seemed more likely to find favour in the Curia (the Papacy's administrative centre) because its acceptance would involve no more than an admission that a clerical error had been made.

However, Catherine of Aragon, who had been aware from the beginning what was happening, had no intention of allowing her marriage to be annulled if she could possibly help it. Her supporters and agents were soon busily at work and were fortunate enough to locate a slightly differently worded version of the dispensation among the royal papers in Spain. What is more, this newly discovered version satisfied the criteria which the copy held in England was argued not to. Much delay, and further frustration, was caused by Charles V (in his capacity as ruler of the Spanish kingdoms) refusing to allow the Spanish version to leave the country. Consequently, the second approach gradually lost its momentum.

The third approach

Wolsey's third strategy was to attempt to persuade the Pope to allow the case to be decided in England. His real hope was that the decision would be delegated to the Pope's representative on the spot – Wolsey himself. It was thought that the Pope might favour such a solution as it would remove from him any personal involvement in the decision reached. On several occasions, when letters were received by Wolsey from his agents in Rome announcing that papers delegating authority in the way requested had been issued, it appeared that success was to come via this route.

However, each time euphoria was to be followed by disappointment as it was discovered on the papers' arrival that they were intentionally deficient in some respect. The normal problem was that the Pope was to retain a reserve power to accept or reject the judgement reached in England as he thought fit. As far as both Wolsey and Henry were concerned, such an arrangement was worse than useless in that it seemed to be no more than yet another stalling device.

Breakthrough?

A breakthrough seemed to have been achieved in 1528 when the Pope at last appeared to agree to a final decision being made in England. The compromise that the English were required to accept was that the judgement would be reached jointly by two papal legates – Cardinal Campeggio as well as Cardinal Wolsey. This arrangement seemed to threaten no danger to the English cause, as Wolsey had worked with Campeggio before (when negotiating the Treaty of London in 1518) and was confident that he would be able to 'manage' this partner whom the Pope was sending from Rome to join him. In addition, Campeggio was already in Henry's pay (as the absentee Bishop of Salisbury) to look after English interests in the Curia. The Pope's offer was therefore speedily accepted, and Henry's spirits rose at the prospect of the imminent resolution of his problem.

Unfortunately for Wolsey's peace of mind, the king's frustration and impatience increased just as rapidly when it became clear that Campeggio did not share the English monarch's sense of urgency. It is true that he was in poor health and that the journey he had been instructed to undertake was therefore most unwelcome, but even in these circumstances his progress northwards was (literally) painfully slow. Frequent breaks were taken for recuperation, and, as these were reported in detail to Henry by his agents, each one worsened the king's temper considerably. And not surprisingly, given Henry's personality, Wolsey was blamed for every new delay.

Campeggio

Matters did not improve once Campeggio finally reached London in December 1528. The speedy decision that had been hoped for was not forthcoming as he insisted that everything be done 'according to the book'. Nothing that Wolsey could do was able to hurry the process as Campeggio proved impervious to all the pressures that normally ensured that Wolsey got his way. There was no threat and no offer that could influence the Roman cardinal for he was tired of life and had no aspirations for the future. His only motivation seemed to be to carry out the Pope's wishes and the fact that he was paid to work in England's interests appeared to be of no significance.

Both Henry and Wolsey soon realised that they had been duped by what was probably yet another delaying tactic, and their suspicions were finally confirmed when work on the case was suspended in July 1529 without a decision being made. Campeggio was insisting that all activity cease for the long summer period during which the courts in Rome were in recess. All concerned realised then that Campeggio would never be prepared to commit himself to a verdict one way or the other. And so it proved. Before the hearing in England could be reconvened in the autumn, the Pope had decided that the case must, after all, be heard in Rome.

This decision was essentially the final nail in Wolsey's political coffin. For more than two years he had been promising a rapid and successful conclusion to the king's 'great matter'. Now it was clear that all his words had been worthless and a very angry Henry was at last prepared to believe the arguments that Anne Boleyn and her faction had been advancing for many months – that the king's chief minister was as responsible for the lack of action as were the men in Rome. It was ironic that Wolsey's arrest and fall from power in October 1529 took place when it did, because at that time he would have been jointly presiding over the continuation of the hearing of the king's case if the Pope had not called the proceedings to a halt.

Key dates

Failed attempt to obtain a divorce using Cardinal Campeggio: 1528–9

Wolsey removed from power: 1529

Wolsey's failure

The lack of conclusive evidence has resulted in historians disagreeing about the part Wolsey played in the failure to secure the king the divorce he so desperately desired. However, the balance of probability now seems to be fairly firmly established. Those who have seen Wolsey as the secret saboteur of the king's plans are probably correct in their assessment of the cardinal's personal feelings about the divorce and the outcome he hoped to see. Their claim is that Anne Boleyn was essentially accurate in her judgement that Wolsey was hostile to her and her cause. There is certainly impressive evidence that there was no love lost between these two very forceful personalities, and that the minister resented the influence the king's second-wife-in-waiting exercised in the political arena.

Key question
Why did Wolsey fail to secure the divorce?

It is almost self-evident that Wolsey had nothing to gain and much to lose from the replacement of Catherine of Aragon (who played little part in day-to-day politics) by Anne Boleyn (who made no secret of the fact that she expected to be the king's confidante in all matters of importance). It was not that he feared a change of policy: rather that he correctly foresaw a significant diminution in his own power and influence if the divorce and remarriage were to go ahead. Thus, it was naturally his hope that the problem would just go away – presumably by Henry tiring of Anne Boleyn and deciding that he would rather leave things as they were. And there was every reason to believe that this would be the most likely outcome. Wolsey had plenty of experience of the king's enthusiasms, which tended to be all-consuming but short-lived, and he knew that the best way of dealing with them was to appear to go along with them until they ran out of steam in the normal course of events.

However, those who have gone on from this to argue that Wolsey acted for most of the time between 1527 and 1529 in line with his personal preferences have been less persuasive. They have managed to show that occasionally the cardinal was less energetic than he would have been had his heart been fully in the divorce project, but they have been unable to establish that he was consistently so. In addition, they have found only one example of his taking action that could be interpreted as being designed to make the divorce less likely to happen. This was when he changed his initial view that the matter could be dealt with by the Church hierarchy in England to a strongly stated opinion that only the Pope could give the necessary rulings.

It is reasonable to suggest that Wolsey, who was not slow to exceed his powers in other matters, would only have done this had his intention been to bog down the matter in the bureaucratic quagmire of Rome. But the case is by no means proven because, on the other hand, it is equally convincing to argue that, in doing this Wolsey was merely protecting himself against difficulties that might have arisen in the future had opponents challenged the validity of a verdict reached in England and thus thrown the legitimacy of any children born to Henry and Anne into doubt.

But the most compelling reason for not accepting the interpretation that Wolsey consistently worked against the divorce (in addition to opposing it privately) is the clear evidence that he soon came to realise that his political future depended on the king's marriage to Catherine of Aragon being dissolved. Some of his letters to Rome reveal a man who was desperately fighting for his survival and who was even prepared to plead for action in order to save his skin.

The air of desperation that surrounded so much of his diplomatic activity in 1528 and 1529, when he was attempting to exert pressure on the Pope to reach an early and favourable decision, does not smack of a man who was merely going through the motions until a change of heart on the part of his monarch freed him from his torment. Thus it seems probable that Wolsey failed to achieve his objective (with which he admittedly had no personal sympathy) despite the fact that he tried hard to be successful and not because he was secretly undermining his public endeavours.

6 | Fall from Power

Praemunire

When the final failure of Wolsey's efforts to secure the divorce became apparent the king turned on his once faithful and most trusted servant. In 1529 Henry decided to use the weapon against Wolsey that had been available to him for more than a decade. A series of acts of parliament in the fourteenth century had created the crime of ***praemunire***, which in essence was any action taken to exercise papal powers in England to the disadvantage of the king or any of his subjects. From the time he had acquired his

Key term

Praemunire
A legal provision, arising from three fourteenth-century laws, which forbade clerics to take any action that cut across the powers of the Crown – especially recognising any external authority without the monarch's explicit permission.

Key question
How and why did Wolsey fall from power?

appointment as *legatus a latere* Wolsey had clearly been open to a *praemunire* charge, and to the punishments associated with it – the confiscation of all property and imprisonment during the king's pleasure.

Arrest and 'exile'

When Henry decided to strike down his minister it was not done decisively. Although Wolsey was arrested and all his possessions were confiscated, he was released and was allowed to live in modest comfort away from court. It was only some months later that he was re-arrested and taken towards London from his archdiocese of York, to which he had been 'exiled' by Henry. But his health was broken and he died at Leicester on 29 November 1530. During the period of his disgrace he had done all he could to engineer his reinstatement. He had sent a stream of pleading letters to the king and had attempted to whip up support among his 'friends' throughout Europe. But all had been to no avail. Henry had slowly become convinced that his long-time leading servant must suffer the only fitting end to his period of dominance – death as well as disgrace. Wolsey's premature end at Leicester had in fact spared him from the show trial and execution that almost certainly awaited him in London.

Death of Wolsey: 1530

Key date

Why had such a successful partnership ended so dramatically?

Undoubtedly, the major reason was Wolsey's failure to secure for Henry the annulment of his marriage to Catherine of Aragon. It seems that this was the issue at the forefront of the king's mind for the whole of the two years prior to Wolsey's fall. The minister had promised that this would be a matter easily resolved because of his influence with the Papacy, from which all annulments of marriages must come, but every attempt had resulted in disappointment.

In the circumstances, Henry had been very patient. Anne Boleyn, his intended next wife, was refusing to have sex with him until he could guarantee to make 'an honest woman' of her by marrying her. It was obvious to everybody at court that this caused Henry great frustration. And Henry was increasingly aware that the passage of time was endangering his aspiration to leave a male heir of adult years behind him when he died. It is an indication of the depth of Henry's faith in Wolsey and the skill with which the minister explained away the delays that the show-down between them was so long delayed. With anybody else it would have happened much earlier.

Historians have disagreed about why the king decided to act against his favourite minister when he did. Although the evidence is far from conclusive, the most plausible explanation appears to be that Henry decided to dispense with Wolsey when he became convinced by Anne Boleyn and her faction that the cardinal was actively conspiring to delay a papal decision – in the hope that the king would tire of his romantic pursuit in the meantime and would be prepared to return to Catherine – thus avoiding the political inconvenience of putting aside a wife who was widely admired and supported at home and abroad.

Of course, it can never be known how much truth there was to this claim (although it is certain that there was some), but Henry seems to have come to believe it, and to have acted on the basis of it. However, the fact that on several occasions during the remaining months of his life Wolsey was given tokens of the king's continuing good will indicates that Henry was not entirely convinced of his minister's faithlessness, and that several times he seriously considered reinstating him in some way. That he did not give way to his doubts was a result of the skill with which the Boleyn faction constantly fed him with anti-Wolsey propaganda. Thus it seems highly probable that there was considerable truth in the contemporary claim that the cardinal was the victim of his political enemies, led by Anne Boleyn.

Although Wolsey's unpopularity was so great that there was general rejoicing at his removal from power, Henry was realistic enough soon to regret that he had allowed himself to be persuaded to destroy the servant who was better able to carry out his wishes than anyone else then available to him. Wolsey may not have been very likeable, but he was certainly a great man according to the criteria most frequently used when such judgements are made. However, many will conclude that a person of outstanding ability who acted in such a self-centred manner throughout most of his life was indeed a wastrel rather than being a man who deserves our admiration.

Assessment

The political situation in England between 1514 and 1529 was very unusual. It appeared, somewhat paradoxically, as if a highly talented and independent-minded young king was very much under the influence of his wily, older minister. But, although this might seem to have been what was happening, historians have generally been unprepared to accept that this was the situation. While it is freely admitted that Wolsey became very skilful in manipulating others, it is maintained that he had met his match in Henry, who was more than able to look after himself in the hurly-burly of political intrigue and who was rarely fooled for long (and certainly not for 15 years). So the conclusion has usually been reached that Wolsey only enjoyed independent decision-making when Henry was prepared to allow him to do so, or for short periods of time when the king was not properly aware of what was happening.

Thus, the relationship between the two was truly that of master and servant, even if the servant was occasionally allowed his head to a greater extent than was normal in such hierarchical relationships. Possibly the most helpful analogy that has been used to describe the situation is that of the senior management of a modern large company, in which Wolsey was the general manager making the most of the important day-to-day decisions, but where Henry was the chairman who decided the policy objectives and devised the overall strategy.

Both men certainly understood that Wolsey was completely dependent on the good will of his monarch and that if this were to be withdrawn his position would be untenable. This was despite the fact that Wolsey worked hard to establish an independent power base within the Church, and felt at times that he had successfully created a position for himself as the spiritual sovereign of England alongside Henry's secular power. But in his heart of hearts he recognised that his *legateship a latere* was only operable as long as Henry agreed that it should be so. Therefore he was normally careful not to go against the king's express wishes even in those aspects of ecclesiastical affairs where theoretically he exercised ultimate authority within the country.

On the one occasion when he did, he had eventually to retract in abject submission in the face of Henry's violent anger. The substance of the incident was relatively petty – the appointment of an abbess to the nunnery at Wilton in Wiltshire in 1528. Henry promised that the nomination should go to one of his courtier's relations and informed Wolsey accordingly. But Wolsey chose not to understand the instruction and awarded the post elsewhere. A second royal instruction was ignored, and a third brought the response that the king's wishes had not been clear. This was too much for Henry, who ranted that he was not prepared to be treated in this way by his servant. Wolsey belatedly recognised the seriousness of the situation and did everything possible to placate his master. A great deal about the relationship between king and minister was revealed in the process, as well as showing that Wolsey was not immune from miscalculations on how much he could get away with.

If the relationship was so dominated by Henry, then how was Wolsey able to establish himself so powerfully in the first place? After all, his position became such that Pollard felt able to describe him as holding 'despotic authority in the state'. The answer is partly to be found in the enormous range and extent of his abilities, and partly in the personality and interests of Henry VIII. Wolsey was undoubtedly one of the most able ministers of the crown in any period of British history. Because of his very rare combination of exceptional brain power, monumental drive and determination and a clear appreciation of how to influence people, he was able to get things done that almost everybody else would have found impossible. Henry was quick to recognise that it was worth paying a high price in order to secure the services of this exceptional man of business. He correctly assessed that, however much power the minister amassed, there was no real danger that he could effectively challenge the king's position. England was a very hierarchical society and base-born subjects had never been able to survive in authority without the support of the monarch. There was no reason why Thomas Wolsey should be any different.

Wolsey also had another advantage in that he could be used to increase the distance between the king and the more mighty of his aristocratic subjects. Although the claim that Henry VIII was strongly motivated by a desire to eclipse the power of those nobles who could be seen as presenting a potential challenge to his régime has long been discredited, there can be no doubt that he enjoyed watching his leading subjects squirm as they were forced to yield pride of place to the son of a butcher who, because of his Church preferments, could demand precedence over them on all formal occasions. For Wolsey to be treated as the superior of the entire nobility of England, while being seen to be totally under the command of the king, meant that Henry could expect to be seen as even more exalted than he might otherwise have been.

Wolsey's explanation for his rise to prominence in the king's esteem was that he alone among the counsellors encouraged Henry to spend his time on his leisure pursuits and to leave the boring work of government to his ministers. Although this account is obviously less than the whole story, it does probably contain a germ of the truth. Henry was delighted to find somebody who could put his ideas into practice for him, without requiring constant instructions or supervision. Such an arrangement allowed him the best of all worlds: he could continue to live his life as he wished, without submitting himself overmuch to the discipline of work, while at the same time being confident that his wishes were generally being implemented.

For Wolsey to achieve a position of dominance in the government was one thing: to retain it for a long period was something very different. It was the difference between climbing a high mountain and remaining camped there during all weathers. As a low-born chief minister serving a master who vigorously and successfully defended his habit of associating with whomsoever he wished, Wolsey had to accept that his motives and actions would be regularly misrepresented to the king by his numerous enemies – despite the fear of reprisal that he created in most people.

Yet Wolsey managed to survive all attacks on his position for 15 years. This was truly a remarkable achievement. It happened both because of the minister's outstanding abilities and because the king was unusually shrewd in assessing the reliability of the information he was given. Thus the relationship between Henry VIII and Wolsey was a real (if very unequal) partnership that depended on the achievements of both parties for its success. Wolsey's failure to deliver the one thing most desired by the king – his divorce – resulted in the dissolution of that partnership.

Summary diagram: Wolsey: government, religion and foreign policy

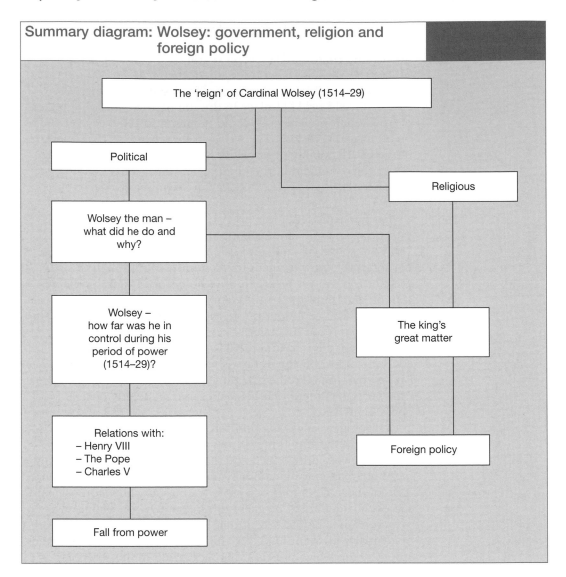

Study Guide: AS Questions

In the style of AQA

Question 1

(a) Explain why Wolsey undertook a range of reforms to the legal system. (12 marks)

(b) How successful was Wolsey in controlling the nobility between 1509 and 1529? (24 marks)

Exam tips

(a) You will need to decide Wolsey's motivation and to assess the competing claims of, for example, his interest in justice, in organisation, in serving his king, in weakening the nobility, and in establishing a personal reputation. Try to pick out which you consider the most important factor and argue accordingly. You should provide a short conclusion summing up your views.

(b) To answer this question you will need to consider the various measures adopted by Wolsey, for example in government, law and finance, and point to the ways in which he succeeded in controlling the nobility and the ways in which he did not. Try to decide what your argument will be before you begin to write and provide a balanced response with a well-supported conclusion. You may wish to comment at the outset about the importance of controlling the nobility, but the main focus of the answer should be on Wolsey's measures.

Question 2

(a) Explain why Henry decided, in c.1527, to seek a divorce. (12 marks)

(b) How far was Wolsey's fall from power brought about by his determination to maintain personal control over decision making? (24 marks)

Exam tips

(a) The obvious answer to this is because Henry wanted to marry Anne Boleyn, but you will need to include a range of factors to gain high marks. You might like to speculate that he had decided before 1527, but the thrust of the answer must focus on why and is likely to include: the need for an heir; Catherine's lack of fertility; the attractions of Anne Boleyn; and the validity of his first marriage. Try to stress the most important factor and provide a linked list of factors leading to a conclusion.

(b) This question invites you to consider the reasons for Wolsey's fall from power and his relationship with the king. You may agree that his desire for personal control was more important in causing the king to tire of him than the scheming of the Boleyn faction or the events of the divorce, or disagree and perhaps emphasise that his relationship with Henry could have survived but for his failure in the divorce case. Whichever way you choose to argue, ensure you support your ideas with evidence and show supported judgement.

In the style of Edexcel
Study Sources 1, 2 and 3.

Do you agree with the view that Henry VIII and Wolsey's foreign policy should be seen as an expensive failure? Explain your answer, using Sources 1, 2 and 3 and your own knowledge.

(40 marks)

Source 1

From a painting c.1520 of the Field of Cloth of Gold.

Source 2

From a letter written to Thomas Wolsey by William Warham Archbishop of Canterbury, 15 April 1525.

It hath been told me secretly that many have repeated what infinite sums of money the King's Grace hath spent already invading France; and little or nothing (in comparison to his costs) hath prevailed: in so much that the King hath no more land in France than his most noble father had.

Source 3

From Henry VIII to Mary I Government and Religion 1509–58, *published in 2008.*

Although there were some obvious large-scale failures, on which between 1525 and 1529, there were many occasions on which both Henry and Wolsey had good reason to think that they had been very successful. After the campaign of 1513 Henry knew that he was internationally regarded as a figure of splendid chivalric kingship and his certainty was increased by events such as those at the Field of Cloth of Gold in 1520. Wolsey was equally successful in creating an outstanding reputation and status for himself (especially in being made *legatus a latere* for life in 1524) which meant that he was treated as being virtually on a par with the leading rulers of Europe. These were no mean achievements to set against the periodic frustrations that beset both men's diplomatic ventures and which became increasingly frequent in the latter stages of their partnership.

Exam tips

The cross-references are intended to take you straight to the material that will help you to answer the question.

This is an example of a (b) question, worth two-thirds of the marks for the unit. You should expect to write a substantial answer to this question and leave yourself about 35–40 minutes to write up your answer after you have analysed the sources and planned a response.

Examiners will award you a maximum of 16 marks for making use of the provided sources and 24 marks for deploying your own knowledge. You must identify points raised by the sources, and then you can use your own knowledge to develop those further and to introduce new and relevant points which the sources do not contain. But you should start your plan with the sources. This will ensure that you do not get so carried away with planning and writing a standard essay answer that you forget to use the sources properly. For the highest marks, you should develop techniques which enable you to use your own knowledge in combination with material from the sources – integrating the two.

Try working with a set of columns, which allows you:

(i) to sort your material into that which agrees with the claim in the question and that which counters it

(ii) to plan in an integrated way where your own knowledge can extend a point found in the sources.

Some examples are given below:

AGREE (evidence from sources)	AGREE (evidence from own knowledge)	DISAGREE (evidence from sources)	DISAGREE (evidence from own knowledge)
Source 2 refers to 'infinite sums of money' spent invading France and no gains of land in France	(i) The misjudged attempt to exploit Habsburg–Valois rivalry after 1521 (ii) War with France and the campaign failures (page 58) (iii) the failed attempt to negotiate the partition of France with Charles after Pavia (pages 58–9)		
Source 3 refers to 'large-scale failures' between 1525 and 1529	Ineffective anti-Habsburg policy: The league of Cognac 1526 Declaration of war 1528 (page 58) Token participation in the negotiations of Treaty of Cambrai, 1529 (page 59)		

AGREE (evidence from sources)	AGREE (evidence from own knowledge)	DISAGREE (evidence from sources)	DISAGREE (evidence from own knowledge)
		International regard for Henry after the campaign of 1513 (Source 3)	The defeat of the French forces and the capture of Thérouanne and Tournai (page 54)
	The Spectacle of the Field of Cloth of Gold was staged at enormous cost (page 55) and achieved little of lasting significance (page 56)	Henry's image as a figure of 'splendid chivalric kingship' was increased by the Field of Cloth of Gold spectacle (Sources 1 and 2)	One of the most spectacular events in modern European history (pages 55–6)

Additional points are given below. Try slotting these remaining points into a plan. You will need to decide into which column they should go and how they should be grouped. Do some of them add to points in the plan above, or are they new points?

- The Treaty of London, 1518, can be seen as triumph for Wolsey (page 55).
- Wolsey gained significant status as *legatus a latere*.
- Was Wolsey following a policy of self-interest rather than national interest in the negotiations of the terms of the Treaty of London (page 55)?
- Habsburg–Valois rivalries offered England opportunities – these were not effectively exploited by Wolsey and Henry in 1519–25 (pages 57–8).

And finally, having sorted and organised your material, what is your decision? Do you agree with the statement in the question?

In the style of OCR

How successful was Wolsey in achieving his aims in domestic administration from 1515 to 1529?   (50 marks)

Exam tips

The cross-references are intended to take you straight to the material that will help you to answer the question.

This question requires you to assess Wolsey's aims in terms of successes and failures. You might begin by identifying his main aims, namely to serve the king and to remain in office as long as possible. To achieve these objectives, Wolsey needed to raise money to satisfy Henry's appetite for grandiose schemes and to wage war. In this respect, apart from the Amicable Grant, he was largely successful (page 59). He was extremely successful at monopolising political and ecclesiastical patronage to enhance his own wealth and power but in so doing, he gained many powerful enemies and, in spite of the Eltham Ordinance, never secured control of the court and royal household (pages 49–50). As papal legate, he introduced some minor ecclesiastical reforms and protected the welfare of the clergy but this attracted criticism, which made the Church vulnerable to attack (pages 41, 60–1). As Lord Chancellor, he enhanced the probity of the common law courts and popularised the use of civil law, especially the courts of Chancery, Star Chamber and Requests. With the exception of the 1525 rebellion, he maintained law and order and kept the country stable (pages 47–8). He was, however, unable to make much headway in implementing economic and social reforms: illegal enclosures remained an insoluble problem and he incurred the hatred of many nobles and landowners through his use of Star Chamber (page 51). You might consider that Wolsey was more of a success than a failure: he stayed in office for 15 years, enriched himself and his family, and only fell because he was unable to give the king a divorce (pages 69–70). Some might argue that Wolsey failed to realise the perils of trying to serve two masters at the same time and actually served the Pope rather better than the king.

Although the question is about domestic administration, it is relevant to consider the impact of foreign relations on Wolsey's handling of the divorce in order to demonstrate that domestic affairs cannot always be separated from foreign issues. However, it is important not to go into the divorce in detail or to get sidetracked by a discussion of foreign issues. Finally, decide which was Wolsey's greatest success and limitation, and ensure that your reasons are supported with relevant and accurate details.

4

Divorce to Dissolution: The Royal Supremacy and the Reformation 1529–40

POINTS TO CONSIDER

This chapter provides an opportunity to investigate the reasons for, and the extent of, change in the English Church between 1529 and 1540. The chapter will assess the impact of the divorce and of both the religious reformers and conservatives on the development of the Church. The changing nature of the relationship between the State and the Church will also be assessed, as will the closure of the monasteries and the reaction of the people. These issues are examined as five themes:

- The divorce
- The Reformation Parliament and the attack on the Church
- The break with Rome and the royal supremacy
- The dissolution of the monasteries
- Opposition to the changes

Key dates

1529–36	Reformation Parliament
1530	Church charged with *praemunire*
1531	Charge of *praemunire* withdrawn in return for a grant of £100,000
1532	Emergence of Thomas Cromwell as the king's chief minister; Supplication against the Ordinaries; Submission of the Clergy; Act in Restraint of Annates
1533	Act in Restraint of Appeals
1534	Act of First Fruits and Tenths; Act of Supremacy; Treasons Act; execution of the Holy Maid of Kent
1534–7	Attack on the Observant Franciscans and the Carthusians
1535	Execution of John Fisher and Sir Thomas More; *Valor Ecclesiasticus*; visitations to the monasteries
1536	Closure of the smaller monasteries; Pilgrimage of Grace; Act Extinguishing the Authority of the Bishop of Rome
1538–40	Closure of the larger monasteries

Key question
Why has the period
1530–1 been
described as 'years of
drift' in the search for
a settlement of the
divorce issue?

1 | The Divorce

Years of drift

The years 1530 and 1531 have normally been described as years during which the campaign to obtain the divorce was conducted in an aimless fashion, with no clear strategy being apparent. It has been likened to a rudderless ship at sea in a storm. In this highly critical portrayal the failure has been seen as being both Henry's and that of his three leading ministers – the Dukes of Norfolk and Suffolk and the Earl of Wiltshire (Anne Boleyn's recently ennobled father). These years have frequently been taken as proving that, whatever other qualities and strengths he might have possessed, the king was no strategist and no 'man of business'. In particular, those who have wanted to show that Henry was as dependent on able ministers as they were on him have made much of the sterility of the period between the fall of Wolsey and the rise of Cromwell. Certainly, there has been no difficulty in establishing that Norfolk, Suffolk and Wiltshire probably had less political acumen between them than even any one of Wolsey's team of 'lieutenants' (which, of course, included Thomas Cromwell) had on his own.

However, this picture is possibly a little harsh on Henry. At least one major initiative was taken in an attempt to win a victory in the debates on the meaning of the Leviticus text and on the Pope's power to issue a dispensation for a man to marry his brother's widow. Henry had already procured an amount of learned support for his case, but now a concerted effort was made to secure formal 'judgements' on the issue from the most prestigious universities of Europe. Large sums of money were spent bribing theologians to vote in Henry's favour and ten verdicts were obtained. But the overall impact of the campaign was minimal, especially as it was widely known that gold rather than conscience had decided many of the outcomes. Some of the participants were even prepared to be bribed by Catherine of Aragon's party (two payments rather than one) to declare publicly that they really believed the dispensation to be valid and that they had only said otherwise because they had been paid to do so. In such ways the credibility of the exercise – which had never been high – was almost totally destroyed.

Yet, unsuccessful as the venture was, it does not seem to indicate a policy without a sense of direction. But it does suggest that the approach being adopted was a mere elaboration of the failed strategy that Wolsey had attempted to implement. The aim was still to persuade the Pope to declare in Henry's favour by convincing him of the rightness of the king's case, despite the clear-cut evidence that the Curia was likely neither to be swayed by public opinion, however eminent were its spokesmen, nor to be unduly influenced by the facts of the case, one way or the other. Henry's agenda and Rome's agenda were poles apart.

But at least these years witnessed one success of sorts. The great fear in London, after the case had been revoked to Rome in the summer of 1529, had been that a verdict in favour of Catherine would be issued. So the English agents in Italy were instructed to reverse the direction of their efforts, and instead of trying to speed up the process they were told to slow it down as much as possible. They undoubtedly managed to initiate some additional delays in what was already a very slow and complicated process, but it is unlikely that, even without their work, any final decision would have been forthcoming for a very long time. Thus there is little credit to be claimed for achieving the 'success', even though the worst outcome had not come about.

So it seems that the 'flavour' of the writers who have judged the time after Wolsey's fall to be the wasted years is correct, even if their case has sometimes been overstated in an attempt to show that a Henry poorly advised was a king who was all at sea. Certainly it would be fair to describe 1530 and 1531, as far as the divorce was concerned, as a period when no strategy that could reasonably have been expected to lead to a successful conclusion to the affair was being pursued. Nobody seemed able to identify the way forward.

Breaking the stalemate: Cromwell's 'new idea'

Rarely is it possible in history to credit anybody with a completely new idea. The greatness of the men and women who have made important discoveries, pioneered new approaches, or carried through significant changes has normally been based on the ability to draw together a number of existing ideas and to refashion them into a way of looking at things that had not been apparent before. The process is so simple that most 'new' good ideas seem obvious once someone else has thought of them. Probably at some time in 1531, Thomas Cromwell hit upon such a new good idea about the divorce. It was that the Pope would never be persuaded to rule in Henry's favour and that the only way forward was to remove the power in such matters from the Pope's hands and to give it to someone or some group willing to be persuaded by the king.

Cromwell's strength was that besides being able to describe clearly what needed to be done he was also able both to indicate how it could be done and to guarantee to do it himself. It seems that, although Henry was quick to recognise the talent of this relatively low-born former lieutenant of his fallen minister and to see that he was a man whose services should be used, he was unwilling to accept the total package that was on offer. It was necessary to persuade him of its good sense and practicality little by little. Therefore there was no sudden change of direction leading to speedy success: rather there was an edging towards a new way forward. This was done with much wavering and hesitation, until events almost took on a momentum of their own and the breakthrough was achieved.

Key question
What was Cromwell's 'new idea' to break the deadlock between the king and the Pope?

Profile: Thomas Cromwell 1485–1540

1485	– Born the son of Walter Cromwell of Putney, a blacksmith and cloth-merchant
1503	– Joined the French army and marched with them to Italy, fighting in the battle of Garigliano
1504–13	– Entered the household of the Italian merchant-banker Francesco Frescobaldi. He later worked as a cloth merchant in the Netherlands
1514	– Stayed in the English Hospital in Rome
1520	– Established in London mercantile and legal circles
1523	– Entered the House of Commons for the first time
1524	– Appointed a subsidy commissioner in Middlesex. Entered Wolsey's service
1530	– Became a member of the king's council
1531	– Took control of the supervision of the king's legal and parliamentary affairs
1532	– Became master of the king's jewels
1534	– Confirmed as Henry VIII's principal secretary and chief minister
1535	– Appointed royal vicegerent, or vicar-general
1540	April – Granted the earldom of Essex
	June – Imprisoned in the Tower of London prior to his trial and execution for treason in July

Cromwell was a dedicated bureaucrat who served Henry VIII well. His greatest achievement was in planning and piloting the legislation responsible for the break with Rome. His survey, closure and eventual destruction of the monasteries represent a model of administrative speed and efficiency. Unfortunately, his skill and effectiveness in government, his promotion of the key aspects of protestantism and his leadership of the religious reform movement at Court caused jealousy and made him powerful enemies. When he made mistakes, such as arranging the marriage between Henry VIII and Anne of Cleves, his enemies pounced and ruined his reputation with the king. Barely three months after being ennobled as Earl of Essex he was executed on trumped-up charges of treason.

Key question

Did the use to which parliament was put amount to a 'revolution' in the relationship between Church and State?

Parliament: revolution in the relationship between Church and State

The key decision was to use parliament to pass laws restricting papal powers by recognising that these powers in fact resided in the Crown of England, and stipulating the punishments that would be meted out to those who opposed or acted contrary to the new arrangements. It is difficult for us, who have grown up in a democracy where parliament has been supreme for centuries, to appreciate the brilliance of the approach suggested by Cromwell and accepted by Henry. At the time it was generally accepted that parliament was a rarely and briefly used component of political life (it had played no significant part in the first 20 years of Henry's reign) whose main functions were to grant extraordinary taxes to the king in times of great national need and to pass new laws covering mainly minor local issues. The idea of using it to bring about a revolution in the relationship between Church and State was highly innovative. It was also very shrewd. It ensured that the representatives of the landed and merchant classes, upon whom the king depended to exercise his authority throughout the country, would be fully implicated in whatever was done.

The crucial action was the passage of the Act in Restraint of Appeals in March 1533. This legislation declared that final authority in all legal matters, lay and clerical, resided in the monarch and that it was therefore illegal to appeal to any authority outside the kingdom on any such matters. The way was now clear for the validity of Henry and Catherine's marriage to be decided finally without the involvement of the Pope or his bureaucracy. And the people were in place who could be relied on to carry out the work speedily and with the desired outcome.

In particular, there was a new Archbishop of Canterbury, the head of the Church hierarchy in England and Wales. The old archbishop, William Warham, who had taken great pleasure in outliving Cardinal Wolsey so that he could prevent the man he so greatly detested adding Canterbury to his many other clerical positions, had finally died in 1532. While he had lived there had always been the possibility that he would summon up enough courage to refuse to do as he was directed by Henry. Certainly, he was not in favour of the divorce and he had proved himself willing to be obstructive to the king, even if his resolve had normally crumbled once pressure had been applied. But with the old man dead, the way was clear for Henry to choose a totally pliable replacement (as long as the Pope could be prevailed upon to endorse the man chosen).

Thomas Cranmer

The choice fell on Thomas Cranmer, who appeared to have all the right attributes. He had shown a marked lack of personal ambition during the 43 or so years of his life so far, much of which had been spent at Cambridge quietly studying and teaching. But he was intellectually very able and had shown himself to be strongly in favour of the divorce. He had already been useful to the king, carrying out his instructions to the letter, whether it was in writing a book supporting Henry's case (in 1529), acting as an agent buying support in European universities (in 1530), or (as now) serving as England's ambassador at the court of Charles V. In addition, he was a very junior member of the Boleyn faction and was thus totally acceptable to Queen Anne-to-be. The only slight problem was that he held no position within the clerical hierarchy, although he was an ordained priest, and it might have proved difficult to justify the meteoric rise of such an outsider when no non-bishop had been elevated to Canterbury for well over a century. But Henry took the plunge

Key question
What role did Cranmer play in the divorce issue?

and much to his relief the Pope, anxious to prove that he could please in some things, confirmed the appointment in record time.

Once the Act in Restraint of Appeals had become law there was a need for rapid action. Anne Boleyn, convinced that the divorce would soon be achieved, had finally consented to share her monarch's bed at some time in 1532. By January 1533 she knew that she was pregnant, and Cranmer was instructed to perform a secret marriage ceremony. It was now important that the divorce be finalised and the new marriage declared legal before the baby (hopefully a boy) was born in the early autumn. Cranmer acted with speed, tact and efficiency. A hearing of the case was arranged for late May and when Catherine refused to attend a judgement was delivered after less than three days of deliberation. It was announced that the papal dispensation had been invalid, that Henry and Catherine had therefore never been legally married, and that the secret marriage of Henry and Anne was in order because Henry had been a bachelor at the time. The king was well satisfied and was not in the least displeased that six years of endeavour on his 'great matter' had ended in such a tame and low-key victory. The anti-climax was to come when the baby turned out to be a girl!

Actions and motives

Key question
What motives lay behind the actions of those involved in the conflict between England and the Papacy?

Although there has been some dispute between historians over matters of detail, there is now general agreement about what happened between 1527 and 1533 in the efforts to secure the divorce and in its final achievement. What has intrigued (and divided) historians much more is the attempt to provide explanations about why events turned out as they did. In particular, the roles and motives of the main participants have been much discussed.

Charles V

The vast majority of writers have judged that the most important person in influencing the outcome of Henry's 'great matter', in the years during which the King of England accepted that the decision on his marital fate lay with the Pope in Rome, was the Emperor Charles V.

Orthodox view

The orthodox view has long been that Charles stopped the Pope from reaching a conclusion that was against the interests of Catherine of Aragon – mainly by making him fear what would happen to him if he did. It has been said that Charles V did this because Catherine was his aunt (his mother's sister) and that his strong sense of family pride drove him to do all he could to protect the honour of such a close relative. In addition, it has often been claimed that Catherine was one of his special favourites and that affection increased his already strong resolve.

With a motive so clearly established, there has been no difficulty in explaining how Charles was able to put his intention into effect. This was possible because, throughout the period

1527 to 1532, the Papacy was diplomatically and militarily at his mercy. The most striking example of this control took place in 1527 when Rome was overrun by his troops and was looted and pillaged for a fortnight with great ferocity. As a result of this unintended action by the Emperor's unpaid and mutinous German soldiers, the Pope, in effect, became for several months Charles's prisoner. Even when papal freedom was restored, the clear message remained that any hostile action would almost certainly be followed by unpleasant repercussions. In similar circumstances, which had occurred several times before during the 30 years of struggle between France and Spain for the control of Italy, papal policy had been predictable. An alliance had been formed with the temporary underdog (France or Spain) and as many other states as could be persuaded to fight to re-establish a balance of power in which they, and the Papacy, could once again exercise some independent influence. But on this occasion the strategy rapidly backfired. A hastily gathered consortium of states, including England and reliant on the military might of France, was discomfited in 1529 when the Emperor's armies were overwhelmingly victorious in battle and Charles was left the undisputed master of Italy. The Pope could now do little but squirm. And, although he could not be forced to take action against his will, he could be prevented from doing anything of which the Emperor did not approve. This, it has traditionally been argued, included granting Henry his divorce.

Revisionist view

It is somewhat surprising that nearly all English-speaking writers about the divorce have accepted this account seemingly uncritically. For, although it rings true in general terms, it appears to be a very simplistic, and therefore partial, explanation of Charles's motives and role. Certainly, his motives are unlikely to have been as straightforward as they are normally portrayed. It is true that he was a committed dynast who was determined to hand on in their entirety the lands and powers he had inherited if he possibly could, and that he made constant use of his relations to help him control his huge and scattered personal empire. But how well he protected (and by implication wished to) their individual interests is more open to question.

There are clear cases where he did not protect their individual interests, especially where it suited him politically not to. The most obvious example is of his mother (Catherine of Aragon's sister) through whom he had inherited the Spanish kingdoms and their empires. Her claims to rule were passed over in Charles's favour and for most of his life she 'existed' in splendid captivity – and all because of her supposed madness brought on by the sudden death of her husband. It is uncontestable that 'madder' male monarchs had often been allowed to rule and that her son showed scant concern for her welfare. Equally, there is little evidence that he cared for Catherine of Aragon in personal terms. Not only did he hardly know her, but he seemingly made no attempt to better the acquaintance during his visits to

England. Thus any claim that she was a special favourite of his seems to have very little justification.

Nor was Charles particularly sensitive to slurs that were cast on his family name, unless it suited him to appear so. He kept his ears firmly closed to the appeals of another aunt when she was 'thrown over' by her royal husband – the King of Denmark – in circumstances that were not totally dissimilar to those affecting Catherine of Aragon. And he did nothing to right the wrongs done to his supposed 'favourite aunt' in the three years between her divorce and her death. In fact, he was very quick to forgive, forget and make up with Henry VIII when it suited him to do so.

Thus it appears that further work needs to be done to disentangle Charles V's reasons for opposing the divorce as strenuously as he undoubtedly did. The answer is likely to lie in a mixture of political self-interest and personal pride. For example, once he had declared himself opposed to the divorce, and once the issue had became a matter of widespread international debate, it is possible that his determination not to be worsted by his highly competitive and often patronising uncle-in-law became the key issue for him.

Equally, the orthodox view that 'Charles V opposed the divorce and that therefore the Pope could not grant it' seems open to challenge. At least it appears valid to contend that the Pope could have acted had he wanted to (at a price), just as he did in 1528 when he allied with Henry VIII and others in a foolhardy attempt to loosen the emperor's grip on Italy. Certainly, the Pope was much more than a pawn in the game.

The Pope

During the whole of the struggle over the divorce the Pope was the same person – Clement VII (1523–34). He was in many ways a pathetic figure. The abiding image of him when dealing with the divorce is the description given by one English envoy of a dithering and distressed old man, wringing his hands in anguish and asking plaintively 'What shall I do?' But his question was not really a request for guidance. He had plenty of that and he did not relish the implications of any of it. Everything that was suggested to him seemed guaranteed to make the situation worse. Whenever he was prevailed upon to do anything affecting the case he was immediately struck by doubts about the decision he had just made. His normal response was to backtrack, at least in part, as quickly as he could. Intense frustration was therefore the lot of those who had to deal with him on the matter.

However, Clement was not consistently indecisive. There were times when he displayed an amazing amount of inner strength and outward certainty. After the **Sack of Rome** in 1527, and again a year later, he was persistent in his determination not to act as a tool of the emperor. He was equally determined not to be bullied by the King of England. These underlying resolves seem never to have deserted him and to have been present even during the periods of weakness when he appeared to be too frightened of everyone and everything to make any decisions at all. Thus, the

Key term

Sack of Rome
Attack on and looting of Rome by Habsburg troops.

man who looked as if he ought to be easily manipulated turned out to be unmanageable.

From what he said and did it appears that Clement resented the divorce issue greatly. He looked upon it as a most unwelcome and insoluble problem, and one that had been thrust on him through no fault of his own. His fervent wish was that it would go away without his having to do anything, although he was hopeful that Catherine would be treated fairly. This could happen by one of the parties dying (not an unreasonable option in an age when life was often short), by Henry tiring of Anne Boleyn and deciding to drop the issue (a distinct possibility given the temporary nature of most infatuations), or by the English taking the law into their own hands. Clement is reported on several occasions as wishing that this would happen. Certainly, it had been done many times before as a face-saving exercise.

In Henry's case it would have meant his marrying Anne Boleyn without having secured an annulment of his existing marriage, and then at some appropriate time in the future (probably after Catherine's death) applying to the Pope for his situation to be regularised and for his children by his second wife to be declared legitimate. It would probably have been possible to do this without difficulty. One other frequently used solution to such problems was suggested as events unfolded. This was to persuade Catherine to enter a nunnery, thus freeing her husband to marry again if he wished. Campeggio arrived in England in 1528 with the instruction to inform Catherine that the Pope advised this. Catherine's response was typically spirited. She thought it was an excellent suggestion which she would be pleased to accept once Henry agreed to enter a monastery!

Much as Clement was indecisive and despondent, hoping to avoid all responsibility over the affair, he was consistent in his determination that no verdict should be forthcoming from Rome while there was still a possibility that the dispute would be settled by other means. Thus, for him, the strategy to be pursued was clear-cut. Delay must be the order of the day, with minimal (and, if possible, illusory) concessions being made only when the pressure on him became intense. So, although he eventually agreed to the case being decided in England, he ensured that Campeggio was in no doubt that under no circumstances must a conclusion be reached. His final ruling, made in Catherine's favour just before he died in 1534, was only issued because Henry had very much taken the law into his own hands by then.

Henry VIII

Henry's motives over his 'great matter' are normally presented as a mixture of lust for Anne Boleyn and concern to provide himself with an acceptable male heir. But, important as these factors were, it would clearly be unrealistic to expect such simple statements fully to reflect the intentions of such a complex and changeable king over a six-year period.

Henry's lust for Anne Boleyn

Contemporaries were amazed that his passion for Anne could remain at such a pitch for so long. The most popular explanation for this atypical constancy was that she had used black magic to bewitch him. This was not as ridiculous a suggestion as it may now seem, because in sixteenth-century England many of the unusual happenings in life were habitually put down to the effects of witchcraft. In reality, Anne did manage her relationship with Henry very skilfully indeed. She made mistakes – especially, on occasions, continuing to press a point beyond the time when the king wished to hear about it – but generally her touch was sure. She worked hard to be good company for him whatever his mood, and she inflamed his passions from time to time by those displays of courtly eroticism which were an accepted part of early modern life in the highest western European societies. She was careful to make certain that he did not forget what would be his once he was able to offer his hand in marriage!

However, it would be inaccurate to think that Henry was consumed by lust throughout the struggle with Rome. His sex drive was insufficiently strong for this to be so, and his affection for Anne had very clear limits. He undoubtedly held concern over his own health as a higher priority than being with the one he loved. He was quick to send her away from court when there was a suspicion that she might be affected by the sweating sickness, a disease that he feared more than anything else. Equally, his departure from London, leaving Anne behind, was very speedy whenever an outbreak of the disease occurred there. Observers at the time were correct in assessing that Anne was of lasting importance in their king's life, but some historians have perhaps been lured by them into exaggerating her role as a driving force behind Henry's actions throughout the struggle for the divorce. The king's love for her was deep and enduring but it only intermittently provided the major motivation for his actions.

Search for a legitimate heir

The same could be argued even more strongly over Henry's desire to procure a legitimate male heir. There is no doubt that this was an issue which concerned him, but there is little evidence that it was at the forefront of his mind except in the months after January 1533 when Anne had told him she was pregnant. Then it was definitely the most important single factor in driving him towards a speedy resolution of the matter whatever the cost. At other times it was probably no more than a background contributory factor which helped to strengthen his resolve. But it would be very difficult to construct a defensible argument in support of a contention that it was an issue of vital importance.

Other motivating factors

If the most frequently offered explanations of Henry's motivation are important but overall not the most important, what then spurred him on over such a long time when he was beset with so many difficulties in continuing with the campaign to have his marriage annulled? In small part, the answer is that often the effort was maintained in response to a combination of motivating forces, including the two already discussed, rather than based on a single all-important factor, and that these combinations varied from day to day and even from hour to hour, depending on what was said to the king and on how he was feeling. Too little has often been made of this variety of factors.

Henry's sense of guilt

It has been common to ignore Henry's sense of guilt over the sinfulness of his marriage which, although self-inspired, was none-the-less ever present and ready to be activated by those who wished to bolster his determination. Equally overlooked has been his ever-deepening and irrational hatred of Catherine as the cause of all his problems, which led him to wish to exact revenge on her as fully as possible. In addition, there was the genuine interest created by the campaign to establish control over the Church within England and Wales which probably began in 1531 and which kept him fully committed to the campaign.

Henry's sense of honour

There was a single factor that seems to have dominated Henry's motivation for a significant part of the time, at least after the early stages of the enterprise. This was the determination to be seen to be right in the stand he had taken over the status of his marriage. The other side of this coin was that he would do everything possible to prevent it looking as if he had come off second best in a struggle with Charles V. This became an enormous point of honour with him – all the more so as he was used to being told by others that he was right and to getting his own way in almost every matter. And the longer the dispute continued and the more public it became, the less acceptable would have been his loss of face had he been seen to give way. It is not possible to identify for certain a date by which Henry was irrevocably committed to obtaining a successful outcome to the venture, but he had definitely placed himself in a position from which there was no going back by the time Cardinal Campeggio had left the country after the abortive legatine court in 1529. Only for such a reason would this pleasure-loving king have allowed a single 'political' issue to have engrossed almost all his attention for months at a time.

This motivation also offers a credible explanation for his maintaining a frontal attack on Clement VII for five unbroken years – long after any uncommitted observer would have judged there to be any realistic chance of success – instead of accepting the 'back door' solution of a clandestine marriage to Anne, as it had been broadly hinted to him that the Pope thought he should. It might also be one of the reasons why he was never prepared to contemplate the other easy way out – the murder of Catherine of Aragon. Such solutions were by no means rare in the early sixteenth century, when the poisoner's art was well developed. Certainly, Catherine's closest friends feared that such would be her fate, and when she eventually died in 1536 there were many who believed, quite mistakenly it seems, that her death was not by natural causes.

In addition, Henry is known on occasions to have commissioned assassins to rid him of opponents whom he could not deal with openly, so he clearly did not object to such methods on principle. There is definitely good reason to believe that for Henry the means by which he was seen to achieve his success was apparently as important as the fact that he obtained his divorce. At least this was so until Anne's pregnancy dictated that a speedy solution must take precedence over one which was resplendent in public celebration of his rightful victory. Perhaps this is part of the reason why he made Anne's coronation a 'no expenses spared' affair only a week or so later.

Catherine of Aragon

Going quietly

Had the queen been prepared to 'go quietly', the divorce would not have been the long-running international scandal that it became. However, Catherine was anything but an Anne of Cleves (four wives later), who was almost pleased to have her marriage annulled in return for a comfortable and trouble-free existence. The first queen was made of much sterner stuff. Henry was surprised as well as infuriated by the unmovable stand that she took, for Catherine had always previously acted as the ideal (from Henry's point of view) submissive wife, accepting her husband's periodic infidelities and more frequent inattentiveness with a good grace and without altering her bearing towards him. But she drew a very definite line when the legality of her long years of marriage (since 1509) and the legitimacy of her only surviving child (Mary) were challenged.

Catherine the 'good wife'

Catherine's position began and remained very clear-cut. As far as she was concerned, there could be no doubts about the validity of her marriage to Henry. She knew that she had been a virgin at the time of her second marriage (although others disputed the fact), she was certain that the Pope's dispensation had removed any impediment that her unconsummated marriage to Arthur might have placed in the way of her legally becoming Henry's wife, and she could see no reason why a marriage that had remained unquestioned for 19 years should now be disputed. In addition and in all modesty, she believed that she had been a very good wife and consort to her royal husband and she felt strongly that natural justice demanded she be allowed to continue in this role.

Catherine's opposition to Henry

This feeling was so strong that she considered herself justified in opposing her husband over the question of the annulment. It was this active opposition (rather than the passive resistance he had expected) that so much surprised and infuriated Henry. He knew that she was writing to the Pope urging him to ensure that she

The trial of Catherine of Aragon, painted by Henry O'Neil in the eighteenth century. Is this painting pro-Henry VIII and anti-Catherine of Aragon or vice versa?

was treated justly in the matter, and that she was in frequent correspondence with Charles V pleading with him to put pressure on the Pope in her interest. But, try as he would, he was unable to block all her channels of communication. Nor was he able to prevent her from winning public relations victories in the contest. The greatest of these was during her appearance before Campeggio and Wolsey's legatine court in June 1529 (she won additional respect by refusing to attend or to be represented at any of the other legal proceedings that Henry initiated in England). Breaking all the rules of procedure, she approached Henry and, on bended knee, pleaded with him to treat her justly and to abandon his attempts to secure an annulment. She then swept from the court, with the judges' demands that she remain ringing in her ears. The king was reportedly nonplussed, while most of the others present were highly impressed. Perhaps Catherine even surprised herself by the boldness of her actions.

Catherine's reputation enhanced

Most historians have commented very favourably on the way in which Catherine conducted herself throughout the divorce campaign and afterwards. Not only did she maintain her dignity in all situations, including a successful resistance to her forced removal from one 'home' to another, but she also set herself strict limits to the nature of her opposition to her husband. She refused ever to say or to write anything that was a direct criticism of him and she declined to be associated with any plan that might result in violence. This was particularly important during the last three years of her life when Eustace Chapuys, Charles V's ambassador in England, was attempting to organise a rebellion on her behalf and to persuade his master to send troops to bolster the native insurgents. Catherine even wrote to her nephew asking him not to listen to such advice.

It is normally said that Catherine was the only person to emerge from the divorce campaign with an enhanced reputation. It is easy to understand why this is so. It is also claimed that her popularity within England was widespread and deep-felt. The spirit of this assessment is accurate, despite the fact that in all likelihood it has been exaggerated somewhat. The most readily available source of evidence about the state of public opinion after 1529 is the large collection of Eustace Chapuys' detailed reports to Charles V, which has long been used by English historians when researching the subject. But sufficient account has not always been taken of the fact that Chapuys was often at pains to stress Catherine's popularity in order to persuade the emperor that if he invaded England he would receive large-scale local support. Perhaps it would be healthier if his judgements had been assessed more critically than they often have been.

However, the fact remains – substantiated from many other sources – that Catherine was generally thought to have been ill-treated and that, once Wolsey was dead, Henry attracted much of the blame for this. But the significance of the Dowager Duchess of Wales, as Henry insisted Catherine be addressed after the annulment of her second marriage, was much greater than her role as the initial cause of the king's growing unpopularity. Unwittingly, she was a major cause of the Reformation in England, because, had her husband not been determined to sever his ties to her, it is very unlikely that the break with Rome would have occurred – at least during the reign of Henry VIII.

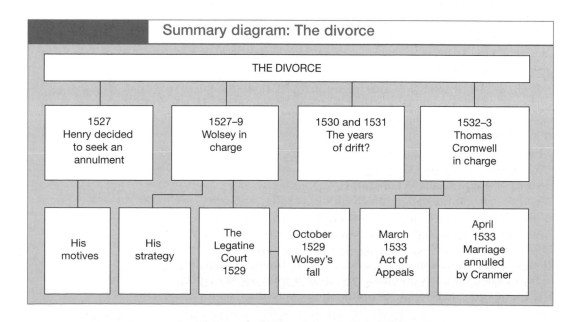

Summary diagram: The divorce

2 | The Reformation Parliament and the Attack on the Church 1529–36

The Reformation Parliament

A parliament was summoned to meet in the autumn of 1529 for the first time in six years. There is no direct evidence to suggest why Henry decided on this course of action. However, it has been claimed that the most likely reasons were that he either intended to use parliament to bring about the fall of Cardinal Wolsey or to increase the pressure on the Pope by demonstrating that the 'political nation' was behind him. Neither of these explanations is very convincing. A more plausible argument is that he had an ill-thought-out plan to use parliament to declare his marriage with Catherine of Aragon invalid. However, it is very unlikely that evidence will ever be found to explain why the action was taken. What is clear is that by the time parliament met Henry had given up whatever his plan might have been, and the session was allowed to proceed in a generally aimless fashion until the approach of Christmas gave reason for activity to be suspended until some unspecified time in the future.

Thus began what has been described as being the most important parliament in the nation's history. Certainly the Reformation Parliament (so named in the nineteenth century) played a central role in the revolutionary events that took place during its lifetime, although its meetings were suspended (in technical terms, it was 'prorogued') for much longer than it was in session (it met for only 484 days in seven sessions over six and a half years), and despite the fact that during the time when Henry VIII was taking the policy initiatives it achieved very little of lasting importance. But during the sessions of 1533, 1534 and 1536, when Cromwell was very influential, legislation was enacted which was of very considerable short- and long-term significance. So, from what appears to have been an abortive initial policy decision, a strategy developed that was to become (in Elton's view at least) the central plank in a revolution in government (see Chapter 5).

> **Key question**
> What was the Reformation Parliament and why is it thought to have been important?

> **Key date**
> Reformation Parliament: 1529–36

Attack on the Church

A second line of policy was also begun in 1529. It was pursued intermittently and with short-term objectives during the next two years, and was finally pushed to its logical conclusion under Cromwell's tutelage. It was the attack on the powers of the Church within Henry's domains.

> **Key question**
> Why did the Crown launch an attack on the Church and what form did that attack take?

The first stage: anticlericalism

The first stage occurred almost by chance. During the first session of the Reformation Parliament a small group of MPs, mainly London merchants and lawyers, launched a planned attack on abuses they claimed were widespread within the Church. Most of the evidence about this comes from the well-known Chronicle of Edward Hall, who was probably one of their number. Hall gives the impression that a wave of indignation swept the Commons over the issue, resulting in demands for major legislation to control the way in which churchmen acted. Although for centuries historians took Hall at face value, it is now generally agreed that he greatly exaggerated both the anger and the actions taken by MPs. Certainly the only concrete outcome of this supposed tide of anticlerical sentiment was the passage of three relatively insignificant bills attempting to limit **pluralism** and **non-residence**.

It has been claimed that Henry allowed this very public attack on the Church to take place because he was pleased to be able to suggest to the Pope that the country was in a state of fervent anticlericalism which could only be controlled by a monarch who had been granted the annulment of his marriage. However, if Hall's account of what happened is somewhat fanciful, this episode must have been rather less significant than it has traditionally been presented as being. Nevertheless, it was noticeable that the king did not instruct those who managed the Commons on his behalf to damp down whatever strength of feeling existed and that he did allow the three anticlerical bills to become law.

The second stage: a three-pronged attack on the Church

It cannot be known how far this episode encouraged Henry to undertake a more general attack on the Church's position. However, what little evidence there is suggests that it was those who 'had his ear' who egged him into taking action. During 1530 there seem to have been three lines of policy being advocated by such people:

- the weakening of the Church's will to resist whatever the king demanded by taking legal action against either a group of its leading members or churchmen in general
- the forcing of the Church to grant the Crown a large sum of money
- the taking of legal control of the Church.

In the end a strategy incorporating all three approaches was adopted, although it was clearly the money which interested Henry most.

Praemunire

Towards the end of the year the churchmen of England and Wales as a whole were indicted on a charge of *praemunire*. This was a catch-all legal provision, arising from three fourteenth-century acts of parliament, which forbade clerics to take any action which cut across the powers of the Crown – especially recognising any external authority without the monarch's explicit permission. The law was so phrased that it was virtually impossible for any churchman to carry out his duties without infringing the terms of the act. It was this law that had been used to topple Wolsey and it was now to be used to cow his former colleagues. The charge was that by recognising Wolsey's legatine powers without Henry's permission all churchmen had transgressed the law and were

Key terms

Pluralism
Term applied to priests who served more than one parish.

Non-residence
Parish priests who did not live in their parish.

Key date

Church charged with *praemunire*: 1530

therefore liable to suffer the penalty of surrendering all their property to the Crown.

'Supreme Head of the Church in England and Wales'

When the Southern Convocation – the parliament of the Church in England and Wales, except the three northern dioceses of York, Durham and Carlisle – met in January 1531, its members were told that Henry would withdraw the *praemunire* charge in return for a grant of £100,000 and the awarding to him of the title of 'Supreme Head of the Church in England and Wales'. With the knowledge of what had happened to Wolsey little more than a year before fresh in their memories, the members of **convocation** (bishops, abbots and other high-ranking clergy) were in no doubt that the king's intentions were serious.

There was therefore little room for manoeuvre and, in the circumstances, they did well to negotiate some significant concessions. They could not achieve a reduction in the sum to be paid but they did extract an agreement that it would be paid over a five-year period rather than immediately as originally demanded. In addition, a qualifying clause – 'as far as the word of God allows' – was added to the king's new title. This made it possible for each person to decide for himself what (if anything) Henry's new honour meant in practice. Traditionally it has been assumed that this change was made at Convocation's request and was therefore a sign that the clergy were willing and able to mount a stout defence of their position. However, this assumption has recently been thrown into serious doubt as it appears that the additional wording may have been proposed by Henry's advisers in order to make the total package less obnoxious to the conservative majority within Convocation.

The pardon of the clergy

Whatever is the truth of the matter, the whole affair was a resounding success for the Crown and demonstrated that little effective opposition was likely to be mounted when, and if, further demands were made. The fact that Henry seemed to lose interest in the issue once an agreement over money had been struck did not lessen the understanding that his advisers had gained of the Church's vulnerability in dealing with the Crown, despite Convocation's attempt to suggest that their 'generosity' was of their own choice and a reward to Henry for the way in which he had protected the Church's interests. **Constitutional historians** have thought it significant that it was decided to confirm both the pardon of the clergy and the terms on which it was granted in an act of parliament. Where the suggestion came from is not known, but it was certainly agreed to by Henry.

The supplication against the Ordinaries

A year later the really telling blows were struck. The episode began in early 1532 when the House of Commons petitioned the king to take action against the way in which churchmen abused their legal powers. The petition is known as the Supplication against the Ordinaries – 'ordinaries' was another word for

Key terms

Convocation
Church equivalent of parliament where clerics meet in two houses – upper house of senior clerics, etc. – to discuss and transact Church affairs.

Constitutional historians
Historians who study political and governmental structures and a nation's laws.

Key dates

Charge of *praemunire* withdrawn: 1531

Supplication against the Ordinaries: 1532

bishops. Historians have continued to disagree over how the Supplication came into existence. Some argue that it arose spontaneously while others maintain that it was engineered in detail by Thomas Cromwell. But there is no dispute over the use Henry made of the document once it came into his hands. He pretended to be the impartial judge in a dispute between two groups of his subjects and passed the petition to Convocation, requesting their response so that he could be informed of the Church's side of the argument before he decided what to do. When he received the churchmen's reply he summoned a deputation of MPs to attend on him and handed a copy of Convocation's defence to them.

But parliament was given no time to act on Henry's broad hint. Almost immediately Convocation was presented with a series of demands by the king. They were to surrender the right to enact new ordinances on their own authority – all future changes in canon law (the legal system followed in church courts) would require the monarch's consent. Existing canon law was to be scrutinised by a committee of 32, half clergy and half laymen, but all appointed by the king, and only those ordinances approved by the committee were to remain in force. This body of law was to stand entirely on the Crown's authority. Thus the intention was that the Church's legal system was to lose its centuries-old independence by being made directly responsible to the king.

Not surprisingly, the members of Convocation were thrown off balance by this bombshell. Most of them seem to have felt instinctively that they must resist this attempt to destroy the Church's legal status as an institution that was parallel to, but separate from, the State. But they were somewhat at a loss in deciding how this could be done. Their leader, William Warham, the aged Archbishop of Canterbury, showed some willingness to fight (possibly because he recognised the approach of death) but he lacked both stamina and a strategy and was soon reduced to virtual impotence by being informed that his monarch was displeased with him. Similar action was used to 'warn off' most other potential opponents, while in a very public display a thinly veiled general threat was issued. Henry summoned a further deputation of MPs to appear before him and pretended to them that he had recently been shown the wording of the two oaths – one to the monarch and one to the Pope – sworn by senior churchmen on taking up a new post.

The submission of the clergy

Were the leading members of Convocation meant to conclude that charges of treason might be in the offing unless the king was given what he wanted? If they were, it was an unnecessary use of such 'big guns' because the clergy's will to resist had already been broken. When the king instructed Convocation to make its decision within 24 hours there was a complete capitulation and a document, the Submission of the Clergy, accepting all that was demanded was voted through without opposition. The fact that a large majority of the members of Convocation chose to

Key date

Submission of the
Clergy: 1532

disassociate themselves from the Submission by being absent from the session at which the vote was taken, so that a minimal number of individuals is recorded as being in favour of the surrender, was of no concern to Henry. He had secured the power he desired. That this was an end in itself, rather than a means to an end, became clear when no action was taken to set up the committee to examine the canon law which Convocation had been forced to accept in their Submission. However, the terms of the surrender were once again confirmed in an act of parliament.

The Church was now virtually powerless to resist further attacks on its position, especially if they were supported by parliament. In 1534 the Act of First Fruits and Tenths established a permanent system of high taxation for the clergy – as opposed to the 'one-off' arrangement of 1531. In future all clerical office holders were to pay the Crown approximately a year's income on appointment (the first fruits) and ten per cent of their income annually thereafter. This system increased the royal revenue by about 40 per cent and was punitive in that laymen were not subjected to taxation on anything like the same scale. The attacks reached their climax when, between 1536 and 1540, the majority of the Church's capital assets were confiscated.

Key date

Act of First Fruits and Tenths: 1534

3 | The Break with Rome and the Royal Supremacy

Introduction

At the same time Henry was increasing his control over the Church in England and Wales, he was also taking steps to reduce the power of the Pope within his domains. His motives for doing so were mixed and often confused. For much of the time his intention appears to have been to exert pressure on Rome in the hope of persuading the Pope to reach a favourable decision over the divorce. However, intermittently to begin with, although more consistently as the years passed, there was a second strand to the policy. Henry was periodically convinced – although he frequently lost sight of his conviction – that his aim should be to re-establish his territories as a 'sovereign empire' within which no other ruler could exercise control of any sort. Much of the force of the argument underpinning this policy lay in the word 're-establish'. Those who urged the king in this direction believed that the rulers of England had enjoyed sole power in their kingdoms until some time in the early Middle Ages when the Pope (unjustifiably in their opinion) had established a variety of legal and financial claims because of his headship of the Western Church. These, it was argued, were all spurious and should be rejected out of hand.

The break with Rome

Henry was frequently undecided whether the actions he took against papal power in England were bargaining counters, liable to be reversed if he was granted his divorce, or permanent steps towards a total destruction of foreign influence in his lands. Because of this, it is impossible to be certain of the significance of

Key question
What part did Henry VIII and others play in the break with Rome?

The 'Seventh Book'.
An allegory of the
Reformation from
John Foxe's *Book of
Martyrs*, a massively
influential piece of
Protestant literature
published during the
reign of Elizabeth I.

much of what happened. However, some aspects of the situation
are clear. Although the king undoubtedly retained the final say in
what happened and was even personally responsible for some of
the initiatives that were taken, his vacillations and lack of clarity
of purpose were minimised by the consistent sense of direction
displayed by a number of his advisers and men of business. This
collection of ministers, junior office holders and advisers was able
to ensure that consistency finally prevailed and that a complete
break with Rome was achieved. Their success, of course, was only
possible because the Pope was unprepared to bow to any threat,
thus enabling Henry to be persuaded that it was only by throwing
off allegiance to Rome that his divorce could be achieved. Once it
had been accepted by the king that there could be no going back,
the task of those who wished to see an end to papal power in
England for reasons unconnected to Anne Boleyn became much
more straightforward.

Thomas Cromwell and Elton's 'new orthodoxy'
Between the early 1950s and the mid-1970s G.R. Elton
established a new orthodoxy to replace the traditional view that
the break with Rome occurred because it was the only way in

which Henry could free himself from Catherine of Aragon. The basic Elton view was that it was brought about mainly due to Thomas Cromwell, for whom it was a vital stage in the development of the sovereign nation state which he aspired to create. Thus, it has become commonplace to suggest that the divorce was the occasion rather than the cause of the ending of papal power in England, and that (by implication at least) it would have happened at about the same time whether or not Henry had had marital problems to resolve.

Although Elton has modified and qualified his views over the years and other historians have chosen to slant their accounts of events slightly differently, the essentials of the Elton orthodoxy remain intact. As a result, the false starts and changes of direction caused by Henry's confusions are thought of as being less significant than they once were.

Cranmer and St German

One important qualification that has been generally accepted since Elton first presented his interpretation is that Cromwell was not the initiator, or at times, even the prime mover of the policy that is so closely associated with his name. Two other men – Thomas Cranmer and Christopher St German – are judged to have played an important role in these events, although it has never been suggested that they should be regarded as challenging Cromwell's claim to be the pre-eminent influence.

Thomas Cranmer

Thomas Cranmer rose to real prominence in 1532 when he was chosen as Archbishop of Canterbury. But even before then he had argued strongly that the king should be the head of all institutions within his realm, including the Church. His reasoning was that God had always intended the rulers he placed in power to have such all-embracing authority and that it was only the usurpations of the popes which had interfered with this divinely ordained system of government. His aim was to see the clock turned back to the time when, he claimed, the situation had been as God intended.

Christopher St German

Christopher St German had for many years been the country's leading theorist about the law and, in particular, about the system of common law. Although he was a very old man for the time (he was in his seventies) when the question of papal influence in England came to be of interest in the highest political circles, he still possessed the energy and the clarity of mind to produce detailed theoretical justifications for the elimination of the Pope's authority outside Rome.

'Caesaro-papism'

The body of ideas put forward by Cranmer and St German is given the name of 'caesaro-papism'. This is because it was advocated that the same person be both the temporal leader (Caesar, as in the Roman Empire) and the religious leader (the

Pope). It is not surprising that Henry, given his enormous ego, should be attracted to such thinking. In 1530 he instructed Cranmer, along with another junior colleague, to gather together all the historical evidence they could to support their case. The result was a handwritten collection of documents known as the *collectanea satis copiosa* (may be translated as the sufficiently large collection). Although it included many items that were (unknown to Cranmer) medieval forgeries, its contents were taken at their face value and were much used to justify the king's case in the years to come. Could there be clearer evidence than this that the Pope should hold no power in England?

Solving the King's 'great matter'

Key question
How was the King's 'great matter' solved and who was responsible?

However, it was not until Cromwell became the major influence on Henry, at some time in 1532, that the decision was reached to break completely with Rome. The new chief minister probably used the twin arguments that this was the only way of being sure that the divorce would be granted and that the king owed it to himself and his successors to regain the powers that had been stolen from his ancestors by fraudulent means. Thus the two strands of policy in dealing with the Pope were brought together – at least, as far as the king's stated intentions were concerned. But Cromwell must have been made very anxious at times over the next year or two when it became apparent that, in his heart of hearts, his master still harboured hopes of reaching some agreement with Rome. Fortunately for Cromwell's plans (and probably for his continued physical well-being), a mixture of papal intransigence and English diplomatic clumsiness meant that nothing resulted from Henry's further attempts to reach an agreed solution in his 'great matter'. Possibly this was Cromwell's first experience of coping with a monarch who was able simultaneously to hold and to act on diametrically opposite views, ideas and policies.

Key dates

Emergence of Thomas Cromwell as the King's chief minister: 1532

Act in Restraint of Annates: 1532

Act in Restraint of Annates

The first official step taken to lessen the Pope's influence in England was the passage of the Act in Restraint of Annates in 1532, which banned the payment of all but five per cent of **annates**. Annates were moneys equivalent to about one-third of their annual income paid to the Pope by all new holders of senior posts within the Church in England and Wales and were the Papacy's main source of income from Henry's kingdom. The fact that the act was conditional – it did not come into effect until the king issued letters patent to activate it – confirms that the measure was part of the programme aimed at making it worth the Pope's while to grant Henry the divorce he sought. Even the provision in the act to remove from the Pope and to give to the king the power to give final confirmation to all senior clerical posts was probably merely intended to deny the Pope an obvious tit-for-tat response.

Key term

Annates
Money equivalent to about one-third of their annual income paid to the Pope by all new holders of senior posts within the Church in England and Wales.

Act in Restraint of Appeals

The really important policy decision was made later in the year at a time when Cromwell's influence was effectively undisputed. The plan was to end the Papacy's right to act as the final court of appeal in most matters governed by canon law, and to legislate that the majority of most legal rulings (including those to do with marriage) were to be made within England. The short-term effect of this was, of course, to ensure that the final verdict on the validity of Henry and Catherine's marriage would be taken out of Rome's hands, but its real significance was that, in order to justify the change, the right of the Pope to make decisions affecting Henry and his subjects had to be denied. It used to be thought that this course of action was only decided on once it was known that Anne Boleyn was pregnant, and that Henry was merely reacting to immediate circumstances in agreeing to this hardening of policy. However, it now seems more likely that Anne Boleyn only began to sleep with her monarch once the policy decision to break decisively with Rome had been made in principle and that the only effect of the pregnancy was to inject a sense of urgency into the work of securing the necessary legislation. In March 1533 the Act in Restraint of Appeals (often referred to simply as the Act of Appeals) passed through both houses of parliament and received the royal assent. Its preamble, which contained the justification for what was being done, argued:

> that this realm of England is an empire, and so hath been accepted in the world, governed by one supreme head and king having the dignity and royal estate of the imperial crown of the same, unto whom … all sorts and degrees of people divided in terms of spirituality and temporality, be bounden and owe to bear next to God a natural and humble obedience to the king…

The act went on to stipulate that it was no longer permissible for any of the king's subjects to appeal to an authority outside the country on a specified list of issues and that the Archbishop of Canterbury would henceforth assume the legal powers over these matters that had previously resided in the Pope. Within two months Cranmer had decided, under the terms of the act, that the papal dispensation allowing Henry and Catherine to marry was invalid and that they had therefore never been husband and wife. It seems that Henry might have been prepared to allow matters to rest there, or even to restore the Pope to his previous position had he, despite the lateness of the hour, been willing to give his blessing to the divorce and to Catherine's replacement by Anne Boleyn. But within a year it was clear that no possibility of a rapprochement remained.

What had seemed to be a promising diplomatic opening engineered via the King of France had come to nothing and in 1534 Clement VII had finally announced that Catherine was legally Henry's wife and therefore still the Queen of England. Cromwell was well pleased. He was able to capitalise on his

Key date

Act in Restraint of Appeals: 1533

master's fury to obtain permission to complete the work that the Act of Appeals had started and to eliminate every trace of papal power in England.

Extinguishing the authority of the Bishop of Rome

Between 1534 and 1536 the Reformation Parliament passed a series of acts to ensure that this was done. All direct payments to the Pope were halted (the money went to the king instead), the Archbishop of Canterbury was empowered to grant the wide variety of dispensations and personal exemptions that had previously only been available from Rome (this probably damaged the Papacy financially much more than the cessation of direct payments), and the Pope's role in the appointment of churchmen and in the definition of beliefs and religious practices was eliminated (these powers now passed to the Crown). The aptly named 'Act Extinguishing the Authority of the Bishop of Rome' (1536) tied up the loose ends and laid down the loss of all property as the punishment for people who defended any of the Pope's former powers. Within two years anyone who referred to the former head of the Church as other than the Bishop of Rome was likely to be suspected of being a traitor, as were priests who merely covered up rather than crossed out the Pope's name in their service books. Although it was Thomas Cromwell who took anti-papalism to such lengths, he was fully supported by a bitter and vengeful Henry VIII.

Key date

Act Extinguishing the Authority of the Bishop of Rome: 1536

The royal supremacy

When the Pope's powers within England were removed, there was no automatic reason why they should have been handed over to the king. There were other options available.

Key question

What was meant by the royal supremacy and how was it achieved?

Options

There was a large number of people, mainly within the ranks of the clergy, strongly opposed to any layman exercising control over the Church. Although they saw no reason why the present situation should be altered, they might have been prepared to lend their support to an arrangement whereby a Church of England was established which owed no allegiance to any authority outside the kingdom but was independent of the temporal state. But Henry VIII had attacked the autonomy of the Church in 1531 and 1532. This had shown that such a solution would be unacceptable to him.

It is probable that Thomas Cromwell favoured a different option. There is considerable evidence that he wished the Pope's former powers to be vested in the king-in-parliament, rather than reverting to the king alone. It has been suggested that it was because of this ministerial desire to see decisions about the new Church of England taken by a partnership of monarch and parliament on a continuing basis that every stage in the transfer of authority from the Pope was authorised by legislation, rather than resting on the will of the king alone. There has even been a claim (no longer taken seriously) that Cromwell was successful in implementing his policy.

However, it is now generally accepted that the king's leading minister failed in his attempt to develop a permanent interdependent relationship between the monarch and the political nation (as represented by parliament). Henry was determined that his authority should remain unrestricted by any such arrangement. His interest was in removing any constraints on his freedom of action rather than in establishing a constitutional partnership with his subjects. As far as he was concerned, the Crown was the only acceptable place for the ex-papal powers to reside.

The Act of Supremacy

This was made very clear by the wording of the Act of Supremacy of 1534 in which the king's supreme headship of the Church was not granted but was recognised as an existing fact. Thus parliament was not giving powers to the Crown (if it had been, it might later have decided to withdraw them). It was merely confirming the situation and defining in legal terms what was assumed to be a God-given authority. The full title of the act carries something of the flavour of what was intended. It was 'an act concerning the King's Highness to be Supreme Head of the Church of England and to have authority to reform and redress all errors, heresies and abuses in the same'. A similar message was contained in the act's opening sentences:

Albeit the King's Majesty justly and rightfully is and oweth to be the supreme head of the Church of England, and so is recognised by the clergy of this realm in their Convocations; be it enacted by authority of this present parliament that the king our sovereign lord, his heirs and successors kings of this realm, shall be taken, accepted and reputed the only supreme head in earth of the Church of England called Anglicana Ecclesia …

Gone was the qualification of the supreme headship to which Convocation had agreed in 1531 (see page 96) and gone was any implication that this was largely an honorific title. It was now made plain that the Church was to be subjected to lay control in matters of its day-to-day management and was not to be left in control of its own affairs, as many clerics had mistakenly assumed that it would be. Before the end of the year Cromwell was appointed as the king's **vicegerent** in spiritual matters. This meant that, as far as the Church was concerned, he was in a position to exercise all the powers that legally belonged to the king. And he was not slow to make full use of his new authority (see pages 108–12), so that bishops and other senior churchmen soon found their work being closely scrutinised and themselves subjected to a steady stream of detailed written instructions about what should and should not be done.

Act of Supremacy: 1534

Key date

Vicegerent Cromwell became the king's deputy in Church affairs.

Key term

Key question
Did the royal
supremacy bring a
change in the English
constitution?

A revolutionary change in the English constitution?

It has often been argued that the coming of the royal supremacy over the Church constituted a revolutionary change in the English constitution. How justified is this claim? In many respects the case has been overstated. It has been customary to contrast a state in which an institution (the Church) with its independent legal system and owning about one-third of the country's landed property was controlled by a foreign power – the pre-Reformation situation – with a modern nation state in which all final authority resided in the monarch – the post-Reformation situation.

However, the difference was not as great as it might seem when described in this way. The difficulty is in the word 'controlled', which undoubtedly gives an inflated impression of the influence that the Papacy exercised over the English Church in the decades before the 1530s. If one discounts the way in which Wolsey used his position as papal legate to establish a virtual dictatorship over his colleagues at all levels (as it seems reasonable to do as Wolsey was hardly a 'foreign power'), it is clear that the Pope played very little part in ecclesiastical affairs on the English side of the cliffs of Dover.

Although his was the final decision in the appointment to senior positions such as bishoprics, there was a long-established tradition that he invariably confirmed the person nominated by the king. Rome was rarely appealed to in cases of canon law, and when it was it was always by the tiny minority of the population which was in a position to pay the high fees (in practice, bribes) required to achieve a successful outcome in the Roman courts. Thus the effect of the appeal system on the English Church as a whole was minimal – although it could be devastating on individuals, as Henry VIII found to his cost. Nor did the Pope tell English Christians what to believe.

The basic teachings of the Church were so well established and unchanging that they required no definition from the centre, and the time had not arrived when it was felt necessary to make rulings on matters of detail. It was left to theologians, mainly studying in universities, to debate the finer points of **dogma** among themselves and to agree or disagree as they chose. It was only during the period of the 'official' Counter-Reformation, after the death of Henry VIII, that Rome felt the need to act as the arbiter on matters of belief and religious practice. Some of the legislation passed by the Reformation Parliament referred to the large sums of money that the Pope gained from England because of his 'usurpation'.

However, these complaints were made largely for propaganda purposes and had little substance in fact. While it is true that the Papacy drained huge amounts of gold and silver from Germany, as was so vociferously complained of by Luther and others, the same was not the case with England where the 'exactions' were hardly noticeable. The only general levy was one of several centuries' standing – Peter's Pence – and it raised no more than a few hundred pounds per year from the country as a whole!

Key term

Dogma
Doctrine or set
belief proclaimed as
true by the State
Church.

If the case for a dramatic extinction of foreign influence within the English state is less than totally convincing, what of the claim that the royal supremacy radically altered the constitution itself? Even here the traditional interpretation appears to be somewhat overstated. The picture has frequently been painted of the pre-Reformation Church forming a state within a state and therefore preventing the development of 'modern' political institutions.

Two aspects of the Church's legal independence,

• benefit of clergy
• sanctuaries

have normally been described as typifying this situation.

Benefit of clergy

Benefit of clergy was the arrangement whereby any person charged in one of the king's courts could claim to be immune from prosecution if he was in holy orders. As all those who played some official part, however minor, in Church life and not just priests were considered to be in holy orders, and as, in the absence of documentation to prove a person's status, those who claimed benefit of clergy had only to be able to read a verse of Latin to escape the clutches of the law, there was an obvious loophole for educated (or even intelligent) rogues to exploit.

Sanctuaries

Sanctuaries were areas of land, ranging in size from the county of Durham to the environs of particular churches or monasteries, which were outside the jurisdiction of the law of the land. People whose normal place of residence was within a sanctuary could claim to be exempt from the normal processes of the law wherever the crime of which they were charged had been committed. Many historians have stated (or at least implied) that while such anomalies existed it would have been impossible for a fully fledged nation state to have developed, and that the royal supremacy, by bringing the Church's legal system under the Crown's control, removed a bar to important constitutional developments.

However, it is doubtful whether the bar was of great significance in reality. Not only had the numbers of people abusing the Church's legal privileges always been small, but legislation in the early Tudor period had also lessened the problem by removing some exemptions entirely – especially for major crimes such as murder and high treason – and by ensuring that those that remained were claimed only once by any individual (claimants were branded on the thumb to prevent them using the same 'escape' a second time). The net result was that the existence of the clerical legal privileges has been assessed as being no more than a minor inconvenience, and certainly not one which would have seriously inhibited the emergence of England as a unitary nation state.

Key question
How significant was
the royal supremacy?

Significance of the royal supremacy

So was the royal supremacy of any great significance? It seems that it was because, with hindsight, historians have been able to detect that it marked a dramatic shift in the balance of power within the state. By the 1530s the secular arm was definitely the dominant partner. This was most graphically exemplified by the fact that, although the Southern Convocation was always summoned to meet at the same time as parliament, it was normally a largely irrelevant side-show.

However, it is clear that the Church was still a major force in the land. But it rapidly declined in both political and constitutional importance after 1534. Church courts continued in existence but they no longer offered any challenge to their civil counterparts, and churchmen largely ceased to play a prominent part in political affairs. With the brief exception of Stephen Gardiner during Queen Mary's reign, Wolsey was the last in a long line of clerical lord chancellors. And, after 1540, with the final disappearance of the monasteries (see pages 108–13), laymen secured a large majority in the House of Lords. Never again would it be possible to think of the Church as providing a potential alternative power base to the monarchy within the state.

Yet even this judgement should perhaps be treated with caution, for there are some commentators who have credibly maintained that the royal supremacy was no more than a symbol of changes that were going to happen in any case, whether or not there had been a break with Rome. Although by their very nature hypothetical arguments can never be proved or disproved, it does seem likely that a mid-sixteenth-century English state remaining within the Roman Catholic fold would have reached an agreement with the Papacy which would have had much the same effect as the legislation of 1534–6. At least, such would have been the case were English monarchs to have acted in much the same way as their powerful continental counterparts had done. Thus, as is explored in Chapter 5, the real significance of the royal supremacy and the break with Rome may in fact have been religious rather than political.

Summary diagram: The break with Rome and the royal supremacy

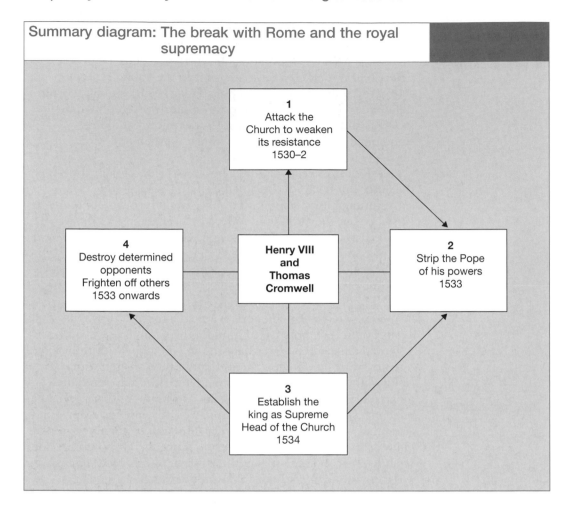

4 | The Dissolution of the Monasteries 1536–40

Background

When Henry VIII came to the throne in 1509 there were more than 850 religious houses in England and Wales. They are nowadays almost always referred to as monasteries, although the word was not common at the time. Many contemporary names were in use, often employed loosely and interchangeably, so that no hard and fast rules on terminology can be established. However, there was a tendency for the larger, mainly rural institutions to be called abbeys, for many of the medium-sized houses to be labelled priories or nunneries, and for the words friary and cell to be used to describe the smaller units.

The houses fell into one of two broad categories:

- There were those that were 'closed', in which the occupants – in theory at least – spent nearly all their time within the confines of the buildings and their adjacent fields and gardens, and devoted most of their energies to attending private religious services within their own chapel.

> **Key question**
> What were monasteries and what was the popular attitude to them in early sixteenth-century England?

- The 'open' houses were the friaries, whose occupants were meant to work in the community at large, bringing spiritual comfort to the needy, be they the poor, the sick or merely those who were denied the services of an effective parish priest.

The two categories were also distinguished by other differences. Whereas the friaries were confined to the towns or their environs, were almost always small, and were universally poor (it was against the rule of each of the four orders of friar to own property other than for their own immediate use), the 'closed' houses – now thought of as the typical monasteries – were more often situated in the countryside than in the towns, were frequently large (in their buildings if not in their number of occupants), and were generally rich.

In fact, the wealth of the 'typical' monasteries as a group was enormous. They possessed most of the Church's riches, normally estimated as including about one-third of the country's landed property. For example, the 30 or so richest monasteries each received an income approximating to that of one of the country's most powerful nobles. This money was derived mainly from 'temporal' sources, but one 'spiritual' source was significant:

- The 'temporal' element was overwhelmingly made up of rents from the agricultural land that they owned.
- The 'spiritual' mainly took the form of profits from the parish priesthoods (benefices) that they held. These arose because very often the monastery would employ a vicar or curate to do the parish work, while retaining the lion's share of the value of the benefice for its own use.

A monastery had often acquired this wealth over several centuries, normally through dozens (in some cases even hundreds) of bequests made in the wills of property owners, large and small, in the hope that their generosity would lessen the time their souls would spend in purgatory.

Most monasteries had been in existence for many generations and were accepted as an integral part of the community by almost the entire population which, mostly disliking change and having grown up with the religious houses, unquestioningly assumed that they were a normal part of life. Although a significant minority of the population lived and died without ever having seen a monastery, most people lived close enough to one, or to one of its outlying estates, to be aware of its activities. And although there were probably no more than a few hundred itinerant preaching friars active at any one time, it is unlikely that many adults would have escaped contact with them at some point during their lives. What evidence there is suggests that in the first half of Henry VIII's reign the popular expectation was that monasteries would always continue to exist.

Wolsey's dissolutions of the 1520s

During the 1520s Cardinal Wolsey was responsible for dissolving 29 small religious houses and for taking over their property with the stated intention of using it to pay for the foundation of a grammar school in his home town of Ipswich and a new college at his old university of Oxford. But there was nothing very remarkable or ominous in this. This was despite the fact that the scale of his activities was much greater than had been that of the bishops who had occasionally taken action to suppress individual religious houses during the past generation.

All of the houses dissolved by Wolsey were 'decayed', in that they had ceased to be viable in the terms envisaged by their founders because of a decline in the number of monks or nuns they contained. Their endowments were to be used for alternative charitable purposes and the dissolutions were carried out totally legally and with explicit papal permission. The fact that the paperwork was not properly tied up by the time of Wolsey's fall in 1529, so that the property was transferred to the king along with all the other possessions of the cardinal, was little known and certainly caused no public consternation. Nor, at that stage, could any significance be read into the fact that most of the detailed work on the dissolutions had been carried out by Wolsey's chief legal adviser, Thomas Cromwell.

Visitation and the *Valor Ecclesiasticus* of 1535

Two overlapping processes, which were historically significant in their own right as well as yielding historians a mass of detailed information about the state of the monasteries at the time, took place in 1535. Cromwell was the king's vicegerent responsible for the day-to-day control of the Church. He planned for most religious houses to be visited by his representatives. Such visitations had long been accepted as a normal, if infrequent, way of ensuring that monasteries were conducting their affairs properly. Traditionally such visitations had been conducted under the authority of the bishop in whose diocese the house lay. In the case of the many houses that had been exempted from such control by a papal dispensation, the visitations had been carried out under the authority of the head of the Order to which the house belonged.

Although Cromwell's programme of visitations was only partial in that it did not include a large number of the smaller monasteries, it was not completed by the end of May as originally intended, and was barely finished by the end of the year. This was because it was interrupted by a second and even more ambitious undertaking, the *Valor Ecclesiasticus*. This was nothing less than an attempt to make a record of all the property owned by the Church in England and Wales, including the monasteries – a colossal undertaking given the lack of civil servants and the primitive state of much estate management at the time.

The work was carried out by unpaid groups of commissioners, mainly local gentry, who, as far as the monasteries were concerned, visited all the religious houses in their county and, by

Key question
How significant was Wolsey's dissolution of the monasteries during the 1520s?

Key questions
How were the visitations carried out and how was the *Valor Ecclesiasticus* compiled? How important were they?

Visitations to the monasteries; *Valor Ecclesiasticus*: 1535

Key date

asking questions and examining account books, built up a picture of the property owned by the monks, nuns or friars. Historians have been lavish in their praise of the completeness and accuracy of the commissioners' work and the *Valor Ecclesiasticus* has been compared to the Domesday Book as an administrative achievement. Certainly, it has proved to be a bedrock for those researching either the dissolution of the monasteries or the subsequent history of the lands that were taken over by the Crown in the process.

However, it was the series of visitations that took place in 1535 that was of the greater significance at the time. Much of the work was carried out by two of Cromwell's trusted 'servants' (a word that would be better translated as 'employees' nowadays), Thomas Legh and Richard Layton. They shared many of the attributes of their master. They were very able (so that the wool could rarely be pulled over their eyes), were prodigious workers (as the speed at which they travelled around the country showed), were highly ambitious (realising that the only way to succeed was to give their superiors exactly what they wanted), and were completely unscrupulous when they needed to be (although they could be humane, and even generous, where their vital interests were not affected).

From the letters they regularly sent to Cromwell describing their activities it is possible both to piece together their itinerary and to assess the way in which they worked. Before they left London they were provided with lists of questions to ask at each house and sets of instructions (injunctions) to issue the monks and nuns they 'visited' – both as appropriate. Although there is no direct evidence for this, it seems that they were also told to make as full a record as possible of all the shortcomings in the lives of the members of the religious houses. Certainly, the detailed *comperta* (lists of transgressions admitted by monks and nuns) that they compiled suggest that this was so.

The short amount of time (often only hours) spent at many houses, the huge quantities of information collected and the many complaints about their bullying tactics, suggests that they were anything but gentle in their work. In the process they acquired a widespread reputation as typifying all that was bad in the government's new ways of conducting much of its business. They were even included in a list of the king's 'evil counsellors' thought to be deserving of special punishment, drawn up during the Pilgrimage of Grace in 1536.

The dissolution of the smaller monasteries 1536

Ever since the visitation of 1535 and the commissions to compile the *Valor Ecclesiasticus* had begun, rumours had been rife that the government's intention was to disband the monasteries and to seize their wealth. These fears were born out in part by an act which was passed by parliament in March 1536. The act stipulated that all religious houses with an annual income of less than £200 (as assessed in the *Valor Ecclesiasticus*) should be dissolved and that their property should pass to the Crown. It

Key question
What is meant by the 'dissolution of the smaller monasteries'?

Key date

Closure of the smaller monasteries: 1536

provided for the heads of the houses to be granted a pension and for other members to be offered the option of transferring to a larger house or ceasing to be 'religious' by going out into the world without being bound by the vows of poverty and obedience that they had taken; although they were expected to continue to honour their vow of chastity and therefore would be unable to marry.

Just over 300 houses fell within the category specified by the act, but by no means all of them were immediately dissolved. The act had given the king power to grant exemptions to individual 'smaller' houses as he saw fit. Evidence has been found that he did so in 67 cases, and it is estimated that there were probably a further ten or more monasteries that escaped closure but whose records have been lost. What is known for certain is that those monasteries whose application for exemption was successful were forced to pay heavily – often in excess of a year's income – for the privilege. The official position was that the houses granted exemption were those worthy of continuation because of the high quality of their performance, but it seems in reality that the escapees were a mixture of those with friends in high places and those with a high percentage of members who wished to remain as monks or nuns. Apparently, the prospect of finding new 'homes' for hundreds of displaced religious was somewhat daunting to Cromwell and his leading assistants.

As soon as the legislation had received the royal assent, commissions, whose task it was to implement the closure of the monasteries affected, were appointed to each county. The urgency was necessary to ensure that as little as possible of the monasteries' movable wealth disappeared before it could be seized for the Crown. In most districts the groups of commissioners acted speedily and efficiently. The monasteries to be dissolved were visited, any inmates who remained were expelled, valuable metal – especially gold, silver, lead from roofs and bronze from bells – was carted off, normally to the Tower of London, any saleable items (even down to hinges from doors) were auctioned locally, and any property that had not previously been let out was offered to rent to a selection of the many people who rapidly came forward with requests for such favours. A large number of the monastic buildings were in such a poor state of repair that by the time locals had helped themselves to whatever the commissioners had not put up for sale, in many cases there was soon little to show that a monastery had previously existed on the site.

However, the 'vultures' did not descend equally speedily in all areas. Particularly in the counties of the north, widespread disapproval of what was happening was more in evidence than individual greed. As a result, commissioners generally acted less energetically and were often willingly prevented from taking action by groups of local people who made it clear that they would offer physical violence to anybody who tried to implement the act. The groups of commissioners who ignored such warnings are thought to have been partly responsible for stirring up the

Lincolnshire Rising and the Pilgrimage of Grace in October 1536. Certainly, once the rebellions were under way no further action could be taken to dissolve monasteries in the areas affected, and some of the houses which had already been closed were even re-opened.

Key question
Why were the remaining monasteries dissolved and what methods were employed to close them?

Key date

Closure of the larger monasteries: 1533–40

The destruction of the remaining monasteries 1538–40

Although most monasteries were careful to remain aloof from the Pilgrimage of Grace, a number were pressured into providing active support. These houses, large and small, were high on Henry VIII's vengeance list once order was restored. The technique used to punish them was thought at the time to be of dubious legality. The head of each house involved was declared a traitor in an act of attainder passed by parliament (there was no trial) and was sentenced to be publicly executed, normally at his own monastery. The possessions of the house were treated as if they had belonged to the abbot personally, and were transferred to the king as was the case with all traitors. Any remaining monks not being punished for taking part in the rebellion, were forced to leave their homes and commissioners disposed of the house's assets in the way that had been normal in 1536.

Of course, this action left hundreds of surviving houses, mainly to the south and west of the River Trent. These included most of the richest and most famous monasteries in the land. However, by early 1540 none remained in existence. The process by which this massive change took place was piecemeal – there was no equivalent for the larger monasteries of the act of 1536. Once, in 1538, the dust from the Pilgrimage of Grace had fully settled, Cromwell sent out pairs of his most trusted servants with commissions to receive the property of the remaining religious houses as free gifts to the king. Each commission was for a specified part of the country, except that for the friaries which applied nationally. In their early 'sweeps' the commissioners were instructed to spend little time on those heads of houses and their communities who seemed prepared to resist strongly. They were merely to report such situations, having created as much fear and discord as possible, and to devote their energies to the vast majority of abbots and abbesses who were prepared to please the king. Many of the heads of houses who initially resisted the 'invitation' of the commissioners were willing to resign their positions when instructed to do so in their monarch's name. They were then speedily replaced by men and women who were known to be more amenable, with the obvious end result.

Part way through the sequence of sweeps there occurred an event of only technical significance. In 1539 an act of parliament was passed stipulating that any voluntary surrenderings of monastic property which had so far taken place, or which were to take place in the future, were completely legal and that no challenges to the validity of the king's title to the possessions – or of those to whom he subsequently transferred them – were to be allowed by the courts. This virtual afterthought had been enacted because some of Henry's legal advisers were fearful that without it the way would be open to potentially embarrassing legal disputes in the future. But, of course, the passage of the act neither speeded up nor slowed down the pace at which the dissolutions took place.

Despite the overwhelming success of the commissioners, there was a handful of individual heads of houses who, with the support of their communities, were not prepared to be cajoled or frightened into compliance. They were the stuff of which martyrs are made, and Henry did not disappoint their expectations. They were tried on spurious charges of treachery – normally for crimes such as secreting items of value so that they would not eventually fall into the king's hands – and were sentenced to death, with the possessions of their houses being forfeited to the Crown. The most famous to suffer in this way were the Abbots of Colchester, Reading and Glastonbury. The latter was the head of one of the richest monasteries in the country. His execution at his abbey, along with the subsequent destruction of one of the finest buildings in England, was for generations to be one of the best remembered 'crimes' of Henry VIII.

The dissolution of over 800 monasteries in less than five years is a remarkably well-documented episode, thanks mainly to the survival of the letters received by Cromwell from the men responsible for carrying out the work. As a result, historians have long been in very general agreement about what happened and when. In recent decades the researches of local historians have usefully filled out many of the details, but they have done little to amend the overall picture. However, the same degree of unanimity has never existed in providing answers to the 'why?' and 'with what effects?' questions. These have for long been part of the battleground of the 'What sort of king was Henry VIII?', 'What was the role of Thomas Cromwell?' and 'Why was there a Reformation in England?' controversies.

Why were the monasteries dissolved?
The early **sectarian controversy**: Catholic vs Protestant interpretation

For about 300 years after the death of Henry VIII this was a hotly disputed question between writers with Catholic or Protestant sympathies.

Catholic interpretation

The Catholics argued that the dissolution had nothing to do with religion. Their contention was that a greedy and wicked king was persuaded by his unscrupulous minister that a major piece of legalised theft would make him wealthy almost beyond his wildest dreams. They made much of a remark in a report of the Emperor's ambassador, Eustace Chapuy, that Cromwell had risen to favour by promising Henry that he would make him the richest king in Christendom. They also attempted to prove that the monasteries were generally functioning well and were respected

Key term

Sectarian controversy The conflict and differences of opinion between Catholic and Protestant historians in the way they interpret changes in the Church.

by the population as a whole at the time of their destruction. They made much of the active support for the monasteries that was forthcoming in the north, especially during the Pilgrimage of Grace, and highlighted the bravery of those who chose to die rather than to comply with the sacrilegious orders of their king.

Protestant interpretation

The Protestants argued that by the 1530s the monasteries were generally corrupt places where sinners and **charlatans** lived in degenerate luxury, paid for by the charitable bequests of earlier generations. In addition, they contended that the very reason for the monastic way of life was based on one of the major lies that the Papacy had long ago promulgated in order to strengthen its own position. This was that merit in the eyes of God (and therefore salvation) was to be gained by good works rather than by faith, and that the highest form of good works was the living of a life devoted to worship, and especially the celebration of the Mass. To this ancient falsehood, they argued, had been added the fictional doctrine of purgatory, by which it was taught that the souls of the dead suffered agonies for a finite number of years before being admitted to heaven, and that the time spent in purgatory could be shortened by giving money to monks and nuns so that they would pray on your behalf. Therefore, their argument was that the monasteries deserved to be dissolved both because the money to support them had been acquired under false pretences and because they no longer carried out the functions that their founders had intended.

Protestant writers were also particularly keen to establish that the dissolution of the monasteries was an integral part of the Reformation in England. This they saw as a coherent process by which a debased form of Christianity emanating from Rome was replaced by a cleansed and revitalised version – the Church of England – thanks to the actions of Henry VIII, two of his children, and their ever more numerous Protestant supporters. In this the destruction of monastic ways of life was seen as important in that it rid the country of the major centres of support for the perverted belief that salvation could be gained by good works alone and, in particular, through a life devoted to worship and the avoidance of the world's temptations by shutting oneself away from them. Thus monasticism was viewed as an open challenge to the central Protestant belief that salvation was freely available to all those who were prepared to accept it by believing in God and his only son Jesus Christ. In these circumstances it was readily assumed that the monasteries must have been dissolved for 'religious' reasons, as part of the cleansing operation of the Reformation.

The later sectarian controversy

As might be imagined, up to the middle of the nineteenth century this controversy generated much more heat than light, with most of those who took part in it being much more interested in defending a pre-determined position than in

Key term

Charlatans
False or untrustworthy people who pretend to be what they are not.

establishing any objective truth. The change during the next
100 years was that, although most writers still maintained an
identifiably Catholic or Protestant position, a genuine attempt
was made to substantiate their claims with facts. But because so
many 'facts' existed that could be used to support either position,
the dispute based on religious affiliation continued for much
longer than might otherwise have been expected. Catholic writers
were able to point to the extensive evidence of thriving
spirituality within the English monastic system at the time of the
dissolution.

In particular they could catalogue the heroic struggle of so
many members of the London Charterhouse and the
complimentary reports about the virtue of much of what they
found that were written by several of the groups of commissioners
whose task it was to implement the closure of the smaller houses
in 1536. They were also able to present further evidence that both
Henry VIII and Thomas Cromwell were primarily motivated by
greed in their decision to destroy the monasteries. In particular,
they took pleasure in drawing attention to the fact that Cromwell
made a conscious effort to enrich himself at the monasteries'
expense. Not only did he accept 'gifts' from many smaller
monasteries in return for supporting their appeals to be exempt
from the terms of the 1536 act, but he also persuaded at least 30
religious houses to grant him an annual payment. The advantage
of these retainers was that he could continue to claim them for the
rest of his life, even after the monasteries involved were dissolved.

However, Protestant authors were able to call upon much more
extensive evidence to support their contention that the
monasteries deserved to be closed. The *Valor Ecclesiasticus* and the
comperta resulting from the visitations of 1535 provided a
massive amount of ammunition. The *Valor Ecclesiasticus*, which
itemised expenditure as well as income, could be used to show a
major misapplication of monastic funds. It was calculated that, on
average, about one-quarter of each monastery's income was paid
directly to the head of the house. This person, normally with the
title of abbot or abbess, was in most cases an absentee leader,
living the life of a country gentleman in a comfortable house on
one of the monastery's manors, while leaving the day-to-day
exercise of his or her duties to a deputy (normally called the
prior or prioress) who was resident in the monastery. It was a
simple matter to contrast this profligacy with the three per cent of
income that the same document showed as being spent on
charitable works.

Even more damning, and certainly more sensational, was the
story of widespread immorality and sexual perversion that could
be extracted from the *comperta*. There were contemporary
reports that it was the reading out of such evidence by ministers
during the debate in the Commons on the legislation to dissolve
the smaller monasteries which provoked angry support for the
government's policy. That hundreds of monks had admitted to
taking part in homosexual practices, often with young boys, while
many others told of their strings of mistresses – accounts

mirrored by the confessions of nuns to bearing children, sometimes several times – seemed to suggest that the isolated anecdotes of sexual laxity or worse that had been in circulation for decades were part of a general picture of moral depravity among the religious.

Writers approaching the issue from a Protestant standpoint have also been eager to establish that the monasteries were unpopular at the time of their dissolution. They have been able to point to general trends such as the decline in the number of men and women wishing to become monks or nuns in the final decades of the monasteries' existence, the hostility shown by MPs to the religious houses and their shortcomings, and the alacrity with which people from all walks of life attempted to acquire the monasteries' possessions once it seemed likely that they would become available.

In addition, it has been possible to argue convincingly that by the 1530s the élite of leading English intellectuals, who might have been expected to feature among the monasteries' principal defenders, had reached the conclusion that the monastic way of life had little to commend it. Erasmus's scathing attacks on the lives lived by the religious had done much to bring about this negative perception of monasticism among the country's intellectual leaders, which seemingly had already percolated down to many of the less-educated members of the ruling élite.

Key question
How and why do modern interpretations differ from those of earlier sectarian interpretations?

Modern interpretations

Most historians writing about the issue since the Second World War have had neither a Catholic nor a Protestant axe to grind and, although there have been clear differences of emphasis between them, a surprising degree of consensus has emerged.

The most significant point of agreement has been that the monasteries were dissolved almost entirely because Henry VIII wished to lay his hands on their wealth. Other contributory factors have been identified (and often disagreed about), but the vital factor – in that without it the dissolution would not have taken place – has generally, and most probably finally, been agreed to be the king's desire to acquire the monasteries' riches. In this the 'top-down' school, led by Elton and Scarisbrick, has been as one with the 'bottom-up' revisionists, including Dickens who was their original inspiration.

The 'top-down' historians reached this conclusion after finding that Henry was solidly behind each of the moves forward in the story of the dissolution, while at the same time accepting none of the doctrinaire reasons subsequently advanced by Protestants to justify his actions. Even more persuasive evidence that Henry's motives were not in the least 'religious' has been provided by the fact that he seems to have believed quite strongly in the traditional values of monasticism. Not only did he insist, against the wishes of his advisers, that the monks and nuns who chose to abandon their vocation when their houses were dissolved must be forced to maintain their vows of chastity, but he even went to the lengths of re-founding two monasteries after the initial batch of dissolutions with the specific purpose of ensuring that frequent prayers were said for him, his wife and the souls of his ancestors.

At the same time, any possibility of the contention being successfully advanced that he supported the dissolution programme for general political reasons has been destroyed. It is clear that by mid-1535 any threat to the acceptance of either the royal supremacy or the new order of succession that the monasteries might have posed had effectively been eliminated. And Henry was clearly not impressed by the argument that, despite the monks and nuns having taken the oaths required of them, the monasteries would constitute a latent source of opposition as long as they were allowed to continue in existence.

The 'bottom-up' writers have reached the same position by establishing that there was very little popular opposition to the continued existence of the religious houses, and that their shortcomings were such that a modest reform programme could have eliminated most of them. In this, by chance, they have found themselves in agreement with some of the arguments previously advanced by Catholic historians. They have been able to prove beyond reasonable doubt that the public attitude towards the religious houses was just on the supportive side of neutral – that in any opinion poll (had such things existed at the time) the 'do not really mind one way or the other' would have been in a majority and that those strongly supportive of or violently opposed to the continuation of the monasteries would have formed small minorities, with the latter probably being the smallest of all.

This lack of strength of feeling against the monasteries is perhaps best exemplified by contrasting what happened in England and Wales with events in Germany. In Henry VIII's realm there were no examples of violence being offered to existing religious houses and their inmates, while in Germany the sacking of monasteries by hostile mobs intent on ending what they regarded as anti-Christian practices commonly accompanied the spread of the Reformation into new districts. It even seems that in England and Wales those who complained about specific abuses which adversely affected them were content merely to grumble and were generally in favour of the monastic system as a whole. They, in common with most of the population, appear to have accepted as a fact of life the way in which the abbots and abbesses took such a high percentage of their houses' income. In short, there was no indication of widespread indignation.

The 'bottom-up' historians have also shown that the state of the monasteries in the 1530s was not nearly as bad as Protestant writers have generally maintained. Their conclusion has been that, although less than ten per cent of houses were centres of spiritual fervour, the vast majority were adequately following the way of life prescribed by the Order to which they belonged. In particular, they have established that the comperta resulting from the visitations of 1535 must be treated with extreme caution. It is clear that the visitors carried out their orders to 'dig up as much dirt as possible' with efficiency and enthusiasm, but with no regard for fairness or presenting a balanced picture.

Although it is not suggested that they went as far as fabricating evidence, there is no doubt that they were prepared to mislead quite outrageously. This can be shown both from internal evidence in their reports and from external evidence that has been unearthed relating to a few of the confessions included in the comperta. It was the reporting of a total of 181 cases of 'sodomy' that gave rise to claims of widespread homosexual practices in monasteries. But a careful reading of the reports shows that the visitors' definition of sodomy was most unusual, in that all but 12 of the cases are described as being instances of 'solitary vice', presumably masturbation.

Thus, in fact, there was one confession of homosexuality for roughly every 30 monasteries visited. There were 38 confessions by nuns that they had had children. But it is now known that one of the pregnancies took place at the beginning of the century, and probably before the nun in question took her vow of chastity. This opens the possibility that many of the other confessions related to similarly ancient falls from grace. It is therefore clear that the religious houses were in no sense the dens of vice that they have sometimes been painted as being.

Thus the currently agreed explanation of the causes of the dissolution of the monasteries is well rounded and convincing in its essentials. It is clear that there was no popular demand for the destruction of the religious houses, that they were not in a terminal state of collapse through decadence and moral laxity, and that they posed no political or religious threat to the king or his policies. However, they did possess enormous wealth, and it was the desire to gain control of this that motivated Henry to allow or to insist that Cromwell and his assistants destroyed the monasteries and transferred their possessions to the Crown.

Key question
What evidence can be put forward to suggest that Henry VIII and Cromwell planned the dissolution?

How far was the dissolution of the monasteries planned?
Older interpretation

For nearly 400 years after the event it was the received wisdom among writers on the subject who were hostile to Henry VIII that Cromwell had risen to power by promising the king to acquire the wealth of the monasteries for him, and that he spent the next seven or eight years putting his plan into operation. Thus, the belief was that the end result was in mind from the outset. It was argued that the proposal's successful outcome was assured once the king had given it his blessing. Such a simplistic view can no longer be supported.

The central, three-stage thread of the interpretation (below) is very much open to question:

- that Cromwell offered
- that Henry VIII accepted
- that Cromwell delivered.

Newer interpretation

Few people would now support the suggestion that Cromwell never made an explicit offer to Henry VIII about the monasteries. The evidence that he did so is highly unreliable, being based on hostile gossip some time after the event, and, in any case, the story portrays Cromwell in a role that was foreign to him. He did not do deals with Henry – the relationship was much too unequal for that – and any planting of ideas that he did was by subtle insinuation, probably in casual conversation, over a period of time, for it was essential that Henry believed any new idea to be his own. Nor is it likely that Cromwell would have needed to introduce the possibility of dissolution to Henry, who was well-informed as well as greedy, and would probably have heard about the seizures of monastic land in Lutheran Germany, Zwinglian Switzerland, Denmark and Sweden before he ever met Cromwell. It is likely that his imagination would have been set racing by such news.

Of course, the truth of what happened will never be known – the evidence does not exist – but a well-informed guess would be that the king and his minister discovered in conversation together that they shared a common perception that there was money to be made from a well-timed dissolution of some monasteries. It is likely that this happened later rather than sooner, probably about the middle of 1535. Certainly, there seems to have been no intention to implement a programme of dissolutions on the part of either man at the beginning of the year when Cromwell initiated the visitation of the monasteries and Henry ordered the collection of the information that was to become the *Valor Ecclesiasticus*.

Cromwell's motives

Cromwell probably had a wide range of motives for deciding to exercise his rights of visitation as vicegerent. Among these might have been a desire to have his powers understood throughout the country (often a slow process in the days before the mass media), a genuine wish to reform the monasteries in an evangelical direction (the fact that he ordered all monks and nuns regularly to listen both to the Bible read in English and to sermons based on it suggests this), and a plan to enrich himself at the monasteries' expense by ordering them to obey impossibly restrictive regulations and then granting them exemptions in return for cash 'gifts'. This much can be surmised from the injunctions that his representatives were instructed to issue to each house. Among these were:

- that no monk or brother of this monastery by any means go forth of the precincts of the said monastery
- that women be utterly excluded from entering into the limits or circuit of this monastery or place unless they first obtain licence of the King's highness or his visitor
- that there be no entering into this monastery but one and that by the great fore-gate of the same

Key term

Lucre
Another term for
money.

- that they shall not show any relics or feigned miracles for increase of **lucre** but that they exhort pilgrims and strangers to give that to the poor that they thought to offer to their images or relics.

Certainly, it is most probable that the instruction to the visitors to gather as much evidence as possible of the monasteries' shortcomings was issued later in the year, suggesting that it was only then that the king had decided that a partial dissolution was soon to take place. And, although the *Valor Ecclesiasticus* was to be a vital tool in implementing the dissolution of the smaller monasteries, it was certainly not designed with this in mind. Its purpose was to provide the information necessary to calculate how much each institution would have to pay as the ten per cent of clerical income that parliament had already granted Henry. Had seizure of property been in mind questions would have been asked about the liquid assets (in cash and kind) held by each monastery.

The fact that Cromwell had not had time to draw together all the evidence against the smaller monasteries by the time parliament came to debate the legislation dissolving them suggests that the minister was not working according to a carefully laid plan. It is much more likely that he was having to react to a sequence of his master's hastily made decisions – even though they were decisions of which he heartily approved and which he had probably done much to encourage.

A one-off 'smash and grab' operation?

A strong case can be made to support the contention that the dissolution of the smaller monasteries in 1536 was envisaged by Henry and Cromwell as a one-off 'smash and grab' operation. In it as much wealth as possible would be secured for the Crown from those religious houses which could be argued to be too small to be truly viable, as proved by the lack of discipline uncovered by the previous year's visitations. They probably judged that this move would be acceptable to the propertied classes, whose support they needed to retain, because it was merely a small extension of the long-held clerical belief that a religious house of less than a head and 12 members was too small to be effective. It was true that the head-count approach was being replaced by a criterion based on income (houses with an income of less than £200 per annum were to be dissolved), but it could be maintained (not very honestly) that the result would be essentially the same.

Certainly, the wording of the 1536 act would lead one to think that a total dissolution of the monasteries was not envisaged, even as a long-term aim. The entire document revolved around the claim that by weeding out the smaller religious houses, in which the monastic life was not and could not be effectively pursued, and by transferring dedicated monks and nuns to the larger houses which were in a good state of spiritual health, any necessary reform of the system would be achieved.

However, this seemingly clear evidence is not to be trusted. Much of the legislation instigated by the government during the 1530s was couched in terms that were mere propaganda, in that the arguments used were those that it was thought would be acceptable. In fact they were often the complete opposite of the government's motivation or of what was intended for the future. This means that the wording of the 1536 act is essentially worthless as evidence of either Henry and Cromwell's motives for dissolving the smaller monasteries or their plans regarding the larger ones.

Nor should the fact that no further action was taken until 1538 be thought to have any bearing on the question of whether or not there was any long-term plan to dissolve all the monasteries. The inaction is totally explicable in terms of Henry's decision to slow down the pace of change and Cromwell's wish to lie as low as possible following the widespread discontent with government policies that had been revealed by the Pilgrimage of Grace in late 1536. But this is not to argue that there was a plan. In fact, both the sequence of events that followed the dissolution of the smaller monasteries and what is known of Henry and Cromwell's methods of working lead to the same conclusion: that, on balance of probability (the evidence will support no stronger claim than this), the government was merely taking advantage of possibilities as they somewhat unexpectedly arose.

Expectation of dissolution

The key to the situation appears to have been the news received by Cromwell that many of the larger monasteries were expecting to be dissolved in the near future and were dispersing their assets among friends and well-wishers so that they would not fall into the king's hands. This seems to have caused Cromwell to amend his judgement that the richer religious houses would be too powerful to destroy without risking widespread political unrest. The 'sweep' of late 1538 and early 1539 was probably a move to test the resolve of the remaining monasteries. When it was found that most were willing to surrender without a struggle, it was an obvious encouragement to press on with the process.

It would have been typical of Henry, now made aware that huge riches were his for the taking, to instruct his minister to complete the dissolution, even if it meant taking violent action against the resisters. He would have found no difficulty in justifying to himself the virtually overnight change from wishing to found new monasteries to pray on his behalf to insisting on the destruction of all religious houses, whatever their spiritual merits. Equally it would have been very typical of Cromwell, the highly skilled, pragmatic politician, both to have seized on a half-opportunity and to have converted it into a huge success, and to have learned from the events of 1536 that it was safer to pick off his intended victims one by one rather than by launching a full-frontal attack.

Of course, it could never be proved that Henry and Cromwell had not planned the destruction of all the monasteries from the outset, but it seems unlikely that they did. Henry's actions, in particular, fit the pattern of the bold adventurer who intended to steal half the apples and then found that the rest virtually fell into his lap. It is more possible that Cromwell dreamt of a complete dissolution from the early 1530s onwards (he had that sort of mind), but he certainly possessed no blueprint for turning such an aspiration into reality. His achievement – if it can be regarded as such – was in taking initiatives whenever the slightest opportunity arose, and following them through with outstanding administrative skill. No one else of his generation could have done it so well.

Key question
What were the short-term and long term effects of the dissolution?

What were the effects of the dissolution?
The debate
For centuries Catholic writers criticised the dissolution for its religious, humanitarian and cultural effects. The word 'vandalism' was much used – 'religious' vandalism because institutions with a proud spiritual tradition going back many centuries were eliminated at a time when they were far from moribund and when there were even signs of a significant upsurge of piety, and 'cultural' vandalism because many of the realm's most impressive pieces of medieval architecture were wilfully destroyed and most of its finest examples of medieval art (the illustrated manuscripts in monastery libraries) were carelessly allowed to be lost because their contents were temporarily out of fashion. Much was also made of the hardships suffered by the occupants of the dissolved monasteries. It was claimed that their ordered way of life was suddenly ended when they were cast out into a turbulent and fast-changing world. It was also said that the many poor people who had depended on the charity disbursed by the religious houses suffered considerable hardship as a result of the dissolution.

Short-term consequences of the dissolution
Modern historians recognise a large element of special pleading in this argument. In particular, the cries of religious vandalism are seen to be largely subjective, being dependent on the writer's value system, and as such worthy of little consideration by professional researchers of history, in whom objectivity is expected to prevail. After all, committed Protestant writers have advanced an exactly opposite point of view. It is, of course, very difficult to make an objective assessment of the religious effect of the dissolution. What criteria does one apply, and what relevant evidence exists? These are issues that have not greatly interested recent historians of the English Reformation, who have generally satisfied themselves with the judgement that the dissolution of the monasteries was probably the part of the Reformation that had the least effect on either the quality or the quantity of religion in England and Wales.

Cultural vandalism?
The claim of cultural vandalism has generally been treated more sympathetically, although probably with more subjectivity than

objectivity. There is a strong streak of 'if it is old it must be worth retaining' sentimentality running throughout the western world, and the sight of the majestic ruins of some of the larger rural abbeys, such as Fountains in Yorkshire and Tintern in Gwent, still elicits criticism of the action that resulted in such a loss of architectural heritage. Of course, it should be remembered that not all was lost. In particular, abbey churches survived to become cathedrals in the new dioceses such as Bristol, Gloucester, Chester and Westminster, while several others were purchased by their local communities to serve as parish churches. It may or may not be a relevant fact that few of the hundreds of monastic buildings that disappeared, leaving no trace above ground that they ever existed, are thought to have possessed any distinctive (let alone unique) architectural merit.

Humanitarian harm?

The claim that considerable humanitarian harm was done by the dissolution has excited considerable interest among modern historians and has been the subject of a large amount of painstaking research. Much of this has taken the form of tracking down what happened to named individuals who were turned out into the world by the dissolution. In their totality, the findings of the researchers have been surprisingly clear-cut, even allowing for their incompleteness and the possibility of a high margin of error. The conclusion reached has been that all but about 1500 of the 8000 monks and friars who were dispossessed by the dissolution managed to find alternative paid employment within the Church with which to supplement their pensions, thus allowing them to live comfortably if not luxuriously. It has been estimated that the majority of the 2000 nuns affected by the dissolution did less well, as they were neither allowed to marry nor were eligible for the priestly posts that were the refuge of many of their male counterparts.

It is not known how many of them were able to return to their original families, but those who could not were probably forced to live at a very basic subsistence level, although there was no need for them to starve. No quantitative evidence is available about either the lay servants of the monasteries or the poor who had benefited from monastic charity on either a regular or a casual basis. However, it is thought likely that the majority of servants would have been able to find employment with the new owners of the monasteries' property, while the disappearance of monastic alms is considered to have added to an already serious problem rather than to have caused a new one. The plight of the poor was already dire on a national scale and it is likely that the ending of the monasteries' charitable activities was merely one of many reasons why the problem was becoming high on the government's list of major worries.

Thus the recent tendency among historians has been to play down the traditional arguments of the Catholic writers about the effects of the dissolution. The same is true of some of the other traditionally asserted negative effects. It used to be claimed that the transfer of the monastic estates to a new breed of capitalist, 'make high profits at any cost' farmers, resulted in thousands of their tenants being squeezed to pay higher rents which they could only do by accepting a significantly lower standard of living for themselves, and that by enclosing large amounts of land in order to make it more profitable to farm they were responsible for causing large-scale depopulation and homelessness.

Modern local and regional studies
Modern local and regional studies aimed at examining these contentions have shown them to be largely unfounded. It has been discovered that not only were the rents charged by the new possessors of monastic estates generally similar to those imposed by the former owners, but also nearly all the enclosure of monastic land took place before the dissolution rather than after it. Similarly, the old contention that the destruction of the monasteries led to the urban decay that was a feature of mid-Tudor England has been shown to be inaccurate. Although it is true that some towns did possess a large number of religious houses – there were 23 in London alone – in every case that has been studied the disappearance of the expenditure generated by the monks, nuns and friars has been assessed as having a minimal impact on the prosperity of the community as a whole. If towns were experiencing problems it was not because the monasteries had ceased to exist. Thus it would seem that recent historians have gone a long way towards discrediting traditional beliefs about the short-term effects of the dissolution.

Long-term consequences of the dissolution
When considering the possible long-term consequences of the dissolution, historians have traditionally focused attention on the effect of the disappearance of the monasteries on the relative wealth of the Crown. This is because the seizures made between 1536 and 1540 had the potential of virtually doubling the king's normal income and of freeing him from any dependence on parliamentary grants, except in very exceptional circumstances. The political significance of this possibility was not lost on those writing after the seventeenth century, when the emergence of a parliamentary monarchy rather than the development of a European-style royal despotism was thought to have largely been the result of the Crown's relative poverty. The orthodoxy became that Henry VIII squandered an opportunity to ensure the Crown's long-term financial independence, where a wiser monarch (such as his father) would not have done.

Flaws in the argument: the dangers of hindsight
There are several flaws in this 'old' view. The most obvious of these is that the writers who have advanced it have been guilty of exercising that most dangerous of tools – hindsight. There is no doubt that Henry was deeply concerned about the future of the monarchy, and of his dynasty in particular. Otherwise his actions over potential rival claimants to his throne and the lengths he went to in an attempt to ensure that he left an adult male heir to

succeed him would make no sense. But he had no reason to imagine that the future of the monarchy might depend on financial independence from parliament. After all, he regarded the institution as a useful and pliant adjunct to his power. His experience was that it always did what he wanted it to, as long as his demands were tactfully presented, and he had no reason to think that the situation would ever change. Certainly, he cannot be blamed for failing to realise that the Commons would ever be a threat to the monarchy.

Flaws in the argument: the contention that Henry squandered a significant proportion of the monastic wealth

The other major flaw in the traditional 'squandering' argument is the contention that Henry gave away a significant proportion of the monastic wealth that should have come to him. Detailed research into what happened to the estates of the dissolved monasteries has proved that this was just not so. The picture that has emerged is of a miserly monarch, encouraged by Cromwell, who gave away virtually nothing. It is true that by the time of Henry's death about one half of the monastic lands had left royal possession permanently, but nearly all of it – even that acquired by his friends – had been sold at a full market price.

It seems that the only favour the king was prepared to grant to those who 'had his ear' was to permit them or their friends to purchase the estates they wanted rather than allowing rival bidders to be successful. At one time it was thought that the existence of buyers who rapidly sold on the estates they purchased proved that the Crown disposed of the land too cheaply – otherwise there would have been no profit for the 'middle man' to make – but even this argument has been shown to be false. It seems that the 'middle men' were merely acting as agents for the real purchasers and were earning no more than a modest fee from their activities.

The real argument that remains is whether Henry was wise in his spending of the half of the monastic wealth he disposed of, given that he and his ministers had already ensured that they maximised the value of the assets they sold. Here there is unlikely ever to be agreement. Most of the money realised from the sale of monastic land was spent on the wars against France and Scotland that were fought in the last years of Henry's reign. We now know that the wars achieved nothing of substance for Henry or his subjects and could have been avoided had the king wished to do so.

In the light of these facts, most commentators will choose to accuse Henry of wasteful folly or worse. However, there is an alternative defensible point of view. This involves making a judgement as if from Henry's point of view at the time. Applying such criteria, would it have been justifiable for Henry not to spend the money as he did, when he believed that a monarch's first duty was to be victorious in battle and when he could see the possibility of adding one or even two kingdoms to the lands he already possessed? And, after all, when he died he did leave behind him about a half of the additional wealth he had acquired.

Social consequences of the dissolution

However, there is one area in which it is now generally agreed that the dissolution had very significant long-term consequences. This is in the social sphere. Because so much of the monastic land was sold by Henry VIII and during the reigns of Edward VI and Elizabeth I (virtually none remained in royal possession in 1603), the number of estates available to be bought was much greater than at any time for centuries. Although many of the manors were purchased by those who already owned considerable estates, many were bought by those who would otherwise have remained 'landless' and therefore inferior to the existing country gentlemen.

Some of these were merchants who had made their money from trade but more were the younger sons of landowning families who, because of the system of **primogeniture** by which the eldest son inherited all the land owned by his father, were otherwise doomed to drop out of the social élite into which they had been born. The effect of this was to increase the number of those enjoying the social rank of country gentleman by several thousand before the end of the century. Some would argue that it was this enlargement of the landowning class which resulted in England becoming a parliamentary monarchy, freer from violent revolution than its European neighbours and with the tradition of slow and peaceful change that is such an important part of our heritage.

Thus it seems that the effects of the dissolution of the monasteries might have been very significant indeed in the long term, but not in the short term and not for the course of the Reformation in England. It has even been suggested that the Reformation could have taken place very well without the dissolution, or the dissolution without there being a Reformation. That this view is widely supported suggests that the 'top-down' historians are very much in the ascendancy in this aspect of Reformation studies.

Key term

Primogeniture
English legal term to describe the right of the eldest male child to inherit land.

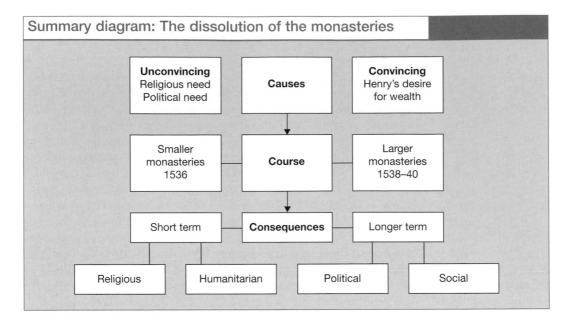

Summary diagram: The dissolution of the monasteries

5 | Opposition to the Changes

The government's strategy

Both Henry VIII and Thomas Cromwell realised that the policies they were pursuing after 1532 were going to be unpopular in many quarters and were likely to be actively supported by very few people. Therefore they consciously developed an approach for dealing with what could have been a very perilous situation indeed. Working from indirect evidence it is possible to identify this approach with confidence. The potential opposition was seemingly divided into two categories:

- those (a tiny minority) who would refuse to accept the changes whatever was done to them
- those (the large majority) who would fall into line provided the stakes were raised high enough.

Given this analysis, the strategy to be followed was clear. The small number of unyielding opponents must be destroyed, partly to act as a warning to others, and the mass of less determined doubters must be forced into positive acceptance of the new situation by threatening them with dire consequences if they did not.

Cromwell believed very strongly that all such action must be legally defensible and it appears that the king agreed with him. So it was necessary to ensure that appropriate legislation was in place to justify whatever action was taken. The traditional way of dealing with traitors, especially where the evidence against them was not clear-cut (as was often the case), was for parliament to pass an act of attainder against them. Such acts were normally passed without there being a trial – a statement by a minister claiming guilt was usually sufficient – which condemned the alleged traitors to death and transferred their property to the

Key question
How did the government deal with opposition to the changes?

Crown. Although such a procedure could be used if necessary, it was clear to Cromwell that it would be a clumsy method of dealing with a number of cases arising over an extended period of time. What was needed was a blanket law which could be invoked as and when the need arose. This was provided by a Treasons Act, originally passed in 1534 and strengthened by amendment on several occasions in the following years. The act specified that any person was guilty of high treason (punishable by death) who:

Key date

Treasons Act: 1534

> do maliciously wish, will or desire by words or writing, or by craft imagine, invent, practise, or attempt any bodily harm to be done or committed to the king's most royal person, the queen's [Anne Boleyn] or their heir's apparent [Elizabeth].

The initial draft of the law had worried many MPs, especially in that it laid open to prosecution anybody who made a hostile comment about the king, possibly in a moment of anger. In order to allay such concerns the word 'maliciously' (implying evil intent) was added in several places. Even so, the act made any expression of dissent about what the king had done (be it the divorce, the break with Rome or the royal supremacy) highly dangerous. In such circumstances a prudent person would be unwise to engage in any discussion of what had happened, especially when life imprisonment was later established as the punishment for anyone who heard treasonable utterances and failed to report them.

Cromwell was rightly confident that everybody who spoke out would be able to be dealt with under such legislation. But silence was not to be allowed to protect the passive majority of dissidents. Within the legislation confirming the break with Rome, the royal supremacy and the new order of succession following the divorce (Anne Boleyn's children to have precedence and Catherine of Aragon's daughter, Mary, to be disinherited), clauses were inserted requiring the entire population, as required, to swear oaths supporting the new arrangements. Death was to be the punishment for those who refused. It was felt in government circles that a sufficient deterrent was in place.

Key question
Why were Fisher, More, the Franciscan friars and Carthusians executed?

Prosecution and execution: Fisher, More and the Observant Franciscan friars and Carthusians
John Fisher

Contemporaries were critical of the way in which two prominent individuals – John Fisher and Sir Thomas More – were treated. Fisher was the one member of the Church hierarchy to remain unwavering in his opposition to what Henry was doing. His position was simple and straightforward. He believed that the powers claimed by the Papacy were genuine and God-given, that anybody who denied them was committing a mortal sin and that it was the duty of the Church to denounce such action. He was so certain of his beliefs that he was prepared to stand by them whatever the cost to himself or to anybody else. There was no room for compromise in this stance.

By the time the breach with Rome occurred Fisher was an old man in his mid-sixties. He had been the Bishop of Rochester in Kent since 1504, and the fact that he had never been promoted from this, the smallest and poorest diocese in England, suggests much about him. He was a very unusual bishop in that he had no worldly ambition, was unskilled in politics and showed few administrative capabilities. His loves were scholarship (he learned Hebrew in his fifties) and prayer (to which he devoted many hours every day). He only became a bishop because it was the wish of Henry VIII's mother, whose spiritual adviser he was, that he do so.

He came to Henry VIII's notice as the most active of Catherine of Aragon's defenders during the struggle over the divorce (see pages 91–3). His outspokenness, both to the king's face and in print, resulted in his becoming loathed by Henry, who seems to have been determined to punish him for his effrontery when the right opportunity presented itself. This seemed to have come in 1533 because Fisher was a declared supporter of the Holy Maid of Kent. But, for some reason, Henry decided to wait a little longer and, although Fisher was named in the act of attainder passed against Elizabeth Barton and her associates, he was allowed to purchase his freedom by paying a relatively small fine. However, the reprieve was short lived. When, in April 1534, he refused to swear the oath accepting the divorce and all that had flowed from it he was imprisoned in the Tower.

Execution of the Holy Maid of Kent: 1534

Key date

The 'politic' thing for Henry to have done would have been to leave him there to die from the harsh conditions in which he was kept. But a year later the king was goaded into giving a public display of his power. The Pope had just announced that Fisher was to be made a cardinal. Henry's response was predictable. The cardinal-to-be was accused of high treason, tried and executed. Although everything had been done according to the law – Fisher was clearly guilty of the charge against him – there was a widespread feeling that spite was the real reason for what had happened. Certainly Henry had provided further ammunition to those who wished to portray him as a tyrant.

Sir Thomas More

Sir Thomas More was one of the most fascinating characters of the early sixteenth century. If writers have found it easy to describe and to agree on the personality and character of John Fisher, as a group they have been perplexed by Thomas More. The result has been that over the centuries there have been almost as many published pages devoted to discussing what sort of man he was as there have been to assessing Henry VIII. And the variety of judgements offered has been almost as large. At one extreme, he has been presented as a flawless saint (he was canonised by the Catholic Church, along with Fisher, in 1935), while his detractors have portrayed him as a confused genius who unnecessarily sacrificed his life for a technicality. So much conflicting evidence exists that there is never likely to be a

A painting of Sir Thomas More wearing his chain of office as Lord Chancellor. Why might More have commissioned this portrait?

consensus among historians about him. This leaves plenty of room for you to exercise an independence of judgement.

However, there is general agreement about the facts of the major events in his life and about many of his dominant attributes and characteristics. He was born in 1478 in London and spent almost his whole life in the city and its environs. He followed his father's footsteps into the law but, although he became expert in it, he was equally interested in all other branches of learning. His intellect and ability to work hard were such that, before the age of 30, he had established a reputation as one of Europe's leading scholars. His well-developed social skills (when he chose to use them) made him highly popular in some circles and the young Henry VIII came to regard him as a friend.

Not satisfied with a successful legal career and an outstanding academic career, More was prepared to be drawn into the political court circle and to act as the king's representative in a wide variety of diplomatic situations. In the process he became thought of as a very able and totally reliable royal servant. His strict moral

Profile: Sir Thomas More 1478–1535

1478	– Born the son of a lawyer, Sir John More, in London
c.1480–90s	– Educated at St Anthony's School, London, and served as a teenage page in the household of Archbishop John Morton
c.1494–6	– Educated at Oxford University
1496	– Admitted to Lincoln's Inn to study law
1501	– Became a barrister-at-law
1504	– Entered parliament and married for first time
c.1505–6	– Became friends with Desiderius Erasmus, an international scholar
1510	– Appointed under-sheriff of London
1511	– First wife died in childbirth. Married for second time
1515	– Joined royal delegation to Flanders to negotiate new agreement on wool trade
1517	– Put down anti-foreign uprising in London
1518	– Admitted to the King's Council as an adviser to the king
1521	– Knighted by Henry VIII. Co-author with the king of *Defence of the Seven Sacraments*, a rejection of Luther and Protestantism
1523	– Appointed Speaker of the House of Commons
1525	– Appointed to government office as Chancellor of the Duchy of Lancaster
1530	– Appointed Lord Chancellor (king's chief minister)
1532	– Resigned from government after refusing to support king's divorce and for opposing the king's attack on the Church
1534	– Refused to swear to the Act of Succession and Oath of Supremacy. Committed to the Tower of London
1535	– Tried and found guilty of treason. Executed by beheading

More was a reluctant martyr and Henry VIII was a reluctant executioner. His last words on the scaffold were: 'I die the king's good servant, but God's first'.

code prevented him from doing the things needed to become a front-line political figure and it was therefore something of a surprise when he was chosen to succeed Wolsey as Lord Chancellor in 1529. This was especially so as he was known by Henry VIII and by his leading courtiers to be opposed to the divorce on principle.

The new Lord Chancellor set himself the task of eradicating heresy in England, following a long period during which his predecessor had virtually turned a blind eye to its existence. As a result of his initiative numbers of both Lutherans and less radical reformers were burned at the stake. Henry's mounting attack on the independence of the Church led More to feel unbearably uncomfortable remaining in office as here was another matter of principle over which he could not agree with his master. His belief was that the Church would no longer be spoken to directly by God if it fell under lay control. Henry finally allowed him to resign once the Submission of the Clergy had been safely made in 1532.

The two men's perception of their relationship was now radically different. More regarded himself as the king's loyal servant who would always obey his monarch to the very limit his conscience would allow and who would never do anything actively to oppose him. Henry thought of his former Lord Chancellor as a dangerous enemy (anybody who was not for him was against him) who had deserted him in his hour of greatest need and who deserved to be punished for what he had done. The hatred he frequently felt for his erstwhile friend was extreme. The collision course had been set.

More tried to retire completely from public life but Henry was determined to corner him. Cromwell would have been satisfied with More's assurance that he would do nothing to aid or assist the king's opponents but his master insisted that the oath, which he knew contained sentiments with which More fundamentally disagreed, must be sworn. More could not be persuaded to do so. He joined Fisher in the Tower, was tried and was found guilty on a legal technicality. He was executed in July 1535, a month after his distinguished co-prisoner. Henry had dealt his own reputation a further unnecessary blow.

Key date

Execution of John
Fisher and Sir
Thomas More: 1535

The Observant Franciscan friars and Carthusians

Less alarming, but still highly irritating to the king, were the criticisms of his treatment of Catherine and of the Pope made by numbers of monks and friars who were closely associated with the Court. What was particularly galling was that they belonged to the two religious orders – the Observant Franciscan friars and the Carthusian monks – which were generally thought to be the most spiritually admirable in the country. In addition, they were geographically well situated to provide hope and encouragement to anyone else who wished to stand up to Henry. The main Franciscan friary was alongside the king's most frequented palace at Greenwich, and the Carthusians' most important centre was the Charterhouse in London. Both were regularly visited by many of the leading figures in society, who were keen to be seen to be associated with such obvious purity of religion.

Observant Franciscan friars

Investigations soon revealed that the Observant friars were united in their opposition to Henry's policies. Therefore the only action open to the government was to close all seven of their houses nationwide and to force their former inmates out of public view. This was done in 1534 and the more stubborn members were imprisoned. It is not clear what happened to them but the probability is that up to 30 of the 200 Observants died in unnoticed captivity.

Attack on the Observant Franciscans and the Carthusians: 1534–7

Key date

Carthusians

However, there seemed to be a possibility of 'dividing and ruling' with the Carthusians. This was because there were some individuals within the London Charterhouse, and many more in the houses in the provinces, who were critical of the uncompromising stance taken by their colleagues. Cromwell hoped to achieve a propaganda victory by showing that the Carthusians had been brought to see reason. But just the opposite occurred. As the leading intransigents were removed to be sent elsewhere, to be imprisoned or even to be executed, a new crop of potential martyrs emerged to carry on the resistance.

Over a period of three years 18 members of the Charterhouse were either executed or starved to death (rather than submit) in prison. In the process many stories of outstanding courage were enacted and have been retold to great effect by Catholic writers over the centuries. In the end the king won a hollow victory when a small group of Carthusians swore the oaths which were demanded of them, and the monastery continued a truncated existence until 1539. But the verdict of history has not been kind and the war of attrition against the London Carthusians has often been judged to be one of Henry VIII's least defensible actions.

Why was there so little opposition to the royal supremacy and the break with Rome?

Although there was a small amount of well-publicised opposition to Henry's policies, the reaction in the country as a whole was one of passive acceptance. Historians have not been slow to speculate about why this was so.

Key question
What explanations for the relative lack of opposition to Henry VIII's actions have been given?

It used to be assumed by Protestant writers that the seeming indifference among the population as a whole was an indication that Christian commitment was at a very low ebb in England and Wales by 1530. The picture painted was of a Church in crisis which had lost the support of the people and which was vulnerable to the least political pressure. A variation on this basic explanation was that an already parlous situation had been made untenable by the activities of Wolsey who had destroyed any spirit of resistance that might have existed among the Church hierarchy. Either way, the emphasis was placed on the Church's deficiencies, in that it was a fruit ripe for the plucking.

In recent decades the explanation has been sought on the other side of the coin. Attention has been concentrated on the way in which Cromwell, with Henry's active support, made it virtually impossible for concerted opposition to form. The most that could happen was that relatively isolated pockets of dissent could arise, only to be eliminated before they could act as a focus for wider discontent. In poker-playing parlance, the good cards were all in the government's hands and when it was time for the

Profile: Reginald Pole 1500–58

1500	– Born a younger son of Sir Richard Pole and Margaret, Countess of Salisbury
1515	– Educated at Oxford University where he received his degree in divinity
1521–7	– Went to study on the continent
1527	– Became Dean of Exeter Cathedral
1529–30	– Went to study in Paris
1530	– Became Dean of Windsor but refused the king's offer of the Archbishopric of York
1531	– Opposed king's divorce policy
1532	– Went abroad to study
1536	– Criticised in print Henry VIII's supremacy of the Church in England
1537	– Summoned to Rome by the Pope who made him a cardinal and papal legate to England
1538	– Henry VIII was furious and had his mother and brother arrested and charged with treason. Brother executed
1541	– 68-year-old mother executed
1547	– Failed to persuade Somerset to return England to Roman Church
1549	– Narrowly failed to get elected Pope
1554	– Returned to England as papal legate and help restore the Church to Rome
1555	– Succeeded Cranmer as Archbishop of Canterbury
1558	– Died same day as Mary I

Pole was a dedicated Catholic who risked his life, and the lives of his family, to oppose Henry VIII's break with Rome. He spent most of his life abroad and was out of touch with the feelings and attitudes of his fellow English when he returned in 1554. His impact on English religious thinking was limited and he failed to turn the clock back to the 1520s. His restoration of the Pope as head of the English Church lasted only three years and did not survive his death. His greatest achievement was to maintain an English presence at the Papal Court.

betting to begin the stakes were made so high that only those with a strong self-destructive urge were prepared to challenge the dealer. After all, it has been argued, the fact that few people were prepared to risk death and the ruin of their family for one part of their traditional faith does not mean that their religion meant little to them.

Key question
What advantages did the Crown have in its dealings with opponents?

Why was there so little opposition to the dissolution?

By the 1530s the general respect ('awe' or even 'fear' would be equally appropriate words) for the power of the monarch, which had been growing since the accession of Henry VII 45 years earlier, had reached such proportions that a determined English king could do virtually whatever he wanted. This deference was even apparent in rebels, such as the leaders of the Pilgrimage of Grace in 1536 (see page 137), and was possibly the major cause of their undoing. This gave Henry a tremendous advantage in his dealings with all of his subjects, the heads of religious houses included. When there is added to this the fact that the king was known to be willing to use the power of the law – in effect, judicial murder – against all who opposed his will, it took very brave and committed people to fail to comply with their sovereign's wishes. And, of course, Henry had the law on his side in another way during his dealings with the monasteries.

Parliament had recognised his position as Supreme Head of the Church in his territories and thus his authority over the religious houses and their possessions. He was therefore within his rights in dealing with them as he saw fit, a position that the monks and nuns had sworn an oath to accept in 1535.

But it was not only the king's exalted position and the might of the law that potential opponents within the monastic system had to confront. After 1536 they also had to overcome the lure of a large element of self-interest. This was because Cromwell was careful to make it financially worth the while of heads of houses to surrender their monasteries into the Crown's hands. It was left to the commissioners negotiating the surrender to agree on the exact terms, but the principle to be followed was that the abbots and abbesses should not be significantly worse off after the dissolution than they had been before. This, of course, was expensive to implement in the early years but as all grants were only for life there was the prospect of the allowances being recovered within a relatively short time.

When the larger monasteries were being dissolved steps were also taken to discourage rank-and-file resistance. If the income of the house could finance it – and in all cases except the friaries it could – the ordinary monks and nuns were to be awarded a pension for life, which in practice was roughly equivalent to the wages of a manual worker. An added advantage of this arrangement was that heads of houses were freed from any feeling that they were sentencing the members of their communities to extreme hardship if they chose to sign the surrender papers when they were invited to do so.

It used to be commonplace to assert that the lay supporters of the monasteries, especially within the court circle, were bought off by the hint that they would be allowed to share in the spoils from the dissolution. While it is clear that such expectations were raised, it is very unlikely that they played a significant part in defusing potential political opposition. Henry ensured that few laymen would seriously contemplate even speaking out about the dissolution of the monasteries by making it clear that the penalty for doing so was likely to be death. In addition, once the opportunity of stopping the dissolutions had been missed in parliament in 1536, Cromwell made certain that by his policy of piecemeal surrenders he denied his opponents an obvious time at which to make a stand. In these circumstances, the hope of financial gain for themselves was merely a sweetener to those who wished the monasteries to remain.

Key date

Pilgrimage of Grace: 1536

Pilgrimage of Grace in 1536

This was a widespread popular revolt that took place between late 1536 and early 1537 in the north of England, particularly Yorkshire and Lincolnshire. Some 40,000 people joined the rebellion which proved to be the most serious outbreaks of violence in the sixteenth century. It was caused mainly by resentment over the changes in the Church and the dissolution of the monasteries. The rebellion never seriously threatened the king but it did threaten the maintenance of law and order in the north.

Summary diagram: Opposition to the changes

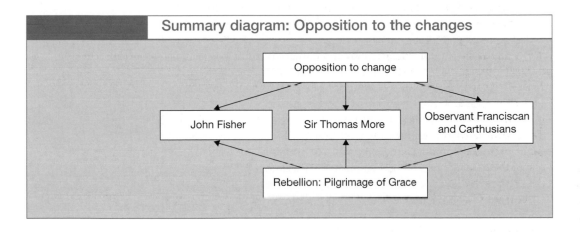

Study Guide: AS Questions

In the style of AQA

Question 1

(a) Explain why the Act in Restraint of Annates was passed in 1532. (12 marks)

(b) 'Royal supremacy had not significantly altered the position of the Church within the state by 1536.' Explain why you agree or disagree with this view. (24 marks)

Exam tips

(a) You would be advised to separate the long-term from the short-term causes here and link the king's desire for a divorce with the difficulties posed by the Pope to the influence of Thomas Cromwell and the decision to break with Rome. Remember that the immediate reason for the Act might genuinely have been to lessen the Pope's influence by removing a source of income, but could equally have been an attempt to 'blackmail' the Pope into granting the divorce.

(b) You will need to decide on a line of argument and balance the points which agree with the statement against those which do not. Obviously there is much that can be said to disagree with this statement: the Church lost its independence, the Pope lost his influence and the monarchy gained supremacy. However, it might equally be argued that the Church continued to exercise a powerful hold over the people, and, for example, Catholic doctrine and Church courts remained. Remember, the question is only concerned about developments to 1536, when the force of change had not yet been fully felt.

Question 2

(a) Explain why the smaller monasteries were dissolved in 1536. (12 marks)

(b) 'The dissolution of the monasteries had limited social consequences.' Explain why you agree or disagree with this view. (24 marks)

Exam tips

The cross-references are intended to take you straight to the material that will help you to answer the questions.

(a) As long-term factors, you will need to explain a little about the context of religious change and the position of the monasteries in England by the 1530s. The immediate reasons are concerned with the visitations and *Valor Ecclesiasticus* and you will need to consider whether religious (perhaps moral) or financial factors provided the greater motivation. Do not get side-tracked into describing what happened, but do show that you understand the interplay of reasons and offer a supported conclusion.

(b) This question is inviting you to debate the social consequences of the dissolution and you will find details on this on page 127. It has been suggested that occupants were turned into vagabonds and that the poor who depended on monastic charity suffered. There is also the view that the sale of Church lands created a new class of capitalist farmers, who enclosed their lands and added to problems of rural depopulation and homelessness, and that where many religious houses in towns closed, there was urban decay. However, the increase in the number of 'gentlemen farmers' may be seen as a positive step – helping to broaden the base of parliamentary government. However, against this view, it might be argued that there was limited evidence of increased poverty and unemployment in the short term and that changes in land owning patterns may not have simply been the result of dissolution, and actually pre-dated it. Decide your view and maintain an argument throughout your answer so as to show some judgement in your conclusion.

In the style of Edexcel

Study Sources 1, 2 and 3.

Do you agree with the view that it was virtually impossible for effective opposition to form to Henry VIII's Reformation? Explain your answer, using Sources 1, 2 and 3 and your own knowledge.   (40 marks)

Source 1

From G. R. Elton, Reform and Reformation: England 1509–1588, *published in 1977.*

The State of the Church was widely believed to be rotten. Popular anticlericalism thrived on tales of gluttonous monks, lecherous friars and dishonest parish priests.

Satirists unquestionably exaggerated the evils in the Church, but they had enough reality to draw on to carry widespread conviction.

Source 2

From Edward Hall, The Union of the Two Noble and Illustrious Families of Lancaster and York. *This book was published in 1548 as a History of the Tudor Monarchy. Here Hall describes what happened in 1536 when rebel forces in the Pilgrimage of Grace met the King's forces at Doncaster, just south of Pontefract. The forces were on opposite sides of a small river.*

But the northern men refused to end their wicked rebellion. But, as if by a great miracle of God, the water suddenly rose to such a height and breadth, so that on the day, even when the hour of battle should have come, it was impossible for one army to get at the other.

Then a consultation was held and a pardon obtained from the King's majesty for all the leaders of this insurrection. They were promised that their petition would be presented to the King and their grievances would be gently heard and their reasonable requests granted, so that by the King's authority all things should be brought to good order and conclusion. And with this promise every man quietly departed.

Source 3

From D. Rogerson, The Early Tudors, *published in 2001.*

The Reformation was opposed by many different people for many different reasons. It was this diversity that probably helped to prevent a major crisis from developing. There was no single obvious issue around which opposition forces could muster. Nor was there an obvious moment (apart from the Pilgrimage of Grace) when opposition could coalesce. The dates of religious changes are clear enough, but it is much less clear when these began to have effects in the localities and when people realised the full significance of what they were living through.

Exam tips

The cross-references are intended to take you straight to the material that will help you to answer the question.

The sources contain the following points:

- There was widespread anticlericalism and criticism of the state of the pre-Reformation Church.
- Many different people opposed the Reformation for many different reasons.
- The Pilgrimage of Grace constituted a violent challenge.
- The rebel army was persuaded to disperse at Doncaster.
- The diversity of opposition to the Reformation may have been its weakness.
- The gradual nature of the changes offered few moments where opposition could coalesce.

How will you organise these points for and against the claim in the question? What key phrases could you select from the sources to develop these points further?

You should use your own knowledge as well to develop or counter these points, and to add new issues. How will you organise the following material?

- The image of a 'Church in crisis' is challenged by recent writing (pages 94–8).
- The Crown had key advantages in dealing with its opponents (pages 134–7).
- Cromwell's policies made it financially worthwhile for heads of houses to surrender their monasteries (pages 136–7).
- Cromwell's policy of 'piecemeal surrender' denied opponents an obvious time to make a stand (pages 121–3).

You will need to reach an overall conclusion. How far do you agree with the statement?

In the style of OCR

Assess why Henry VIII was able to dissolve the monasteries so easily. (50 marks)

> ### Exam tips
>
> *The cross-references are intended to take you straight to the material that will help you to answer the question.*
>
> In order to score high marks, you need to give a number of reasons and evaluate them, before reaching a conclusion on the most important. Some of the following explanations are likely to be considered:
>
> - The monasteries were wealthy institutions and offered easy pickings for the king, government and landed groups who would benefit from the dissolution (pages 108–11).
> - The Papacy was unable to protect the monasteries from dissolution; indeed, resentment of the Papacy may have spurred on its enemies (pages 115–16).
> - The monks and nuns offered little resistance: they were transferred to larger houses in 1536–7 and offered pensions in line with their income at the dissolution in 1539 (pages 124–5).
> - The monasteries were dissolved in stages, small then large, by acts of parliament. The process was therefore legal and any resistance was treason (pages 122–3).
> - There was little popular sympathy for the continuation of most monasteries and nunneries; many were in rural and isolated areas, and their closure only affected a small number of people, mainly in the north of England (page 137).
> - Widespread anticlericalism in the 1530s meant that there was little support for an outmoded and corrupt institution that according to the government was beyond reform (pages 108–9).
> - Henry's execution of Carthusians in 1535 and his severe treatment of the Pilgrims of Grace in 1537 convinced clerics and laity that continued opposition would be foolhardy. The king was a formidable opponent (pages 136–7).
> - Many abbots and abbesses were bribed by Cromwell and his agents to surrender their houses voluntarily and without resistance (page 113).
> - Cromwell's administrative skill, exemplified by his management of the visitations, the compilation of the *Valor Ecclesiasticus*, control of commissioners sent on circuits around the country, and his management of parliament ensured the dissolution was a smooth and largely unopposed operation (pages 110–11).
> - Henry declared that he would put the monastic wealth to educational and social uses, which won over critics and cynics who suspected that the king was simply motivated by greed. In practice, Henry did not keep his word and spent the money on war.

5 The King's Faithful Servants: Cranmer, Cromwell and the Revolution in Government

POINTS TO CONSIDER

This chapter concentrates on the career, character and achievements of two of Henry VIII's key advisers – Thomas Cromwell and Thomas Cranmer. Cromwell's remarkable legacy as defined by Sir Geoffrey Elton as the Revolution of Government is debated and evaluated. Cranmer's importance and influence on the changes in religion and the Church are assessed. These issues are examined as three key themes:

- Thomas Cromwell
- A Revolution in Government: the Elton thesis
- Thomas Cranmer

Key dates

1532	Cromwell appointed master of the king's jewels; Thomas Cranmer appointed Archbishop of Canterbury
1533	Cromwell appointed Chancellor of the Exchequer
1534	Cromwell appointed Henry VIII's Principal Secretary
1536	Cromwell appointed Lord Privy Seal; publication of the Ten Articles; Durham's County Palatine status ended. The county became an integral part of the English state; So-called Act of Union integrated Wales into the English state
1537	Publication of the Bishops' Book
1539	Act of Six Articles
1540	Cromwell executed on a charge of treason

1 | Thomas Cromwell

Introduction

Before the 1950s almost all historians portrayed Thomas Cromwell as a somewhat shadowy and unpleasant figure: as Henry VIII's unscrupulous hatchet man – willing to do anything – of the 1530s who received his just deserts in 1540 when he was abandoned and judicially murdered by his master. He was normally presented as the ambitious go-getter who gained Henry's favour by offering to make him the richest ruler in the

Key question
Who was Thomas Cromwell?

world, and who then went on to make good his promise by despoiling the Church in the dissolution of the monasteries. It was argued that in order to control public opposition to this campaign of state vandalism he erected a ruthless system of repression that rested on spies and informers and resulted in hundreds of innocent victims being executed for largely imaginary crimes. He was thought of as being a thoroughly 'bad thing'.

This perception was dramatically altered by one of the outstanding British historians of the second half of the twentieth century. Professor Sir Geoffrey Elton had devoted the major part of a prodigious research career spanning more than 40 years to a detailed investigation of the central government of England in the 1530s, and in the process has advanced a very different picture of the leading minister of the decade. He has also made and maintained a case for the period being one of the most important in the development of government in England – in

A portrait of Thomas Cromwell. Explain the significance of the book and letters in this portrait.

fact, as being revolutionary. These claims have provoked an enormous amount of historical debate and have stimulated large numbers of researchers to undertake further work on the topic. As a result, the 1530s are possibly the most researched period in English history. Although the focus of the debate has shifted somewhat over the decades as the emphases of interpretations have been amended, the controversy continues to provoke widespread interest and attention – as well as a considerable amount of heat and animosity.

Rise to prominence

The precise date of Thomas Cromwell's birth is uncertain, but is unlikely to have been after 1485. Very little is known about his early life in Putney apart from his own declaration to Archbishop Cranmer much later as to what a 'ruffian he was in his young days'. He may even have been imprisoned for a time. Whether it was his own bad behaviour, an argument with his father, or some other reason which prompted his decision, Cromwell left England to travel the continent. Accounts of what he did and where he went are both sketchy and contradictory, but it is likely that he first joined the French army and fought in the battle of Garigliano, Italy, in December 1503.

At some point after this he left the French army, settled in Italy and entered the household of the merchant banker Francesco Frescobaldi. On leaving Frescobaldi's service Cromwell journeyed to the Netherlands where he worked as a cloth merchant. There he learned his trade living among the English merchants and was able to develop an important network of business contacts, as well as learning several languages. He returned periodically to Italy where he may have received some training in the law.

Some time after 1515 Cromwell returned to England where he married Elizabeth Williams with whom he had his only surviving son, Gregory. By 1520 Cromwell was firmly established in London's mercantile community as a business agent, a role which included legal work and moneylending. It was while acting as a legal agent for Charles Knyvett, formerly surveyor to Edward Stafford, third Duke of Buckingham, that Cromwell came to the attention of Cardinal Wolsey.

In 1523 Cromwell entered the House of Commons for the first time which was followed a year later by his being appointed Wolsey's legal adviser. Throughout the 1520s his enormous energy allowed him to do all that his master asked of him as well as building up a thriving private legal practice on his own account. Between 1526 and 1529 Cromwell had risen to become one of the cardinal's most senior and trusted advisers. His instinct for survival ensured that he left Wolsey's service before his master's sudden fall from power in 1529. Indeed, Cromwell revealed a great deal about himself by his reaction to Wolsey's fall. He behaved in a very different manner from most of those around him. He neither became dispirited and inactive nor attempted to distance himself from the calamity by joining in the general attacks on his former master. He summed up the

Key question
What factors promoted Cromwell's rise to prominence?

situation rapidly and acted decisively by busying himself to secure his nomination to a currently vacant seat in the parliament that was about to gather at Westminster. His intention in doing so was two-fold.

- He wanted to advance his own claims to preferment by bringing himself to the attention of the king and whoever were to be the new leading figures at Court.
- He also wished to be in a position to defend the interests of his former master.

This display of loyalty to Wolsey during the cardinal's last months, as well as the skill with which he conducted the business involved in disentangling many of the fallen favourite's complex legal affairs, resulted in his coming favourably to the notice of Henry VIII, who was soon pleased to recruit him directly into his service.

Clearly, Cromwell was not a meek and mild yes-man who was content to be a back-room boy merely carrying out the instructions that were handed down to him. In short, he was anything but a passive conformist.

Serving the king

Key question
In what ways did Cromwell serve the king?

Despite all the research that has taken place in recent decades, it has still not been possible accurately to chart the stages by which Wolsey's legal adviser became Henry's leading minister. There is just not sufficient evidence for it to be done. But however it happened, it was certainly not a rapid process, for it was not until the spring of 1533 that the major influence over the king was clearly his. Nevertheless, because it is known how the rise to prominence was not achieved, it is possible by a process of elimination to make informed guesses about the way in which it came about. Cromwell did not secure his promotion by successive appointment to a series of important state offices. In fact, at no point during the whole period of his ascendancy did he acquire any of the major offices of state, and during the years in which he was manoeuvring himself into power all he managed to acquire was a selection of minor offices which brought him no more than a modest income and the opportunity to find out exactly how the existing administrative system worked (however badly) in practice.

Thus Cromwell's rise must have been by informal means, much as Wolsey's had been 20 years earlier. It is very likely that he won the king's favour by showing that he could think his way through problems and come up with solutions where more senior advisers (in terms of both experience and social status) could not. Of course, the seemingly insoluble problem of the time was how to bring the king's marriage to Catherine of Aragon to an end so that Anne Boleyn could become his second wife. It seems that Cromwell's emergence was the result of his ability to propose a realistic way forward and his possession of the administrative skills needed to put the policy into practice.

However, Cromwell was a very shrewd politician. He recognised that while his position relied entirely on the good opinion of his monarch, he was extremely vulnerable to the political in-fighting with which the court was rife. One serious mistake, or even the appearance of one, could bring his official career to a premature close unless he had influential friends to protect him or a power-base from which he could mount an effective counter-attack. There was little prospect of securing the former, as Wolsey, his long-standing patron, had recently died in disgrace and he had no relatives in high places to whom he could attach himself. He did make attempts to win the favour of the rapidly emerging Boleyn faction, but it was not surprising that his approaches were not warmly welcomed by a group that was deeply suspicious of anybody who had been connected with the cardinal, and which in any case wanted followers rather than additional leaders. So Cromwell set about the task of establishing a stronger position for himself.

Although there is no direct evidence to indicate that this was so, it seems likely that he was the first person to recognise the massive potential of the minor post of Principal Secretary to the king, which was at the time little more than a highly confidential clerical position. Certainly he seems to have worked very hard to obtain his own appointment to the post. At first he substituted on a voluntary basis for the existing secretary who was on business for the king abroad, and he then elbowed aside others who aspired to the position and prevailed upon Henry to dismiss the current incumbent and to appoint him in his place. As the appointment depended entirely on a word of mouth instruction from the king – there was no documentary evidence to confirm what had happened – there can be no certainty about when this took place, but the most probable date is April 1534.

Cromwell in power

Cromwell utilised his position at the centre of affairs, with so much information and so many instructions literally passing through his hands, to create a situation in which anybody who wanted a favour from the king or who wanted something to be done was more likely to be successful if he gained the Principal Secretary's support first. Although he was never able to secure a stranglehold on the channels of royal patronage and decision-making of the type that Wolsey had established, he was able to build up a position in which hundreds of people depended on his good will for the furtherance or maintenance of their ambitions. This was especially the case in the years following the disgrace of the Boleyn faction in the spring of 1536, by which time he had secured the appointment of many of his own servants to key positions throughout the administration.

Some sign of his increased dominance came in July 1536 when he was raised to the peerage as Baron Cromwell followed by his appointment as Lord Privy Seal. The latter appointment meant that a large majority of the king's most legally binding instructions only took effect once he had endorsed them. But the significance of the change should not be exaggerated. Most people had already become used to accepting that when

Key dates

Cromwell appointed master of the king's jewels: 1532

Cromwell appointed Chancellor of the Exchequer: 1533

Cromwell appointed Henry VIII's Principal Secretary: 1534

Cromwell appointed Lord Privy Seal: 1536

Key question
How powerful was Cromwell?

Cromwell wrote or said 'His Majesty wishes that', the communication was virtually a royal command. Elton long ago showed in detail the extent to which Cromwell's word had become administrative law within the government.

Architect of the Henrician Reformation?

Described by his enemy, Cardinal Reginald Pole, as 'an agent of Satan sent by the devil to lure King Henry to damnation', Cromwell, in his role as the king's vicegerent in religious affairs, had exerted the greatest day-to-day influence of any individual on the life of the Church. During this time the impact of the decisions he made and the actions he took was considerable and, some have argued, of lasting significance. Nevertheless, denying that Cromwell held genuine evangelical convictions, Cardinal Pole claimed that he was moved instead by greed and a **Machiavellian** desire to serve the king. Indeed, Cromwell may even have agreed in part with Pole's assessment for he maintained to the end that his beliefs always took second place to his loyalty to his master, and that he would have followed whatever religion he had been instructed to. It seems that within months of his minister's death Henry VIII was convinced of the truth of this claim, and most historians have subsequently come to the same conclusion.

However, this is not to suggest that Cromwell was not interested in religious issues for their own sake, because he clearly was. It is just that his first priority was always to prove his unswerving loyalty to Henry by carrying out whatever instructions he was given, even if these ran counter to either his policy objectives or his personal beliefs. Sufficient evidence exists for us to be able to identify Cromwell's religious preferences with a fair degree of certainty. The strategy he adopted in attempting to further his desired religious policies is also apparent. The result is that it is probably accurate to describe Cromwell as a moderate Lutheran who frequently attempted to use the fact that the king's attention was focused elsewhere to 'slip through' religious changes about which he knew his master would not have been enthusiastic had he been fully aware of what was happening. But, given his attitude towards Henry, he was always prepared to back-track or to take actions that were inconsistent with his previous decisions if this was necessary to satisfy the king's demands.

Cromwell utilised his position as vicegerent to the full. At the level of major policy, he attempted to manipulate the bishops as a group into devising detailed statements of belief that could be issued in the king's name and which would be binding on the entire Church. He also tried to secure their agreement to the publication of a Bible in English and to its distribution nationally. In addition, he issued several sets of highly detailed injunctions. His justification for doing this was that he was attempting to ensure that there was uniformity of beliefs and practices within the Church. These injunctions were instructions to those in positions of authority within the Church to ensure that certain practices ceased and that others were followed.

Key question
Can Cromwell be fairly described as the architect of the Henrician Reformation?

Key term

Machiavellian
Cleverly deceitful and unscrupulous. Named after an Italian political writer and thinker.

In the process he – no doubt knowingly – gave the status of policy to numbers of practices that had never been agreed by either the king or any representative group of churchmen. He backed up his injunctions with circular letters to Justices of the Peace (JPs) instructing them to check that the bishops were carrying out their duties of enforcement vigorously, and to bishops to ensure that they monitored the effectiveness of JPs in reporting any failure to comply with his instructions. Given the inability of the central governments of most states at the time to arrange for their policies to be put into effect in the localities, Cromwell's record as vicegerent was remarkable. It was, of course, merely one facet of his outstanding administrative achievement as the king's chief minister.

The years 1537 and 1538 were undoubtedly the years of Cromwell's greatest success in securing a movement away from the existing beliefs and practices of the Church of England. Some progress had already been made with, for example, the publication of the Ten Articles in 1536, a brief statement of the Church's beliefs which had been as significant for what it left out as for what it included. The Catholic Church practised seven sacraments (activities which, it was claimed, conferred God's grace on the participants or on those in whose names the sacrament was performed). Protestants argued that only those sacraments which had been authorised by Jesus, as reported in the New Testament, were valid. The Ten Articles included only these three sacraments (baptism, the Eucharist and penance): the other four were not rejected, they were merely 'lost'.

Key dates

Publication of the Ten Articles: 1536

Publication of the Bishops' Book: 1537

Cromwell's plan seems to have been to follow up the Ten Articles with a much fuller explanation of what was to be believed and practised and what was not. His strategy was for this to be devised by a group of bishops and theologians under his tutelage and for the end product to be agreed by Henry 'on the nod'. The first part of the plan worked well and a draft text had been completed by the bishops after six months' work in July 1537. Among other things, it showed Cromwell adopting the orthodox Lutheran position that only those beliefs and practices that were based directly on the authority of the Bible were justified.

As perhaps Cromwell had hoped, Henry was too busy even to read the draft document that was submitted for his approval. But he was too shrewd a politician to allow the work to be published in his name before he had scrutinised it carefully. He therefore instructed that the book be clearly marked as carrying only the bishops' authority. Hence when the Bishops' Book, as it was popularly known, appeared in September 1537 it was not the definitive statement that Cromwell had sought. In fact, it was not until 1543 that such a document was prepared. This was the King's Book, so-called because it had been vetted in detail by Henry and reflected most of his conservative prejudices.

Nevertheless, the reformers could count the publication of the Bishops' Book as being another significant move in the right direction. This was despite the fact that, in some ways, it was a retreat from the gains reflected in the Ten Articles. Thanks to the strong opposition to Cromwell mounted by a group of conservative bishops, the four 'lost' sacraments were found and were included, although it was explicitly stated that they were of lesser value than the other three. But the document as a whole reads like a continuing slide away from the orthodox Catholic position and towards Protestantism. This was mainly as a result of the Bishops' Book's failure to confirm many traditional Catholic beliefs and practices – transubstantiation was not mentioned, the Mass was largely glossed over, the special status of priests was understated, and purgatory was only present by implication. Only a few clearly Protestant statements were made – such as that the main duty of priests was preaching – presumably so as not to alert the potential opposition to what was happening. In fact, the publication bore all the signs of being a step in the 'softening up' process that was such a typical and successful strategy of Cromwell's.

A more definite step towards Protestantism was also witnessed in 1537. It was ordained, thanks to the vicegerent's efforts, that within two years every parish church must possess a copy of the Bible in English and that it must be kept openly available for parishioners to read. Cromwell took upon himself the task of ensuring that the requisite number of Bibles was available. This involved him in almost as much work as it took to mount a military campaign, but he was determined to be successful, and he was.

With hindsight, Protestant historians have felt able to judge this achievement to be one of the most significant in the whole story of the English Reformation. The argument has been two-pronged:

- that once the population as a whole was put in a position to find out what the Bible actually said the victory of Protestantism was assured
- that Cromwell's Bible (a translation by Miles Coverdale which was based substantially on William Tyndale's work), only slightly modified as the Authorised version 70 years later, became the cornerstone of an English Protestant literary and linguistic culture that survived nationwide well into the twentieth century and was thus massively influential.

Revisionist historians have not been slow to challenge this verdict. They have convincingly maintained that the first argument is highly speculative and lacks solid evidence to support it, while the second argument does nothing to explain the success of Protestantism but rather is a result of that success.

In 1538 Cromwell published his second general set of Injunctions as vicegerent, following those issued to religious houses in 1535 (see pages 110–11) and the first general set which had appeared in 1536. The Injunctions were detailed instructions to bishops about the policies they should implement in their dioceses. Whereas the orders given in 1536 had been rather vague (and therefore easy to ignore by those who did not welcome change), those of 1538 were much more specific and reformist in a Protestant direction. Instead of merely stipulating that superstitious practices should be discouraged, they stated that objects of dubious veneration, such as the relics of saints, should be removed from churches and that people should be actively discouraged from undertaking pilgrimages.

Although many bishops dragged their feet over putting these policies into effect, not all did. Catholic sympathisers have written with great feeling about the cartloads of precious objects being transported to the Tower of London when the shrine to St Thomas Becket, one of the most famous pilgrimage sites in Europe, was removed from Canterbury Cathedral. One of the injunctions was subsequently of special significance to research historians in general and to genealogists in particular. This was the instruction that a register of births, marriages and deaths should be kept in every parish. The intention at the time was seemingly to ensure that evidence was available to decide whether a couple should be barred from marriage because of the closeness of their blood relationship, but the unintended consequence has been the accumulation of one of the richest sources of evidence for the study of family history.

However, even before Cromwell was executed in July 1540 the drift towards Protestantism had been reversed, making it clear that it would have been very unlikely that he would have been able to manipulate Henry into a position of openly avowed Lutheranism however long he had remained in power. The little-by-little, 'slide' policy that was so effective when adopted by the monarch and the minister in concert could not be operated by Cromwell against Henry. Thus it appears justified to argue that Cromwell's strategy could have had little long-term effect on the struggle between Catholicism and Protestantism in England and that therefore his impact on the religious Reformation was doomed to be as temporary and potentially reversible as that of Anne Boleyn.

Fall from power

In June 1540 Cromwell was arrested and charged with treason. He was executed the next month. Some historians have expressed surprise and even revulsion that this should have happened. However, given the relative insecurity of the minister's position, despite his best efforts to make it otherwise, and the increasingly fickle nature of a master whose limited constancy was frequently undermined by lengthy bouts of excruciating pain and their accompanying anger and frustration, it was almost certain to happen at some stage. The question for the historian to answer is not why the blow was struck but why it happened when it did.

Despite the fact that it has not proved possible to disentangle all the plotting and counter-plotting that took place, it is certain that events reached their climax very speedily. While it is true that Cromwell's position had been less strong since he began his support of the disastrous marriage to Anne of Cleves in 1539, he had subsequently been successful in recovering much of the lost ground. It was, for instance, a mark of very special favour when, a few months before his fall, Henry had created him Earl of Essex –

Key question
How and why did Cromwell fall from power?

Cromwell executed: 1540

Key date

a very rare elevation to the senior peerage of a man who had not even been born into a family with noble connections. This would certainly not have been done had Henry at that stage had even the remotest intention of cutting down his leading minister.

It seems as if the most influential of Cromwell's opponents – the re-formed Boleyn faction led by the Duke of Norfolk – had been able to produce a trump card that the new earl could do nothing to counter. They dangled before Henry a second niece of Norfolk's (Anne Boleyn had been the first) and mixed poison about the minister with the cup of sweetness about the 19-year-old Catherine Howard. The king was beguiled and agreed to believe the lies and misrepresentations about Cromwell as the price to be paid for securing the vivacious young woman who was to become his fifth wife. The grounds on which Cromwell was charged are not to be taken too seriously by searchers after the truth: first the decision was made to destroy him, then suitable grounds were sought. The charge most likely to impress Henry was that Cromwell had secretly been plotting to introduce a fully blown version of Protestantism, of the Anabaptist type, in the face of the king's known aversion to radical changes in the theology of his church.

There was sufficient evidence of Cromwell's personal sympathy for Protestant beliefs for such a charge to seem credible – except that there could be little doubt that he was genuine in his frequently repeated assertions over the years that he would do or believe whatever the king instructed him to. To execute such an obedient servant for treason defied all logic, a realisation that Henry rapidly came to once his infatuation for his new wife-toy had rapidly run its course. Among the most striking ironies of a most bizarre episode were the almost simultaneous execution of Cromwell and the marriage of Henry and Catherine (emphasising the impression that they were mutually dependent events), and the recognition by Henry that Cromwell's enemies had duped him, as he unwillingly became convinced that not only had Catherine been free with her favours before her marriage, but that she had also regularly contemplated committing adultery once the reality of marriage to a physically repellent man about 30 years her senior had become clear to her.

But there was little that the king could do to exorcise his remorse, except to consign Catherine and her closest associates to the same fate that had so unjustly befallen Thomas Cromwell. That, of course, could not bring back to life the only man who might have guided England successfully through the turbulent later years of Henry's reign.

Cromwell reassessed

Key question
How and why have historians changed their opinions of Cromwell?

Since Elton pioneered the radical re-evaluation of the life and career of Thomas Cromwell dozens of other researchers have made contributions that have fleshed out our understanding of this remarkable man. The result of all this endeavour has been the creation of as full a picture of a common-born Englishman who died more than four-and-a-half centuries ago as could realistically be expected. And it is a picture about which there is a surprisingly large degree of consensus among academic writers on the period.

For example, few would now dissent from the view that Cromwell was the best minister that any English monarch was fortunate enough to be served by in the sixteenth century. The force of 'best' is both that he was extremely good at the work he did and that he was dedicated to serving his master's interests. Wolsey, of course, was difficult to better in terms of application and political skill – although Cromwell may not have been far behind him in either of these respects – but his actions were so influenced by self-interest that Henry invariably paid a high price (always financial and sometimes political) for the service he received.

With Cromwell there was no such problem. Among both contemporary commentators and modern researchers there is agreement that Cromwell's first thought was always how to achieve what his master wanted. On numerous occasions he abandoned a policy he favoured or reversed a decision already made if it became clear to him that this was not favoured by Henry. He seems never to have employed Wolsey's strategy of purposely misunderstanding an instruction in order to continue to pursue a cherished policy. However, it has often been suggested that Cromwell's loyalty to Henry was the result of his fear of the king rather than of a genuine devotion to his master. A contemporary visitor to court reported that:

> the king beknaveth him twice a week and sometimes knocks him well about the pate; and yet when he has been well pummelled about the head and shaken up as it were a dog, he will come of the Great Chamber shaking off the bush with as merry a countenance as though he might rule all the roost.

But this description should not be taken too readily at face value, as it is suspected that the account is merely a repetition of a greatly exaggerated story that was circulated by hostile courtiers who wished to undermine the minister's authority. Yet it should be remembered that there was often at least a germ of truth in even the most improbable stories of the time that received widespread circulation among those who were close to the events they described, and the account does fit in well with what we know of both Henry's bullying tactics and Cromwell's proven willingness to put up with whatever was necessary to retain the king's favour. Certainly it seems safe to conclude that Cromwell did not manage to acquire a fraction of the room for manoeuvre that Wolsey created for himself.

Cromwell and Wolsey were very similar in the qualities they brought to the task of carrying out the king's business. They both possessed minds of very high quality that were well able to formulate large-scale plans and to evaluate the advantages and disadvantages of the options that were open to them. Although Cromwell had received little formal education, he had read extensively and had, for example, mastered several languages by his own efforts. He possessed a powerful memory – it is said that as a young man he memorised the entire New Testament while riding across France on his way to Italy. Because he very much enjoyed discussing problems and possibilities with other men of ability his powers of reasoning were constantly enhanced, so that by the time he rose to prominence he was generally recognised as being able to hold his own with the most skilful advocates in the land, such as Sir Thomas More. He was, therefore, regularly able to make the best possible decisions based on whatever evidence was available to him. Both men were also prodigious workers who not only devoted long hours to their duties but also transacted business at an unusually rapid rate.

Thus Cromwell was able to supervise most details of government personally and to ensure that all decisions of significance received his careful consideration before going to the king for final approval. This should have allowed him to ensure great consistency of policy but this did not happen. This was largely because he tried never to present to Henry a proposal with which he was unlikely to agree. Hence he allowed himself to be deflected from persisting with policies when he suspected that his increasingly moody and changeable master was hostile to some part of his intention.

Summary diagram: Thomas Cromwell

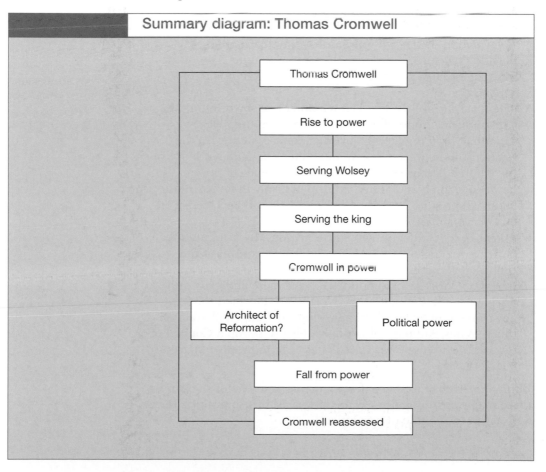

2 | A Revolution in Government: The Elton Thesis

The debate: a Tudor revolution in government?

Elton began by identifying what he termed 'a Tudor revolution in government' as taking place between 1532 and 1540, when Cromwell was Henry's chief minister. His main contention was that during these years a series of changes was made that in their totality marked the change from medieval to modern forms of government. Allied to this theory was the significance Elton attached to the part played by Cromwell in these 'revolutionary' changes in government.

Elton's theory can be broken down into four component parts:

Key question
What did Elton mean by his use of the term 'revolution in government' and how significant was Cromwell's part in it?

- The structure and organisation of central government. The 'administrative revolution' was responsible for a radical change in the structure and organisation of central government. The major part of this recasting of central administration revolved around the reorganisation of the financial departments and the creation of the Privy Council. The result was that *government by the king* was replaced by *government under the king*.
- The role of parliament and the scope and authority of statute law. The essential ingredient of the Tudor revolution was the concept of national sovereignty and the creation of a sovereign law-making parliament. In using parliament to enforce the Reformation the Crown was emphasising that nothing lay outside the competence of parliamentary statute. The result was that *king and parliament* had been replaced by *king-in-parliament*.
- The relationship between Church and State. By bringing the Church firmly under the control of the king the royal supremacy had initiated a 'jurisdictional revolution' in the relationship between Church and State. The independence of the Church had been quashed and the balance of power between Church and State had tipped firmly in favour of the latter. The result was that *Church and State* had been replaced by *Church in State*.
- Extension of royal authority in the regions. By bringing the outlying regions of the kingdom under the control of the central government Cromwell was aiming to create a nation that was a jurisdictional entity. He gave more authority and purpose to the Council of the North and reformed the government of Wales by empowering the Council of Wales and the Marches. Although short-lived, he also set up a Council of the West. The result was that a *fragmented polity* was replaced by a *unitary state*.

Elton argued that, as these developments were one of the two or three major turning-points in the history of British politics, they well deserved the title of revolution.

The structure and organisation of central government

Elton's argument turned on his definition of medieval and modern forms of government and his assessment of what happened in the 1530s. He was quite specific about the features that typified medieval government:

> In every way, then, the great restoration of government after the civil wars of the fifteenth century, the work of Edward IV and Henry VII, represented the restoration of medieval government at its most efficient. A financial administration based on the king's chamber and the somewhat informal means adopted for audit and control, the extended use of the signet [the king's private seal] and the rise of the secretary, and government through individual councillors rather than a council, all these marked the triumph of household methods in administration.

Elton argued that modern forms of government were the antithesis (opposite) of medieval methods, in which administration was based on the monarch's household. Modern systems of government were bureaucratic, being based on properly constituted 'departments' that worked according to agreed rules and procedures and which were therefore less open to the influence of any one individual. In this way the bureaucratic 'departments' could function efficiently without the constant supervision of the monarch, who might be lazy or weak. Therefore, the 'system' was paramount.

Elton maintained that in the 1530s sufficient changes took place in the structure of government for the Henrician state to be considered to have crossed the line that divides the medieval from the modern. He identified two changes as being of particular significance.

First change: the replacement of a household system of finances by a bureaucratic system

The old system

In the old system most of the king's income was received by individual officers whose conduct was not regulated by clearly formulated procedures and whose accounts were not properly audited.

The new system

In the new system legally constituted departments received money from pre-specified sources, paid out money for properly sanctioned reasons and were efficiently audited to ensure that they were acting as they should.

The departments

Apart from the long-established Court of Exchequer (this dealt with income that came in from sheriffs and customs duties), the departments did not have titles that identified them as being financial bodies.

The Duchy of Lancaster was an existing 'department' that administered the extensive lands and rights that had come to the crown from the house of Lancaster, and it was the model for a number of new 'courts' which were established to administer most of the crown's other sources of income.

The most famous of these new 'courts' were the Court of First Fruits and Tenths and the Court of Augmentations, set up to handle the Church wealth that was newly coming to the king. They were called courts because they also had the legal power to determine disputes over what was owed to the government or what should be paid out by it.

In addition, the household, particularly the King's Chamber (this dealt with the income coming in from royal estates), was subjected to close regulation related to the monies it still controlled so that it virtually became one of the new breed of financial departments.

Apart from efficiency, Elton argued that one of Cromwell's aims was to reduce the role of the King's Chamber (i.e. to reduce it to its original function of Court Treasury) and to increase the authority of the Court of Exchequer, a non-household bureaucratic institution of which he was Chancellor.

Second change: the establishment of the Privy Council

Elton argued that at some unidentifiable time in the 1530s (but probably in 1536) the informal medieval system of a large council, with between 70 and 90 members, most of whom rarely attended, was replaced by a more formal Privy Council system in which an élite group of about 20 trusted permanent councillors assumed responsibility for the day-to-day running of the government. As the informality of the medieval system had normally resulted in one or two councillors (such as Cardinal Wolsey) gathering most power into their own hands, the change was seen as the movement of control away from a small number of influential individuals to a powerful bureaucratically organised group.

According to Elton the Privy Council's small size and the eminence and competence of its members enabled it to function effectively during periods of crisis such as the rebellion known as the Pilgrimage of Grace and even during the royal minority of Edward VI. The creation and importance of the Privy Council by 1540 is not in doubt but some historians have rejected Cromwell's part in its creation. Responding to criticism from historians who claim that the Privy Council was structured along lines prefigured by Wolsey in his Eltham Ordinance of 1526, Elton pointed out that the Cardinal's chief adviser at the time was none other than Thomas Cromwell.

The role of parliament and the relationship between Church and State

Elton claimed that Cromwell's work radically enhanced the power of the State and the competence of parliament within the state. It is claimed, with some justification, that Cromwell not only paved the way for royal government to take control of the English

Church, he masterminded the method through which this could best be achieved: by means of parliamentary statute. By making Henry VIII the Supreme Head of the Church in England Cromwell had effected a revolution in the relationship between Church and State. In using parliament to enforce the Reformation, Cromwell had established the principle that king-in-parliament constituted the highest form of authority in the kingdom. To support his case Elton compared the volume of legislation passed during Henry VIII's reign, some 37 years, with that passed between 1258, the middle of the reign of Henry III, and 1509, some 251 years. For example, in the printed *Statutes of the Realm* the laws passed by Henry VIII filled 1032 pages but the laws passed between 1258 and 1509 filled 1094 pages. Clearly, the workload of parliament had increased dramatically.

Extension of royal authority in the regions

It is perhaps in the area of regional and local government that Elton's thesis is most vulnerable to criticism. Elton's argument here turned more on what Cromwell intended than what he achieved. Cromwell may have intended to extend royal authority into the wilder and remoter parts of the kingdom but his success in this field was limited. He had no choice but to depend on the unpaid co-operation of local gentry acting as JPs and on the willingness of powerful noble landowners or influential clerics who invariably filled the offices of president of the regional Councils of the North, West and Wales.

Only in respect of his reform of the government and administration of Wales and the Marches can anything approaching an Eltonian 'revolution' be detected. Between 1536 and 1543 the semi-independent power of the Marcher Lordships was swept away, Wales was divided into shires as in England and the Welsh were given representation in parliament for the first time. In addition, the Council of Wales and the Marches, which had been a household institution of the Prince of Wales, was bureaucratised and given statutory authority to govern this region of the realm whether there was a Prince or not.

Key date
Durham and Wales integrated into the English state: 1536

Key question
How have historians challenged Elton's thesis?

A 'revolution' in government: the critics' response

It is a curious fact that many of the 'revisionist' historians who have challenged Elton and the revolutionary nature of the 1530s were once his pupils. David Starkey is perhaps the most ardent opponent of the 'revolution' theory but even he acknowledges that change did happen. For example, Starkey admits that in the debate on the structure and organisation of central government Elton's argument that there was a shift away from 'medieval' household government is valid but not because of a Cromwellian master-plan for reform. Starkey believes that the change was a result of Cromwell's reaction to conflict between court factions. In an effort to protect his position and power, Cromwell weakened the influence of the King's Chamber, which was at the heart of the royal household, because he could not control it. This was practical politics and not a preconceived plan for reform. To prove his point Starkey claims that in the 1540s household government once again dominated, thus making the Edwardian protectorate possible.

As far as the Privy Council is concerned, John Guy denies that Cromwell had a hand in its creation. He is supported by Starkey, who states that in an effort to limit his authority it was Cromwell's opponents, and not Cromwell, who set up the Privy Council in 1540. According to Dale Hoak, the Privy Council was created as an emergency response to the danger posed by the Pilgrimage of Grace and that once this crisis had been resolved it largely disappeared, to be revived during the reign of Edward VI under the presidency of Northumberland.

In the debate on the role of parliament Jennifer Loach does much to confirm Elton's arguments on the value of parliament to the Crown and the enhanced status of statute law. However, she maintains that the institution itself was still largely the same as its medieval forebears, that it had no will of its own and could not act independently of the Crown. Loach argues that the 'revolution' here lay not in the role of parliament in government, which remained occasional and at the discretion of the monarch, but in the implication that parliaments were competent to deal with any matter.

While the Elton controversy was at its height some historians also developed an argument that the final years of Henry's reign and those of his children Edward VI and Mary, c.1540–58, were of significance because they ushered in a near 20-year period of instability in England that they termed 'the mid-Tudor crisis'.

Cromwell: architect of a 'revolution' in government?

Although he spent a significant part of his time in the decades following the publication of *The Tudor Revolution in Government* in 1953 explaining, refining and defending his main thesis, Elton also found time to continue the investigation of Thomas Cromwell that his first researches had suggested might be fruitful. He had come to the conclusion that the traditional view of the minister was dramatically flawed, and he was anxious to prove his point.

He wanted to replace the picture of the selfish and unscrupulous go-getter with one of an outstanding public servant who, although ambitious and willing to make unpopular decisions when he had to, was a great believer in the rule of law and was a dedicated reformer for the public good. He was sure that sufficient evidence existed for this to be done, as, when Cromwell was arrested in 1540, all his papers had been impounded and still remained available for the researcher to examine. The archive was very extensive. Cromwell had been a meticulously organised preserver of documents – perhaps the first Englishman to be so, and certainly in marked contrast to Wolsey. He had even retained the scraps of paper on which he jotted down *aide memoires* of the things to be done in the immediate future. All this was in addition to the many less complete collections of contemporary papers that existed elsewhere.

> **Key question**
> Can Cromwell be fairly described as the architect of a 'revolution' in government?

The final task to be undertaken was to debunk the tradition that Cromwell had acted as a brutal tyrant. This was effectively done in *Policy and Police*, published in 1972. The myth that Cromwell had established and maintained a network of paid spies and informers was exploded. It was clear that he had almost totally relied upon the traditional channels of communication – from witnesses to treasonable events, to local members of the élite (especially JPs), and on to the Council in London.

Equally, the allegation that Cromwell had been responsible for securing the execution of large numbers of potential opponents based on little evidence and by utilising questionable legal proceedings was shown to be almost totally untrue. A detailed analysis of the cases of all those charged with treason during Cromwell's period of ascendency was carried out. Of the 883 people charged, only 329 (about 40 per cent) were actually executed. As over half of these followed the Pilgrimage of Grace, this was hardly evidence of a concerted reign of terror.

More revealing still was the evidence that Cromwell was not only prepared to abide by the normal legal processes, but was frequently insistent that this should be done. As a result, many of the 60 per cent of unsuccessful prosecutions failed because of legal technicalities, which Cromwell readily accepted – although he was sometimes furious at those whose incompetence had resulted in cases being lost. The few examples that were found of him 'bending' the rules so as to secure convictions were cases in which Henry took a personal interest and over which he presumably made it clear to his minister that nothing less than a conviction would be acceptable.

However, Elton did not pretend that Cromwell had been all sweetness and light as he worked to maintain law and order. The king and his minister were not men of gentle kindness. They were riding a revolution [the Reformation] and they needed drastic instruments of repression.

There was no doubt that the powers with which they equipped themselves by acts of parliament were extremely draconian. Not only was speaking out against the king as head of the Church punishable by death, but failure to report anybody who did so (known as misprison) was also treason and could result in imprisonment for life and the confiscation of all property.

Yet, while Elton freely admitted that the general fear created by the existence of misprison could be construed as being almost a reign of terror in its own right, he stoutly maintained that Cromwell exercised his extensive powers with a general lightness of touch. He convincingly showed that the minister was quick to recognise that many of the supposed traitors who were reported to him were harmless cranks and posed no threat whatever. Some of these featured in reports over several years without action being taken against them.

The other side of this coin was that he was quick to take action against those whom he felt could be influential with others. At least, Elton felt that this was a fair interpretation to place on the fact that about half of those prosecuted were clerics who, as a group, accounted for only five per cent of the population. So the impression was confirmed that Cromwell was an energetic hunter-down of possibly dangerous opposition. He kept this aspect of the government's work under his personal control, sending and receiving hundreds of letters every year on the subject of breaches of the peace, interviewing many of the suspected traitors himself, and deciding which cases to proceed with and which to abandon. But he was never bloodthirsty, taking lives almost for the fun of it. Those he acted against all seemed as if they were or could become the instigators of rebellious activity.

Cromwell: a 'commonwealth' man?

Another element in Elton thesis was the attempt to establish Cromwell as one of the 'commonwealth' men. The commonwealth men were a collection of individuals who held similar views about the need for the government to take action to reform aspects of the country's social and economic life in the interests of the common good. They were not an organised group, but were actually part of a general western European movement of thinkers who advocated the novel idea that rulers could and should improve the lives of their subjects by introducing laws and regulations to maximise social harmony and to minimise selfish divisiveness.

Before Elton's work, it was generally accepted by historians of the early modern period that such ideas were present but were of little practical effect in the England of the 1520s and 1530s, before blossoming briefly during the reign of Edward VI (1547–53). Elton's contention, most extensively spelled out in *Reform & Renewal: Thomas Cromwell and the Commonwealth* (1973), was that Cromwell built up a group of commonwealth men around him and used them to prepare programmes of legislation for him. These proposals formed the basis of a legislative programme which he attempted to implement, only to be frustrated by both the unwillingness of the commons to support him and by his fall which interrupted his efforts mid-term.

Conclusion: reviewing Elton's assessment of Cromwell and the Revolution in Government

When, in future generations, writers come to analyse what were the outstanding qualities that made Elton one of the remarkable historians of the twentieth century, they are likely to make mention of his facility both in dealing with obscure but significant points of detail and in charting the broad sweep of events. It is rare for a writer to be equally at home while discussing the implications of a scribbled note on the back of an otherwise unimportant document and in connecting events

Key question
Was Cromwell a 'commonwealth' man and what is meant by this term?

Key question
How has Elton's assessment of Cromwell and his role in the 'revolution' in government been challenged by historians?

together in imaginative new ways so as to create an original perception of a period. But this is what Elton has managed to do during the decades of his intermittent work on Cromwell. In the process he has made many sweeping claims for the previously underrated leading minister of the 1530s. For example,

- Cromwell was 'the most successful radical instrument at any man's disposal in the sixteenth century', and 'the most remarkable revolutionary in English history'
- he was 'an administrator of genius' who displayed great 'dexterity in constructing afresh'
- because of the way in which he handled parliament during his period of ascendancy he was judged to be 'the country's first parliamentary statesman'
- but perhaps the most significant claim was that Cromwell was 'a man who knew precisely where he was going and who nearly always achieved the end he had in view'
- this was not intended to mean that Cromwell saw things in terms of personal goals; rather that he had a coherent vision of the revolution he wished to implement, that he was 'engaged on refashioning the very basis of the state'.

This was Elton's overview statement into which all Cromwell's endeavours could be accommodated – his remodelling of the king's finances by bureaucratic procedures, his creation of the Privy Council as the body collectively responsible for executing the king's policies, his methods of containing opposition while the revolution took place, his attempts to introduce social and economic reform along the lines advocated by the commonwealth men, his establishment of the king in parliament as the highest authority in the state, and his destruction of the Church's position as a state within a state.

However, some historians continue to challenge Elton's assessment of Cromwell. Professor Euan Cameron firmly holds to the belief that:

- Cromwell's 'creation of the courts of revenue now looks more like wasteful inflation of his own patronage than modern "bureaucratic" innovation'
- the Privy Council was 'conjured up to throw a smoke-screen over the Cromwell clique's role in government in 1536, rather than to create an efficient executive committee of the Crown'.

The debate begun by Elton is unlikely ever to be resolved as a new generation of historians comes to the fore with fresh ideas and more challenging interpretations.

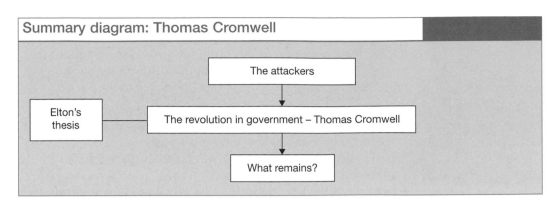

Summary diagram: Thomas Cromwell

3 | Thomas Cranmer

Cranmer and historical controversy

For nearly 400 years Thomas Cranmer was one of the most controversial figures in sixteenth-century English history. Dozens of Catholic writers castigated him as the weak and changeable leader of the Church in England who, alone, had been in a position to save his country for Rome but who had been too cowardly to do so. In stark contrast, generations of defenders of the Protestant cause lauded him as one of their faith's foremost martyrs (he was burned at the stake during Queen Mary's reign). The hostile commentators generally had the best of the argument as no convincing justification was ever forthcoming for either Cranmer's rejection of the Pope's authority so soon after swearing, on taking up his duties as Archbishop of Canterbury in 1532, to obey him, or his attempt, as martyrdom beckoned, to reject Protestantism in a fruitless attempt to save his own life.

However, in recent decades historians have become less and less interested in the sectarian battle and in the making of moral judgements – in deciding whether Cranmer was the champion of Protestantism or the betrayer of Catholicism and in determining whether his actions were right or wrong. Instead they have concentrated both on trying to explain how, although he was in a highly vulnerable position, he managed to survive throughout the Henrician Reformation while many others did not, and on assessing what influence he had on events between his surprise elevation in 1532 and Henry's death in 1547.

Rise to prominence

Of all the leading political figures of Henry's reign Thomas Cranmer was perhaps the most 'human'. He was in no sense 'larger than life' and was certainly no hero. In many ways he was very ordinary. He began life with the advantage of being the son of a gentleman but with the disadvantage of being a younger son, who would have to make his own way in the world. However, his ambitions were very modest and he sought no more than a comfortable existence with no great stresses. Up to the age of 40 he managed this successfully, living most of his adult life as a relatively undistinguished member of staff at Cambridge

---

Key question
Why was Cranmer's career thought to have been so controversial?

Cranmer appointed Archbishop of Canterbury: 1532

Key date

Key question
What factors promoted Cranmer's rise to prominence?

Profile: Thomas Cranmer 1489–1556

1489	– Born in Nottinghamshire, the younger son of a lesser gentry family
1520s	– Studied at Cambridge University where he joined the 'White Horse' group to discuss the new ideas coming from Europe such as Lutheranism
1526	– Became a doctor of divinity
c.1529	– Became chaplain to Thomas Boleyn, Earl of Wiltshire, father of Anne. Supported Henry VIII's divorce
1530	– Appointed ambassador to Charles V (1530–33)
c.1532	– Secretly married the niece of the Lutheran church leader of Nuremberg in Germany
1533	– Chosen by Henry VIII to succeed William Warham as Archbishop of Canterbury
1533–4	– Presided over Henry VIII's divorce from Catherine of Aragon, promoted the marriage with Anne Boleyn and declared Henry VIII Head of the Church in England
1536	– Presided over Henry VIII's divorce from Anne Boleyn, promoted marriage with Jane Seymour
1536–8	– Worked with Cromwell in government and in turning England towards Protestantism, e.g. responsible for the 'Bishops' Book' of 1537
1539	– Unsuccessfully opposed the conservative Act of Six Articles. Forced to separate from his wife but refused to resign his offices
1540	– Took no part in the destruction of Cromwell
1541–7	– Became leader of reformist party at Court. Henry VIII's support enabled him to survive conservative attempts to destroy him
1547	– Took leading part in the Edwardian regime both in government and in the Church. Issued Protestant Book of Homilies
1549	– Issued the blandly reformist First Book of Common Prayer
1552	– Issued the more extreme second Book of Common Prayer
1553	– Stripped of his title as Archbishop of Canterbury
1554	– Arrested and imprisoned for heresy
1556	– Burned at the stake for withdrawing an earlier promise to accept some key Catholic doctrines

Arguably, Cranmer played a greater role than any other single churchman in establishing and shaping the Church of England. He was not as timid as some historians believe but was willing to accept gradual change in the Church. He was fiercely loyal to the Crown and he proved to be an able government minister and Churchman. His greatest strength lay in his refusal to support religious extremism; he advocated toleration and preached against persecution.

University. Then a series of accidents shattered his peaceful existence.

The skill with which he carried out a request to write in support of the king's divorce in 1529 brought him to the notice of Anne Boleyn. As a very junior, but seemingly very reliable, member of her faction, he was then persuaded to become the king's representative at the court of Charles V (a highly sensitive appointment at this juncture of affairs). On the long-awaited death of William Warham, the Archbishop of Canterbury, he was recalled to England and, to his and most other people's amazement, was asked by Henry to become the new Archbishop of Canterbury. It was made clear to him that refusal was not really an option.

Comparing Cranmer and More

The centuries-long running battle between Catholic and Protestant writers over Cranmer did much to cloud our understanding of his personality and character. Both the blackness and the whiteness of his many portrayals were equally unreal and essentially hid the true nature of the man. Perhaps the clearest appreciation of him can be gained by contrasting him with a contemporary such as Sir Thomas More. Both men held principles, but whereas More hung on to his with an unshakeable grasp (even if that resulted in his own death), Cranmer followed his as far as his courage would allow (and certainly sometimes to his own disadvantage), but he could be pressured into abandoning them when the threat was great enough.

Key question
Why have historians tended to compare Cranmer and More?

Both men took life seriously but Cranmer lost little sleep over either the decisions he had to make or the actions he had already taken. He was able to rationalise away most of the guilt he might have felt. More was almost the opposite. He agonised over almost every decision, and was frequently filled with self-loathing over sins he suspected he had committed.

Their attitudes to their own sexuality were particularly revealing. Cranmer accepted his periodically strong sex drive as a natural occurrence and generally handled it with mature responsibility. As a young man he even resigned his comfortable position at Cambridge (where celibacy was the rule) in order to marry the woman, Joan, with whom he had formed an attachment. In similar circumstances many men merely arranged to have a live-in housekeeper, but Cranmer's principles would not allow him to do this. As it turned out, his principles cost him little as his wife soon died (in childbirth along with his child) and he was reinstated to his old position.

While he was at Charles V's court in Germany he was persuaded by Lutherans that it was acceptable for a priest (as he by then was) to marry, and in 1532 he took a second wife. On his return to England he found Henry VIII taking a strong public line against such heretical practices. Cranmer admitted his 'fault' to his monarch, who allowed him to keep his partner with him as long as this was done in complete secrecy. For obvious reasons little evidence has survived about how this was achieved, although rumours did circulate about the Archbishop transporting a woman in a large box during the frequent moves of his household from residence to residence! However, it is known that Cranmer sent his wife out of the country in 1539 when it was explicitly made illegal for priests to continue living in a married state.

Sir Thomas More believed that sexual desire was the work of the devil. He hated himself for allowing his lust for a woman to prevent him becoming a monk as a young man (he always believed that monasticism was his true vocation), and he customarily wore a hair shirt partly to subdue and partly to punish himself for his sexual desire. It was with some pride that he could claim that his second marriage had never been consummated.

Both men were highly intelligent (although More was clearly the only one with touches of genius) and both were excellent public speakers. But in private conversation they were poles apart. More could charm if he wanted to, but he could also be biting and sarcastic, especially to those of only limited intellect. Many people found him difficult to talk to. On the other hand, Cranmer is universally reported as being a pleasure to be with. He was always cheerful and friendly, never had an ill word to say about anybody, and had a self-effacing modesty of manner that placated the haughty and flattered those with lesser pretensions. He could speak his mind without giving offence and could diffuse the anger of others without causing them a loss of dignity. In modern parlance it would be said that his inter-personal skills were outstanding.

Cranmer and the king

Key question
How well did Cranmer get on with the king?

Many historians have identified this as one of the main reasons Cranmer was able to retain Henry's favour for so long. There is no doubt that the king liked him very much and was always predisposed to interpret what he said and did in the best of lights. This made it virtually impossible for those who wished to discredit the archbishop, because their views differed from his, to win Henry's sympathy. It seems that attempts to undermine Cranmer were always laughed at by the king. But there were other important reasons why the archbishop retained his monarch's confidence.

Henry trusted him as far as he ever trusted anybody. He was confident not only that Cranmer would always do what he was told, whatever the circumstances, but also that he would never act independently in a manner of which his monarch would disapprove. It was Cranmer's lack of policy objectives of his own that probably set him apart from Cromwell in Henry's estimation. With Cranmer, Henry was confident that what you saw was what you got – there was no hidden agenda – whereas with Cromwell there was always the suspicion that there was something you were not being told.

Some writers have been tempted to dismiss Cranmer as nothing more than the king's yes-man. Such a verdict is misleading. It is correct that Cranmer's belief was that his loyalty to his king demanded that he accept whatever decisions Henry made and that he try his utmost to implement them, but he saw his duty as extending beyond this. He believed that he was called upon to offer his master the best advice he could at all times, even when he knew it was likely to be met with either disfavour or anger. Thus, for example, he pleaded with Henry not to allow Anne Boleyn's disgrace to damage the Reformation and he argued that leniency should be shown to Cromwell.

The extent to which he was prepared to take his duty to advise fearlessly is recorded in the written response he made in 1538 to the more than 200 amendments Henry suggested be made to the Bishops' Book when he eventually found time to study it closely. Cranmer dealt with each point in detail and explained why most of Henry's proposals were either inappropriate or ill-founded. The fact that he took it upon himself to correct the king's grammar in places suggests much both about the archbishop and about his relationship with his master.

Cranmer and the Henrician Reformation

During the time Cranmer served Henry he was widely believed to be either a Lutheran or a Lutheran sympathiser. Although his views fluctuated over the period as the influences on him changed (this inconsistency is partly what makes him so human), it is clear that he was always more of a Protestant than the king would have wished him to be. But, even more than Cromwell, he distinguished between his personal faith (which he openly declared to the king) and the policies he was helping to implement. Thus, at the extreme, he was prepared to pass judgements of heresy (leading to death by burning) on individuals whose beliefs were no different to his own when the king instructed him so to do. Those who have been revolted by such 'hypocrisy' have perhaps not thought deeply enough about what could lead a man to act in this way.

While the sectarian debate about Cranmer raged few writers were in any doubt that his influence on the Henrician Reformation was great, but a closer investigation of the facts suggests otherwise.

If the question asked is, 'In what ways would the Henrician Reformation been different had Cranmer not been the Archbishop of Canterbury?', answers are difficult to find. For example:

* In 1537–8 he supported Cromwell's attempts to move the theology of the Church towards Protestantism and in the years after 1543 he pursued a similar policy when invited to do so by the king.
* But his efforts were of no lasting significance, and one is really left with the highly intangible (and therefore essentially unquantifiable and unprovable) claim that his mere presence as the most senior cleric in the Church of England acted as an encouragement to those who wished to see Protestantism triumphant.

Key question
What part did Cranmer play in the Henrician Reformation?

Yet, however one argues the case, it is impossible to escape the conclusion that, although Cranmer's significance in the Reformation after 1547 was very considerable, up to 1547 it was minimal in comparison to that of the man he served.

Shaping future Reformation 1540–53

Key question
What part did Cranmer play in shaping future Reformation?

After Cromwell's execution Cranmer emerged as one of the leading reform-minded councillors. With the king's support Cranmer survived the so-called 'Prebendaries' Plot' of 1543 (orchestrated by a combination of disaffected Canterbury Cathedral clergy and their conservative allies at Oxford University) and was allowed to promote his own English Litany and King's Prymer. Shortly after Henry VIII's death Cranmer issued his Book of Homilies, a set of official model sermons, followed by his English prayer book. Issued in March 1549, Cranmer's Book of Common Prayer has been described as his greatest achievement but it was too conservative for the reformers and too radical for the conservatives – it even provoked the Western Rebellion. This was a rebellion of commons and some landowners in Cornwall and Devon who were protesting about the religious changes. Undaunted, Cranmer set to work on a more radical edition of his prayer book which he issued in 1552. The Second Book of Common Prayer was explicitly anti-Catholic and was adapted and adopted by the Elizabethan regime to become the standard work available to an increasingly Protestant clergy.

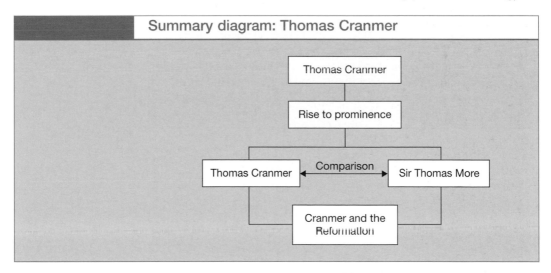

Summary diagram: Thomas Cranmer

Study Guide: AS Questions

In the style of AQA

(a) Explain why, in 1537, Cromwell ordered the Churches to make a copy of the Bible in English available to parishioners.

(12 marks)

(b) 'Cromwell planned and carried out the English Reformation to 1540.' Explain why you agree or disagree with this statement. (24 marks)

Exam tips

(a) You would need to explain something of the context of religious change and the position of Cromwell so as to provide the long-term factors here. Cromwell's Protestant convictions, and his desire to ensure uniformity of beliefs and practices are important. The immediate reasons are connected with the need to build on the Ten Articles and the Bishops' Book and to try to win over the mass of the population, perhaps trying to push through change before the king and conservatives could prevent his doing so.

(b) This question is asking you to assess the part played by Cromwell in the English Reformation. In your answer you will need to define what you understand by the English Reformation. If you take it to mean everything that happened after the Act of Supremacy, clearly Cromwell played no part in the early stages, whereas if you take it to mean the changes that occurred in doctrine, belief and the impact of the Church in people's lives, clearly Cromwell's influence would be keenly felt. You can, of course, take issue with the idea that the changes were 'planned' and you might also suggest that Cromwell had alternative motivation. You also need to balance Cromwell's role against that of others – particularly the king and Cranmer.

In the style of Edexcel
Study Sources 1 and 2.

Do you accept the view that the fall of Thomas Cromwell in 1540 was primarily the work of his enemies at Court? Explain your answer, using Sources 1 and 2 and your own knowledge.

(40 marks)

Source 1

From the Parliament Roll of 1540, listing the charges made against Thomas Cromwell in the Act of Attainder, used to avoid the necessity of a trial.

Thomas Cromwell, contrary to the trust and confidence that your Majesty had in him, caused many of your majesty's faithful subjects to be greatly influenced by heresies and other errors, contrary to the right laws and pleasure of Almighty God. And in the last day of March 1539 when certain new preachers, such as Robert Barnes, were committed to the Tower of London for preaching and teaching against your Highness's proclamations, Thomas Cromwell confirmed the preacher to be good. And moreover, the said Thomas Cromwell, being a man of very base and low degree, has held the nobles of your realm in great disdain, derision and detestation.

Source 2

From A. Anderson and A. Imperato, Tudor England 1485–1603, *published in 2001.*

Cromwell accepted his defeat on religious policy and might have survived if his enemies at Court had not made good use of the collapse of the Cleves marriage. Henry's distaste for Anne was heightened by his growing desire for Catherine Howard, the pretty, young and flirtatious niece of the Duke of Norfolk – Cromwell's bitterest rival on the Privy Council. The Protestant alliance, Cromwell's religious preferences and the Cleves marriage created a suspicion in Henry's mind that his chief minister was pursuing his own interests rather than his king's. This was a suspicion that Cromwell's enemies were well placed to exploit, and on this occasion Henry's anger and desire seems to have clouded his judgement.

Source: Edexcel, 2007.

Exam tips
The cross-references are intended to take you straight to the material that will help you to answer the question.

The key issues raised in this question are the reasons for Cromwell's fall from power, and the role of Court faction in bringing it about. The sources provide the following points.

Cromwell was charged with heresy and betraying the king's wishes (Source 1). The reference in Source 2 to the suspicion in Henry's mind that Cromwell was 'pursuing his own interests' links with that. This is developed in Source 2 by reference to a Protestant marriage and alliance, and to Cromwell's own religious views. Your own knowledge here can be used to add depth to these points by reference to Cromwell's religious policies (pages 150–1) and the disastrous Cleves marriage (pages 150–1). Your own knowledge can also be used to support the suggestion that Cromwell's policies went further in the direction of Protestantism than the king's own religious preferences (pages 147–9).

Sources 1 and 2 and your own knowledge therefore allow you to counter the claim in the question and to argue that Cromwell fell from power because of significant political and religious differences with the king.

In support of the claim, however, you could take into account the nature of Source 1 to challenge the validity of the evidence: this is a document put together by Cromwell's enemies and intended to justify his execution. There is also an indication of haste in the whole procedure and the device to avoid examination of evidence in a trial.

Sources 1 and 2 also provide evidence of the work of Cromwell's enemies at courts. The reference at the end of Source 1 to Cromwell's origins and attitude towards the nobility hints at the personal motives of his enemies. Source 2 directly refers to the work of Cromwell's enemies at court, the significance of Catherine Howard and her relationship to Norfolk.

Source 2 also suggests that the king's judgement was clouded. These points can be further developed from your own knowledge using pages 150–1.

How strong in your view is the evidence that Cromwell's fall came primarily because his enemies were able to exploit certain errors of judgement and that Henry was manipulated by faction?

In the style of OCR

Assess the claim that reform of the Privy Council was the most important achievement of Thomas Cromwell in government and administration. (50 marks)

Exam tips

The cross-references are intended to take you straight to the material that will help you to answer the question.

The focus of this question is on Cromwell's reform of the Privy Council, which most historians consider evolved in the course of the 1530s (page 156). Within the Privy Council the office of Secretary of State became crucial and, though it was discontinued at the fall of Cromwell, it was restored under Edward VI and became one of the key officials thereafter (pages 146–7). The role of the select council in central government and administration, which was one of Cromwell's bureaucratic reforms, could be usefully discussed and compared with the royal household, which it principally displaced (pages 145–7). The advantages need to be assessed to explain why the council was created in the first place, and Cromwell's relationship to it.

An argument can also be made that the Privy Council was not Cromwell's greatest achievement. You could discuss the growth in centralisation exemplified by the creation of six financial departments of state, the development of the councils in the north, Wales, the Marches and Ireland, Cromwell's use of parliament and reliance on statute, and the extension of royal power, for example, the removal of franchises (pages 156–7). You could also argue that Cromwell's administration of the Church as vicegerent after 1535, in particular his creation of the Court of Augmentations, which handled the finances and legal issues arising from the dissolution of the monasteries, was another considerable achievement (pages 46–7 and 156).

Though students will disagree about the most important achievement, and some may even reject Cromwell's involvement in the establishment of the Privy Council, the best answers should prioritise their argument, support their interpretations with factual evidence and reach a clear conclusion.

6 Crisis, What Crisis? Henry's Final Years 1540–7

POINTS TO CONSIDER

This chapter discusses the problems that faced Henry VIII's regime in the last seven years of his reign. These include the succession, foreign relations, politics, finance and religion. The chapter also discusses why many historians have described the final years of Henry's reign as a time of failure. These issues are examined as three key themes:

- Politics, government and the succession
- Religious and diplomatic legacy
- Henry the tyrant?

Key dates

1542		Armed raid on Scotland led by Duke of Norfolk
	November	Battle of Solway Moss – heavy Scottish defeat – James V died a fortnight later; succeeded by his baby daughter, Mary
1543		Treaty of Greenwich with Scotland
1544		Invasion of France, Boulogne captured
		Act of Succession passed in parliament
1545		Attempted French invasion of England failed
1546		Treaty of Ardres between England and France
		Henry drafted his last will
1547	January	Henry VIII died

1 | Politics, Government and the Succession

Introduction

Henry VIII died on 28 January 1547. It was not a sudden event. He had been seriously ill on and off for a decade and many had been the times when both his doctors and his court had expected that their patient and monarch would soon be dead. He was, after all, no longer young. The fact that he survived into his 55th year meant that he had already outlived many of his contemporaries in a period when a person at 40 was thought to be entering old age rather than middle age. And he was not a well man for his years. He suffered from excruciatingly painful swelling of his legs (some writers maintain that the evidence suggests that only one leg was affected) which periodically broke out into horrible sores, the discharging of which, paradoxically, brought him considerable relief. He was massively overweight, with a waist of over 50 inches, and other parts in proportion. This huge bulk seems to have increased the severity of the pain that he would, in any case, have suffered.

The political situation

Key question
How have historians changed their views about the political situation in the final seven years of Henry VIII's reign?

The orthodox view used to be that the period from the fall of Cromwell to Henry's death was a time of steady decline in the affairs of both the king and his country, so that a desperate situation was left for his child-heir and his leading subjects to attempt to resolve. The last six years of his reign were typified as being a time of recurring crises which were largely caused by the over-reactions and growing eccentricities of an increasingly tyrannical and pain-maddened ruler. Henry was seen as wavering between lengthy periods of black despair and depression and shorter interludes of unrealistic optimism.

- During his periods of 'black despair', his decisions were likely to be so slow in emerging that their delay caused chaos in the affairs of state.
- During his periods of 'unrealistic optimism', rapid decisions were made based on totally unrealistic premises, with equally disastrous results.

However, revisionists have reassessed the political situation and the idea of recurring crises is no longer popular. There were disruptions and there were problems but the machinery of government continued to operate normally. Indeed, although Henry VIII's final years were marked by the king's failing health and power, he managed to maintain the authority of the Crown and preserve the unity of the realm.

The succession

Key question
Why was the succession such a problem and how was it resolved?

Key dates

Act of Succession: 1544

Henry drafted his last will: 1546

Apart from the wars with Scotland and France which had begun in 1542 and 1544, Henry VIII's major concern in his last years was the succession. Since 1527 he had been obsessed with the need to safeguard the dynasty by leaving a male heir to succeed him. The birth of Prince Edward in 1537 had seemed to achieve this objective. By 1546 the king's declining health made it clear that his son would come to the throne as a minor. To avoid any possible disputes Henry made a final settlement of the succession in his will of 1546. This replaced the Succession Acts of 1534, 1536 and 1544, although the terms of the will were similar to the Act of 1544.

In the event of Edward dying without heirs, the succession was to pass first to Mary, the daughter of Catherine of Aragon. If Mary died without heirs her sister Elizabeth, daughter of Anne Boleyn, was to succeed. The major change to the previous settlement was that if all Henry's children were to die without heirs, the throne was to pass to his niece Frances Grey. Lady Frances was the elder daughter of Henry VIII's sister Mary, who first had married King Louis XII of France and then Charles Brandon, Duke of Suffolk. This clause meant that the other possible claimant to the English throne, the infant Mary Queen of Scots, was excluded. Mary was the descendant of Henry VIII's sister Margaret, who had married James IV of Scotland. Henry was anxious to preserve the royal supremacy, hence the inclusion of the Protestant Grey family and the exclusion of the Catholic Stewart dynasty. Although the will had replaced the earlier succession settlements, the Acts of 1534 and 1536, which had made Mary and Elizabeth illegitimate, were not repealed.

Henry's major concern in his will was to secure the peaceful succession of his son and safeguard the royal supremacy. By 1546 it had become clear that the surest way to achieve this, and to prevent any power struggle, was to give authority to Seymour and the reform faction. The disgrace of Howard and Gardiner had made the position of Seymour and his supporters more secure, and this was strengthened by adjustments to the terms of the will right up to the time of Henry VIII's death. A Regency Council was nominated consisting of Seymour and 15 of his most trusted allies. Members of the Council were to have equal powers, and were to govern the country until Edward reached 18 years of age. In order to secure the loyalty and co-operation of the Council its members were to be rewarded with new titles, and lands taken from the monasteries and the Howard family.

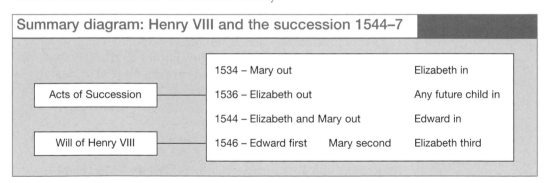

Summary diagram: Henry VIII and the succession 1544–7

Acts of Succession	1534 – Mary out		Elizabeth in
	1536 – Elizabeth out		Any future child in
	1544 – Elizabeth and Mary out		Edward in
Will of Henry VIII	1546 – Edward first	Mary second	Elizabeth third

Henry and government

Key question
How effective was government in the last few years of Henry's reign?

The traditional interpretation claims that in the final stage of his reign Henry acted as his own chief minister, attending to the minutiae of government in much the same way as Wolsey and Cromwell had done in previous times. This allows it to be maintained that the king played the factions off one against the other – that he literally did divide and rule.

However, the evidence that has emerged as the period has been more extensively researched can be used to suggest that the factions manipulated the king at least as much as they were manipulated by him. The core of this alternative interpretation is that, although the oft-quoted evidence has been accurately reported, it is not representative and therefore should not be used to generalise from. This is said to apply to the whole of the period

Profile: Sir William Paget 1505–63

1505	– Born in Wednesbury in Staffordshire
1529	– Entered parliament as MP
1530	– Employed by Henry VIII and Archbishop Cranmer to persuade the universities of northern Europe to support the king's divorce from Catherine of Aragon
1541	– Appointed ambassador to France (1541–3)
1543	– Appointed to the Privy Council (1543–death)
c.1545	– Became, with Edward Seymour, Henry VIII's chief adviser (1545–7)
1547	– Supported Seymour's protectorate with whom he became close friends
1549	– Created Baron Beaudesert. Supported Seymour against Northumberland. After initially being arrested was allowed to return to government office
1551	– Arrested on a charge of conspiring against Northumberland
1552	– Released from prison and forcibly retired from government
1553	– Invited to return to government by Northumberland who sought his help in proclaiming Jane Grey queen. Initially supported Jane Grey but soon deserted her for Mary. Appointed to lead Mary's government along with the Earl of Arundel
1554	– Rewarded for supporting and negotiating Mary's marriage with Philip of Spain
1554–5	– Refused to support Gardiner's religious legislation which angered the queen
1556	– Given the less important office of Lord Privy Seal. Virtually ignored in government
1558	– Served on the Privy Council of Queen Elizabeth
1560	– Virtually retired from government
1563	– Died

Paget was probably one of the most able and influential men in government. He was trusted by Henry VIII and the Duke of Somerset, Edward Seymour, but not by Northumberland who distrusted his loyal support of Somerset in the *coup d'état* of 1549. Nevertheless, Northumberland initially employed him for his talent as a minister. His religion was not known to contemporaries who thought him variously a Protestant reformer and Catholic conservative. The truth is he kept his religious convictions very much to himself. His support of Mary earned her trust and gratitude and his handling of the marriage negotiations won the admiration of Philip of Spain. However, his opposition to what he regarded as extreme religious legislation drawn up by his one-time friend Gardiner, with whom he quarrelled quite violently, led to his losing his leading place in Mary's government. For the last three years of her reign she all but ignored his advice.

under discussion, when Henry's forays into the detailed business of government were unsustained and were mainly restricted to foreign policy, thus leaving ample scope for his leading servants to exercise the major control of events. But the interpretation is most convincing when applied to the final months of the king's life.

In this process of re-evaluation, two previously shadowy figures have emerged as men of considerable political influence. They are Sir Anthony Denny and Sir William Paget.

Sir Anthony Denny

Denny has remained the less understood of the two. He was in charge of the king's Privy Chamber – those rooms where Henry spent much of his time during his last years, and to which others could only gain admittance with Denny's agreement. He was therefore able to control who had access to the king, especially during those long periods when Henry was depressed and was less likely to assert his wishes. It is clear that Denny used his power both to keep out those whom he did not want to have an opportunity to influence the king, and, during their frequent conversations, to present Henry with the information he wanted him to know. It has not yet proved possible to reach a convincing assessment of the cumulative effect of Denny's exercise of his power, but it was clearly substantial.

Sir William Paget

More is known about Paget, although the evidence about him is open to several interpretations. He was Henry's Private Secretary (the post that had been used by Cromwell from which to build his power base) during these years and, somewhat similar to Denny, was able to control the flow of written information that reached the king. He was an unscrupulous self-seeker and was probably instrumental in deciding which of the factions should finally emerge triumphant. He could have sided with either group, but was seemingly made the best offer by Seymour, and therefore facilitated the victory of the 'progressives'. In this he was assisted by Denny, who was almost certainly also part of the plot.

Henry's last will and testament

The vital controlling mechanism in the plot to ensure the success of the 'progressives' was Henry's last will and testament. It seems probable that Paget drew up the first (and uncontroversial) part of this with the king's knowledge in December 1546, and arranged for it to be witnessed at this stage – the witnesses signing where plenty of space was left for further additions to be made. The details about the Regency Council were then added when the king was sufficiently near to death not to be able to do anything to alter them.

Close examination of the relevant wording shows that, with Norfolk in the Tower awaiting execution and Gardiner excluded from court in disgrace for failing to accept the king's instruction on the exchange of some diocesan land, the 'progressives' would be able to dominate the Council and would be able to utilise a

The last will and testament of Henry VIII. Why has Henry VIII's will been described as one of 'extraordinary political significance'?

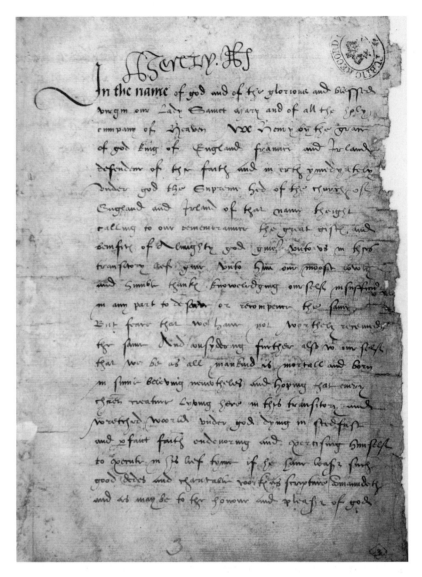

loop-hole whereby Seymour would be able to exercise virtually full monarchical power. It was not even necessary for Henry to sign the will himself because Denny had control of the 'dry stamp' that for the past year had stood in place of the weakening king's actual mark.

Although this version of events will never be able to be proved beyond doubt, it does ring the truest of all the scenarios so far offered by researchers. Thus there is room to believe that the wicked old tyrant of tradition was frequently (especially latterly) a pathetic old man who was shamelessly exploited by those who were entrusted to serve him.

As neither the 'orthodox' nor the 'revisionist' picture is very flattering to Henry VIII, it is difficult to escape the conclusion that the final stages of the king's life were very damaging in one form or another to his reputation. It was undoubtedly a tragedy that a reign that had begun with such high expectations should have ended in such political squalor.

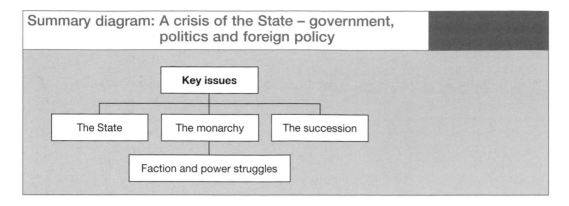

Summary diagram: A crisis of the State – government, politics and foreign policy

Key issues

The State — The monarchy — The succession

Faction and power struggles

2 | Religious and Diplomatic Legacy

The place of religion in the Henrician Reformation

There is wide agreement that Henry VIII's motives in breaking away from Rome were much more political than religious. The English Reformation put the Church firmly under the control of the State. It also removed England from the authority of the Pope; a source of outside interference which was highly resented among the English ruling élites. The resulting royal supremacy made Henry VIII more independent and more powerful than any monarch in English history. It enabled him to rule an undivided kingdom where Church and State were merged into a single sovereign state. Henry VIII was able to reduce the political power of the Church and exploit its vast wealth. Ecclesiastical wealth replenished the Exchequer, which had been almost bankrupted by Henry VIII's unsuccessful wars of the 1520s.

On the surface, the Crown was the main beneficiary of the English Reformation. Yet, once religion had come to the forefront of the political arena, it created problems for the monarchy. Religious differences deepened the rift between political factions at Court. Henry VIII had to tread a cautious path between the conservative Catholic and reforming Protestant parties. By 1547 he had decided that the safest way to protect the succession and the royal supremacy was to give control of the Privy Council to Somerset and the reformers. However, the fall of Somerset in 1549 triggered a renewed power struggle for political power between the Catholic conservatives and the Protestant reformers. Some of the leading Catholic conservatives were able briefly to regain their positions in the Privy Council. However, once Northumberland had consolidated his position, they were expelled.

The power struggle between the conservatives and reformers resurfaced again in 1553 with Northumberland's attempt to change the succession. Northumberland's action was prompted not only by personal ambition, but also by the desire to prevent the Catholics regaining power under Mary Tudor. Even so there was still a great deal of toleration and Catholic politicians were not excluded from government purely for religious reasons.

Key question
Where does religion fit into the Henrician Reformation?

Stephen Gardiner, the leading Catholic bishop, spent most of Edward VI's reign in prison, but this was largely because he refused to co-operate in any way with the Privy Council. Unlike the hard-line Gardiner, a majority of the ruling élites favoured moderate reform.

The doctrinal position in the Church of England during the 1540s

From the time Henry had made himself Head of the English Church in 1534 he had been under pressure to formulate an acceptable doctrine. The reform party led by Cranmer had advocated the introduction of moderate Lutheran ideas. On the other hand, the pro-Catholic, conservative faction led by Gardiner had favoured a policy of minimum change to the basic Catholic doctrines.

During the period 1534 to 1546 royal favour swung between the two groups. The first major statement of doctrine, the Act of Ten Articles, came in 1536. This Act was passed when the reformers were in the ascendancy, and introduced a number of Lutheran doctrines into the Church of England, e.g. belief in **consubstantiation**. Three years later the conservatives regained royal favour and the Act of Six Articles was passed to remove many of the Lutheran beliefs. Such shifts of policy meant that by 1547 the doctrines of the Church of England were a compromise and contained many inconsistencies which were unacceptable to reformers and conservatives alike.

Catholic doctrine in the Church of England

When Henry VIII died, the main articles of faith in the Church of England were in line with traditional Catholic orthodoxy:

- The Eucharist was clearly defined in the Catholic form of transubstantiation. The Lutheran form of consubstantiation was no longer accepted in the Church of England.
- Only the clergy were permitted to take communion with both the bread and the wine, while the laity were again restricted to taking only the sacramental bread.
- The Catholic rites of confirmation, marriage, holy orders and extreme unction had been re-introduced, alongside the previously recognised sacraments of the Eucharist, penance and baptism.
- The laity were still required to make regular confession of sins to a priest, and to seek absolution and penance.
- English clergy were no longer allowed to marry, and those who had married before 1540 had had to send away their wives and families, or lose their livings.
- Although there was no specific statement on the existence of **purgatory**, the need for the laity to do 'good works' for their salvation had been reinstated.
- The singing of masses for the souls of the dead was held to be 'agreeable also to God's Law'. It was for this reason that the chantries, where a priest sang masses for the souls of the

Key terms

Consubstantiation
Belief that the wine and bread taken at communion represent the blood and body of Christ.

Purgatory
In Catholic belief, occupies the middle ground between heaven and hell.

founder and his family, were not closed down at the same time as the monasteries.

- Paintings and statues of the saints were still allowed in the churches, although the laity were instructed not to worship them.

Many of the processions and rituals of the Catholic Church were still practised, because it was maintained that they created a good religious frame of mind in those who witnessed them.

Protestant doctrines in the Church of England

Although the Church of England remained fundamentally Catholic in doctrine, it had adopted a number of Protestant practices by 1547:

- Services were still conducted in Latin, but Cranmer's prayers and responses of the Litany in English had been authorised in 1545.
- Greater importance was attached to the sermon, and the Lord's Prayer, the Creed and the Ten Commandments, all of which had to be taught in English by parents to their children.
- Similarly the Great Bible of 1539 was the authorised English translation which replaced the Latin Vulgate Bible. Moreover, the élite laity were allowed to read the Great Bible in their own homes, unlike on the continent where often only the Catholic clergy were allowed to read and interpret the Bible.
- The practice of the Church of England with regard to some Catholic doctrines was ambiguous. Saints could be 'reverenced for their excellent virtue' and could be offered prayers, but the laity were forbidden to make pilgrimages to the shrines of saints or to offer them gifts, because it was maintained that grace, salvation and remission of sins came only from God.
- At the same time, the number of Holy Days – days on which, like Sundays, the laity were expected to attend church and not to work – had been reduced to 25.
- Finally, in sharp contrast to Catholic countries, there had been no monasteries in England since 1540, when even the larger monasteries had been closed by royal order, and their possessions had been transferred to the Crown.

Attempts between 1534 and 1546 to establish a uniform set of articles of faith for the Church of England had only succeeded in producing a patchwork of doctrines that often conflicted. Until 1547 this ramshackle structure was held together by the Henrician treason and heresy laws. Anyone breaking, or even questioning, the statutes and proclamations defining the doctrines of the Church of England was liable to confiscation of property, fines, imprisonment or execution. Similarly the censorship laws prevented the printing, publishing or importation of books and pamphlets expressing views contrary to the doctrines of the Church of England.

Key question
Why are historians divided over Henry's foreign policy during the 1540s?

Foreign relations

Historians are divided about Henry's intentions at this late stage of his reign:

- It is felt by some that his main aim was to unite Britain by the conquest of Scotland.
- Others think that he was more concerned with his earlier ambition of claiming the French throne, or, at least, reconquering some of the former English territories on the continent.

Consequently, historians have either made a case for or against his conduct of foreign policy in the final stage of his reign:

- The case against Henry's conduct of foreign policy is that he failed to achieve the successes that were available to him, while squandering his wealth and endangering the financial strength of his successors by attempting to win military glory on the continent.
- The case for Henry's conduct of foreign policy is that he succeeded in maintaining England's position as a major player at the centre of international diplomacy, while securing (i) the northern frontier by defeating the Scots and (ii) Calais by capturing Boulogne.

Key dates

Armed raid on Scotland led by Duke of Norfolk: 1542

Battle of Solway Moss: November 1542

James V died; succeeded by Mary: December 1542

Treaty of Greenwich: 1543

Invasion of France, Boulogne captured: 1544

Attempted French invasion of England failed: 1545

Until the 1530s, when the English Reformation had soured relations with the Catholic Empire, the most useful ally for Henry had been the Emperor Charles V. By 1542, mutual fears over France had restored good relations between England and the Empire. In particular, Henry VIII had seen the Franco-Scottish alliance, created by the marriage of James V and Mary of Guise in 1538, as a major threat to English security.

In 1542 an alliance was agreed by which there was to be a joint Anglo-Imperial invasion of France. This alarmed the Scots, who began to launch raids across the border into England. Henry sent a strong army under the Duke of Norfolk into Scotland, and the Scots were decisively defeated at the Battle of Solway Moss in November 1542. This Scottish reverse was followed by the death of James V in December. Mary of Guise was left as regent for the infant Mary, Queen of Scots, and was forced to make peace by the Treaty of Greenwich in 1543. Under the terms of the treaty, the Scots had to agree to a future marriage between Mary of Scots and Henry's son Edward. Mary of Guise and the Catholic party in Scotland soon rejected the marriage agreement.

In 1544 and 1545 Henry sent Edward Seymour (later to become the Duke of Somerset) to ravage the Scottish Lowlands. This 'rough wooing' did little to encourage the Scots to support the marriage proposals. At the same time, an English army had landed in France to support an invasion by Charles V. This meant that England had to fight a war on two fronts. Consequently, Seymour was given too few troops to do anything effective in Scotland, while the English army in France was too small to do more than capture the port of Boulogne. Even so the cost of the war was enormous, and by 1546 over two million pounds, mainly raised by the sale of monastic lands, had been spent.

Charles V withdrew from the conflict and Henry VIII, plagued by ill-health and worried about the cost of the war, was left to make peace with France. It was agreed, under the terms of the Treaty of Campe (sometimes known as the Treaty of Ardres) in June 1546, that England should hold Boulogne for eight years.

When Henry VIII died in 1547 he left behind him a very uncertain diplomatic situation. The uneasy peace with France and Scotland was further undermined by the renewal of the Franco-Scottish alliance, which left England exposed to the danger of invasion from both north and south. England was in a precarious position, especially as the succession of the young Edward VI, a minor, could be exploited by the two main continental powers to strengthen their own positions in their dynastic wars. Furthermore, the Catholic nations were watching with interest to see if the religious compromise in England would survive the death of Henry VIII.

Lord Paget, England's ablest diplomat, summed up the whole position very clearly for the new Regency Council. He thought that England was not strong enough to defend Calais and Boulogne against the French. On the other hand, Charles V was a threat because of his support for the Catholic religion. However, he felt that it was too dangerous for England to risk assisting the Lutheran princes in Germany. Consequently, he recommended that the alliance with Charles V should be maintained, and that all efforts should be made to promote hostility between France and the Holy Roman Empire.

Key dates

Treaty of Ardres: 1546

Henry VIII died: January 1547

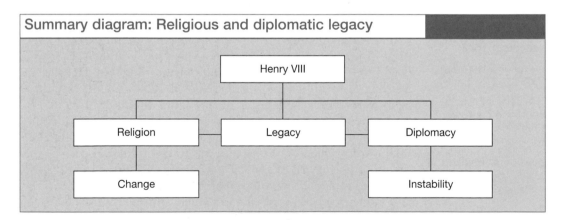

Summary diagram: Religious and diplomatic legacy

Henry VIII

Religion — Legacy — Diplomacy

Change

Instability

3 | Henry the Tyrant?

Introduction

Arguably the most damning indictment on Henry VIII is the way in which he ruled the country in the years before his death. He has been described as being a typical tyrannical bully who abused his authority by punishing not only those who dared to disagree with or to oppose him, but also many of those whom he only suspected of wishing to do so. He has been said to have operated

Key question
Why have some historians described Henry as behaving like a tyrant in the 1540s?

a primitive reign of terror in which everybody spied on everybody else and in which fear of having one's words or actions misrepresented sapped initiative at all levels of government, as officials remained inactive unless they received specific instructions from an authorised superior. What is worse, it has been maintained that Henry took a perverted pleasure in watching his subjects squirm, for he let it be known that he was likely to forgive those who made a full confession of their faults and pleaded for his mercy. Sometimes he even set up situations seemingly for the sole purpose of causing maximum embarrassment to those who were attempting to carry out his instructions.

However, research in recent decades has thrown the greatest doubt on the view of Henry as an ageing tyrant. It is still generally accepted that this is how he thought of himself, and how he performed on well-publicised occasions. But what has been quite effectively challenged is the idea that this is how things were for most of the time between Cromwell's fall and the king's death.

A portrait of Henry VIII painted by Cornelys Matsys in 1544.

The arrest of Catherine Parr

One of the incidents that has most often been recounted to illustrate these facets of Henry's kingship is the attempt made in 1546 to arrest Catherine Parr, his sixth wife, on suspicion of heresy. Henry had married Catherine presumably to bring him comfort rather than excitement. He probably learned of her 'advanced' religious views after she had become his wife. The 'conservative' faction at court (of which the Duke of Norfolk was a leading member) attempted to do to Catherine Parr what the 'progressives' had previously done to Catherine Howard. But this time the charges were based on religious rather than sexual misconduct.

There was unambiguous evidence that in her beliefs and practices Queen Catherine was closer to the Protestants than she was allowed to be by law at the time. Wriothesley, the Lord Chancellor, was chosen by his colleagues to present the evidence to the king. He must have done his work well because Henry agreed that his wife should be arrested and taken to the Tower for questioning. It seems that he then ensured that Catherine was told about what had been arranged, because within hours she had sought her husband's presence and had won him over by her promises that she would believe and do whatever he, in his superior wisdom, instructed her to. Henry pronounced himself satisfied that all was well but, presumably on purpose, 'forgot' to tell Wriothesley that the situation had changed. When the Lord Chancellor duly appeared the following afternoon with a contingent of guards to arrest the queen, he was treated to a torrent of abuse from the king for daring to attempt such a stupid and possibly treasonable act. Henry had well and truly displayed the fullness of his power.

Key question
What motives lay behind the arrest of Catherine Parr?

Attacks on Archbishop Cranmer

A similar incident had previously occurred with Archbishop Cranmer, whom the 'conservatives' also accused of being a secret Protestant. On this occasion Henry took obvious pleasure in instructing Cranmer to investigate the charges himself. The accusers were thereby confronted with the prospect of being judged by the very person they hoped to discredit. It is little wonder that no evidence was found to be forthcoming! And Henry had shown that there was little point in attempting to attack the only one of his senior office holders whom he trusted completely. Cranmer had shown over more than a decade that he had no personal ambition and that he was prepared to do whatever his monarch required of him.

Key question
Why did Cranmer suffer personal attacks?

The execution of Surrey and the arrest of Norfolk

The Duke of Norfolk had established a somewhat similar reputation for subservience to his royal master. He had survived several highly dangerous situations – especially at the time of the disgraces of his nieces Anne Boleyn and Catherine Howard in 1536 and 1542 – by throwing himself totally on his sovereign's

Key question
Why was the Earl of Surrey executed and the Duke of Norfolk arrested?

mercy and by proving that he would carry out whatever duties were assigned to him. But his good fortune appeared to have run out at the end of 1546 when he was implicated in the treason of his eldest son, the Earl of Surrey, who had unwisely hinted that his ancestry gave him as much right as anyone else to be a future king of England.

Henry showed his paranoia about any possible challenge, however distant, to his dynasty, by having Surrey executed. It is thought that had the king lived for one more day, Norfolk would have shared his son's fate. As it was, a mixture of good fortune and timely subservience had allowed him to live long enough to see another reign.

Henry VIII's legacy

Key question
What was Henry VIII's legacy?

However, it has been Henry's desire to control events even from the grave that has provided historians with their most quoted evidence of the king as a megalomaniac during his final years. The issues have been the contents and the timing of his last will and testament. There was never any doubt that Henry's successor would be his only son, Edward. But once it was recognised that it was highly likely that Edward would still be a minor when his father died (he could not be declared 'of age' until the mid-1550s at the earliest), all interest at court centred on the arrangements to be made for the government of the realm in the years before the new king attained adult status. It was well understood that whichever faction secured the dominant position during Edward's minority would be able both to exercise enormous power and to acquire considerable wealth at the expense of the monarchy.

The two contending factions, although they were anything but settled in their composition, were the 'conservatives', headed by the Duke of Norfolk, and the 'progressives', led by Edward Seymour, Earl of Hertford, who was Edward's dead mother's brother. The 'conservatives' have been so-called because they both favoured keeping the teachings and practices of the Church of England as traditional as possible and believed that the king should seek his advice from his leading nobles rather than from men of common birth as had tended to happen since 1485. The most politically able of their active members was Stephen Gardiner, the Bishop of Winchester, whose plottings had been behind most of the attempts to discredit individual 'progressives' ever since he had lost the struggle with Thomas Cromwell to win the king's favour in the early 1530s.

The 'progressives' had been identified with Cromwell during his period of dominance. Since his fall in 1540, they had naturally been somewhat in disarray. Perhaps their obvious new leader would have been Thomas Cranmer, Archbishop of Canterbury, as he had long been known to be sympathetic to their leanings towards Protestantism in religion. But Cranmer was interested neither in politics nor in seeking greater power for himself. His competitive spirit was minimal. It was therefore left to Edward's relations on his mother's side to set about rebuilding the fortunes of the faction that favoured change.

The historians who have seen Henry as the villain of the piece claim not only that he was well aware of the struggle for power that was taking place around him, but that he actively encouraged it so that he could play off one group against the other, and thereby retain effective control himself. It is in this light that his final will and testament has most often been interpreted. In it Henry specified that the country should be ruled after his death by a Regency Council, whose members were named by him and who could not subsequently be changed. It was also stated that the Council's decisions must be corporate, with no member being given greater prominence than any other. This attempt to stop the emergence of a leader, together with the fact that the Council appeared to be composed of equal numbers of 'conservatives' and 'progressives', has resulted in the claim that Henry was trying to ensure that politics remained 'frozen' in their existing state until his son was old enough to decide for himself what changes, if any, were to be made.

The timing of both the drawing up and the signing of the will have also been used to support the case that Henry was a tyrant who used particularly unpleasant methods during the latter part of his reign. The evidence has generally been thought to show that the will was drafted towards the end of December 1546 but that it was not authorised to be signed until a month later, when the king knew that he was about to die. The explanation that has most often been given for this sequence of events has been that the existence of the unsigned will, of which those named in it were aware, was a ploy by Henry to intimidate his leading subjects further. The fact that the document was unsigned was a clear threat that if those named in it did not please him in every detail, the wording of the will would be altered to their disadvantage before it was made final.

Thus the traditional interpretation has been presented, with minor variations, over many years. Henry has been described in the final stage of his life – and up to within hours of his death – as a selfish and unscrupulous tyrant who stumbled incompetently from disaster to disaster, harming the interests of his office, his subjects and his country in the process. It has been maintained that he left behind him serious difficulties that his immediate successors barely survived, and then only with a modicum of good fortune. The implicit judgement has often been that it would have been better for the interests or the reputations of all concerned had he died somewhat earlier than he eventually did.

Summary diagram: The final stage

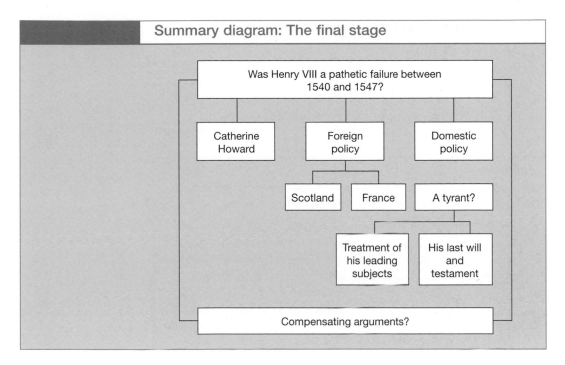

Study Guide: AS Questions

In the style of AQA

(a) Explain why there was much faction-fighting at court in the years 1542–7. (12 marks)

(b) 'By 1547, the Church in England was a Protestant Church.' Explain why you agree or disagree with this statement. (24 marks)

Exam tips

The page references are intended to take you straight to the material that will help you to answer the questions.

(a) You should try to identify a range of factors. Henry's own failing health and his concern for foreign, rather than domestic policy should be considered as crucial context and the question of the succession must also be considered a key point. Religious differences were obviously of key importance and they are also linked to the contemporary and future control of government. More specifically, you should refer to the disgrace of Howard and Gardiner and the ascendancy of the Seymours and to the influence of Denny and Paget. Try to show how your factors link together and provide an overall conclusion.

(b) You will need to consider evidence that both supports and disagrees with this statement. You might, for example, point out that by 1547, the English Church had been removed from papal authority and a number of practices, for example the worship of saints, or the reading of the English Bible by the laity, had been established in line with Protestant thinking (see page 149). However, you will also need to argue that many practices and doctrines remained a compromise and that there were many inconsistencies. Since the main articles of faith were still Catholic (as given on pages 156–7), you are likely to want to argue against the quotation, but you must show balance and supported judgement in your answer.

In the style of OCR

How 'Catholic' was England at the end of Henry VIII's reign in
1547? (50 marks)

Exam tips

*The cross-references are intended to take you straight to the material
that will help you to answer the question.*

Candidates are not expected to know or offer a definitive response
to this question but they should be aware that different historical
judgements may be made. As such, there is no 'right' answer.
Arguments that support the view that England was a Catholic
country in 1547 might include:

- Henry VIII's attachment to several orthodox Catholic views and
  practices such as his belief in purgatory and masses for the dead.
- Henry favoured the Catholic Duke of Norfolk (until 1542) and
  Gardiner (until 1546) after the fall of Cromwell.
- Strong support for Catholicism in the north, west and south-west
  of England.
- The retention of traditional paintings, statues, altars, processions
  and clerical celibacy.
- The Act of Six Articles (1539) that affirmed the seven sacraments
  and re-introduced the burning of heretics was the official faith
  (pages 166–7).
- Chantries continued to be popular at a parish level, although
  founders endowed their prayers with goods rather than property.
- From 1543 restrictions were placed on access to and reading of
  the Bible.

A counter-argument might suggest:

- There were many inconsistencies between the Church's teachings
  and the Act of Six Articles, e.g. more emphasis was put on the
  sermon than the service, pilgrimages were discontinued and the
  number of holy days was reduced (pages 163–6).
- Cranmer favoured Protestant reforms (e.g. The King's Prymer in
  1543 and the Litany in 1545) and was protected by the king from
  his enemies (page 167).
- There was strong regional support for Protestantism in the east
  and south-east of England, especially in Essex, Kent and London.
- Prince Edward was educated by Protestant tutors, and his
  Protestant uncle Edward Seymour was politically pre-eminent in
  1547.
- In 1545 Henry VIII dissolved a number of chantries; and in the
  1540s monastic land was sold off and no new monasteries were
  founded.

You might conclude that it is impossible to gauge popular feeling
although, unlike in the period 1536–9, there were no rebellions
against the religious reforms, there were very few burnings, and there
was no iconoclasm and no vocal support to return England to Rome.
This may suggest a general sense of indifference, a desire to obey
the law or tacit support for the Church's condition in January 1547.

7 Edward VI: Somerset and Northumberland 1547–53

POINTS TO CONSIDER

This chapter is designed to help you to understand the key features of the reign of Edward VI through the experiences of Somerset and Northumberland, who ruled the kingdom on behalf of the boy-king. The chapter examines the political, religious and economic problems that faced the Edwardian regimes. These issues are examined as two main themes:

- Protector Somerset
- Lord President Northumberland

Key dates

1547	January	Death of Henry VIII and accession of Edward VI
	February	Edward Seymour created Duke of Somerset and Lord Protector
1549		Rebellion in East Anglia and the West Country
	October	Fall of Somerset
1550		Emergence of John Dudley, Earl of Warwick, as the most powerful man in England
1551		John Dudley created Duke of Northumberland and Lord President of the Council
1552	January	Execution of the Duke of Somerset
1553	May	Northumberland's son, Guildford, married Lady Jane Grey
	June	Edward VI changed line of succession in favour of Lady Jane Grey
	July	Death of Edward VI, brief reign of Lady Jane Grey, and succession of Mary
	August	Execution of Northumberland

1 | Protector Somerset

Government and administration

Key question
How effective was Somerset's government and administration?

Somerset's government and administration was not markedly different from that of the last years of Henry VIII. The Privy Council was made up of men who had risen to power under Henry VIII and who were using the same methods and machinery of government to cope with similar problems. The real differences were the lack of effective leadership, and the fact that existing problems had grown worse. Economic and financial expedients and a half-hearted religious reform policy only created confusion and uncertainty among both the landed élites and the general public.

It has been suggested that Somerset was neither more nor less to blame than his aristocratic colleagues. But whether this was because he was unwilling, or unable, to change their attitudes is uncertain. While there is no evidence that he tried to corrupt the government, it is equally true that he introduced no reforms. What can be said is that he failed to show the leadership

Key dates
Death of Henry VIII and accession of Edward VI: January 1547

Edward Seymour created Duke of Somerset and Lord Protector: February 1547

A portrait of Edward Seymour, Duke of Somerset.

necessary to compensate for the absence of an adult monarch. Whether this was because of his preoccupation with the war effort, or because of his stubbornness and inability to adjust to new conditions is difficult to judge. Some evidence exists to support each interpretation, but it is not conclusive.

Somerset and the problems of government

The new regime inherited three pressing short-term problems from the previous reign. Immediate decisions had to be made about:

- whether or not to continue the wars against Scotland and France
- the question of religious reform
- how to find ways of raising more revenue.

As well as these immediate political and administrative difficulties, the government faced a number of serious long-term economic and social problems. Population continued to increase, and this presented a major threat to the government. Increasing population was the main cause of inflation because greater demand for goods pushed up prices. Not only did this add to the cost of administration, but it also threatened most people's living standards at a time when wages were not increasing. In addition, it meant that more people were available for employment. This, in turn, caused more poverty because it also raised the number of vagrants looking for work.

The main objective of domestic policy appears to have been the prevention of public disorder, which the ruling élites regarded as a threat to the whole structure of society.

Therefore, Somerset and the Privy Council were faced with a considerable dilemma. They had to continue the war for the sake of national prestige and to retain the support of a large section of the élites. If they maintained the war effort the country would be plunged further into debt. However, if they raised taxes this would be unpopular with the élites and other taxpayers.

At the same time they had to take some action over religious reform if they were not to lose the support of the Protestant activists. Such a loss of support might allow a Catholic revival which would endanger their hold on power. Yet if they went too far the reformers might provoke the Catholics into open rebellion.

The administration was well aware that there was rising popular discontent over the worsening economic conditions. They feared that this might lead to popular uprisings, but they were uncertain how to tackle the economic problems. Therefore, whatever action the government took it was likely to cause as many problems as it solved. In the event, it appears from its actions over the next two years that the government's main objective was to continue the wars. At the same time it cautiously introduced some religious reforms and tried to damp down popular discontent.

Laws and proclamations 1547–8

When the government had established itself parliament was summoned to meet in November 1547. One of its first actions was to pass a new Treason Act. This repealed (did away with) the old heresy, treason and censorship laws and the Act of Six Articles which had maintained doctrinal orthodoxy since 1539. The removal of the heresy laws allowed people to discuss religion freely without fear of arrest, while the ending of censorship on printing and publishing enabled the circulation of books and pamphlets on religion, and the importation of Lutheran and Calvinist literature. A whole mass of unpopular legislation passed during the previous reign was thus swept away. In the past this has been seen as clear proof of Somerset's tolerant attitude, although it could equally well have been interpreted as the normal action of a new regime trying to gain popularity by abolishing the oppressive legislation of its predecessor. However, closer examination suggests that the government was clearing the way for religious reforms.

The Treason Act

Whatever prompted the government to pass a new Treason Act, it immediately created problems for itself. The removal of the restrictive laws encouraged widespread debate over religion (see page 129), particularly in London and other towns. Public meetings frequently ended in disorder and riots, with attacks on churches to break up statues of saints and other Catholic images. At the same time, the repeal of the old laws left the county and urban authorities with much less power to deal with such situations. Consequently the government had helped to promote the very disorder that it was trying to avoid. In the process, it had undermined the confidence of the ruling élites, who now felt themselves powerless to enforce order.

The new Treason Act also repealed the Proclamation Act of 1539 which stated that royal proclamations should be obeyed as if they were acts of parliament, providing that they did not infringe existing laws. Although Tudor monarchs had used, and would continue to use proclamations, the Proclamation Act had been regarded with suspicion because it was feared that it would allow the monarch to rule without parliament. However, the repeal of the Act did not mean that proclamations could not be used. Indeed, because the limitations previously imposed by the 1539 Act had been removed, it has been suggested that Somerset was trying to give himself more freedom to rule without parliament.

There is no evidence to suggest that this was his real intention, although there was a considerable increase in the use of proclamations during his period of office. Under Henry VIII proclamations were, on average, used six times a year. During Edward VI's reign they averaged 19 per year, and of these, 77 – well over half – were issued by Somerset. This increase is now seen as a strategy adopted by a government, faced with severe difficulties, which needed to react as quickly as possible to changing circumstances. Certainly contemporaries did not seem to think that Somerset was trying to corrupt the constitution. There is no evidence that he did not have the backing of the Privy Council, and there was no sign of protest from parliament about their use.

The Chantries Act

The Chantries Act of 1547 might be seen as another measure of religious reform. Undoubtedly it was a logical step, after the dissolution of the monasteries, to close the chantries. Yet, in reality, this Act was a device to raise money to pay for the wars. A similar plan had already been discussed by Henry VIII and his advisers in 1545. Commissioners were sent out early in 1548 to visit the chantries, confiscate their land and property, and collect all the gold and silver plate attached to them. The latter was then melted down to make coins. Simultaneously the royal mints were ordered to re-issue the coinage and reduce the silver content by adding copper. The coinage had already been debased in 1543 and there were to be further debasements until 1551, by which time the silver content had been reduced to 25 per cent. Although these measures provided much needed revenue, they created further problems. By increasing the number of coins in circulation the government was adding to inflation. Prices, particularly for grain, rose rapidly, fuelling discontent among the poor.

The Vagrancy Act and Public Order

That the maintenance of public order was very much in the mind of the administration is shown by the Vagrancy Act of 1547. The harshness of this legislation shows little concern for the poor and needy. The earlier Poor Law of 1536 did recognise that the able-bodied were having difficulty in finding work, and ordered parishes to support the impotent poor. The 1547 Act was a savage attack on vagrants looking for work, who were seen by the government as a cause of riots and sedition. Under the new law, any able-bodied person out of work for more than three days was to be branded with a V and sold into slavery for two years. Further offences were to be punished with permanent slavery. The children of vagrants could be taken from their parents and set to work as apprentices in useful occupations. The new law was widely unpopular, and many of the county and urban authorities refused to enforce it. Although it also proposed housing and collections for the disabled, this measure does little to support Somerset's reputation for humanitarianism.

It is clear that the level of popular discontent was rising by the middle of 1548 because the Privy Council was forced to take measures to appease public agitation. It used to be suggested that this legislation formed part of a reform programme put forward by John Hales at the Treasury and the so-called 'commonwealth men', supported by Somerset. In the light of the evidence now available this interpretation is currently regarded as being very suspect. There are even increasing doubts about whether such a group ever existed. It seems more likely that growing discontent over rising prices and local food shortages forced the government to take some piecemeal action. Here again Somerset's reputation as a reformer and a friend to the people is very much open to question.

The trouble was that the government blamed all the economic problems on enclosure. It was felt that the fencing-off of common land for sheep pasture and the consequent eviction of husbandmen and cottagers from their homes was the major cause of inflation and unemployment. Proclamations were issued against enclosures, and commissioners were sent out to investigate abuses. The main effect of these measures was to increase unrest. Hopes were raised among the masses that the government would take some decisive action, which it did not. At the same time, fear grew among the landed élites that the authorities would actually prevent this form of estate improvement. Further measures limiting the size of leaseholds and placing a tax on wool only made the situation worse by increasing these fears. In any case, many of the élites evaded the legislation which, consequently, fell most heavily on the poorer sections of society it was supposed to protect.

It is reasonable to suggest that the government was more concerned with avoiding riot and rebellion than with helping the poor and solving economic problems. This suspicion is supported by three proclamations issued in 1548 aimed specifically at maintaining law and order. A ban on football was rigorously enforced on the grounds that games usually ended in riots and disorder. It also became an offence to spread rumours, as they were likely to create unrest. Finally, all unlawful assemblies were forbidden. Anyone found guilty of these offences was to be sent for varying periods to the galleys – royal warships propelled by oars. These seem like emergency measures passed by a government which realised that the economic position was getting out of hand, and which feared the consequences.

Fall from power

Key question
Why did Somerset fall from power?

It appears that these attempts to control the situation were ineffective because in 1549 the country drifted into what was potentially a major crisis. Somerset seemed unable, or unwilling, to take decisive action to suppress well-supported popular uprisings in the West Country and East Anglia. His unwillingness to act has traditionally been interpreted as showing sympathy. However, it seems more likely that the initial delays were caused by the reluctance of the local ruling élites to intervene without government support. Lack of money made it difficult to raise a new mercenary army, and Somerset, as Commander-in-Chief, was reluctant to withdraw troops from his garrisons in Scotland and France. It was only when the Privy Council realised the seriousness of the situation and provided additional troops that Lord Russell in the West Country and John Dudley, Earl of Warwick, in East Anglia were able to defeat the rebels.

A major consequence of the rebellions was the fall of Somerset, whose colleagues quickly abandoned him as a man who had failed to prevent anarchy and revolution. When his chief rival, John Dudley (later to become Duke of Northumberland, and hereafter called Northumberland to avoid confusion), fresh from his victory in Norfolk, engineered Somerset's arrest in October 1549 there was no opposition. Although Somerset was released early the following year and rejoined the Privy Council, within a year he was accused of plotting against the government. He was executed in January 1552.

Key dates

Fall of Somerset: October 1549

Execution of Somerset: January 1552

Foreign policy

Foreign policy during the first part of Edward VI's reign was strongly influenced by the situation left by Henry VIII. The young king's minority created fears over national security and the succession. There were major concerns over the possibility of renewed French intervention in Scotland and the end of the fragile peace. Affairs in Scotland were of paramount importance because of Henry VIII's desire to see his son Edward married to the infant Mary, Queen of Scots. Under the terms of his will Henry had set aside the English claim to the Scottish throne. This might be seen as a way of encouraging the Scots to accept the proposed marriage between Edward and Mary. On the other hand, Mary Queen of Scots, as a legitimate claimant to the throne, could be used by either the French or the Habsburgs as a means of gaining control of England in the cause of the Catholic faith.

Key question
Why did Somerset follow Henry VIII's foreign policy and what problems did he face?

Scotland and France

Somerset decided to try to isolate the Scots by negotiating with France for a defensive alliance. However, the death of Francis I and the accession of the more aggressive Henry II ended any hopes of a compromise with the French. Somerset strengthened the defences at Calais, Boulogne and Newhaven, and the fleet was sent to patrol the English Channel. Henry II renewed the Franco-Scottish alliance, and in June 1547 sent a fleet of galleys with 4000 troops to Scotland. Somerset was left with no alternative but to intervene directly in Scottish affairs on the pretext of arranging the marriage between Edward and Mary agreed in 1543.

In September 1547 a joint land and naval invasion of Scotland was launched. Somerset and Dudley led an army to Berwick. In the west Lord Wharton raided into Scotland from Carlisle with 2000 troops supported by 500 cavalry.

The main English army occupied Preston Pans and advanced towards Edinburgh to confront the Scots. At the battle of Pinkie they were cut to pieces by the English cannon and cavalry. After this victory Somerset was able to occupy all the main border strongholds. This gave England control of the border, but the success was not as decisive as it appeared because the English army was not strong enough to occupy the rest of Scotland.

Defeat united the Scottish nobles, and they supported Mary of Guise in her opposition to England. While Somerset was in London, the Scottish Council decided to ask the French for more help. It was suggested that, in return for French military aid,

Mary Queen of Scots should marry Henry II's eldest son, Francis. Meanwhile, England continued to negotiate with France. However, it soon became obvious that war would break out and that France was going to intervene in Scotland.

In June a French fleet landed an army in Scotland, and by August, Mary Queen of Scots had been taken to France to be educated. Henry II proclaimed that France and Scotland were one country.

Meanwhile Somerset was preoccupied with domestic issues. He was unwilling to leave London, and was worried by the French build-up of forces around Boulogne. Finally, judging correctly that Henry II would not attack Boulogne for fear of drawing Charles V into the war, he sent the Earl of Shrewsbury north with an army which succeeded in securing the border. As the French tired of the expense of the war and the Scottish nobles came to resent the French presence in Scotland, Franco-Scottish relations deteriorated.

In January 1549 Somerset appointed Lord Dacre and the Earl of Rutland to guard the border, while the Earl of Shrewsbury was made Lord President of the Council in the North. However, before these changes had had time to take effect, affairs in the north were overshadowed by the peasant uprisings in England. Here again Somerset showed indecision. He was unwilling to withdraw troops from the border garrisons, and this delay allowed the situation in England to get out of control.

Finally, in August, he was forced to withdraw troops from the north, and to recall the fleet to guard the English Channel against possible French attack. This caused the English to abandon Haddington and the other strongholds north of the border. Fortunately for England the French had already decided that the war in Scotland was too costly, and had redeployed their forces on the siege of Boulogne. Without support the Scots were too weak to launch any major attack on the north of England.

Somerset's leadership qualities

Key question
How effective a leader was Somerset?

Opinion among historians in their judgement of Somerset as a diplomat and a military commander is divided. It is widely agreed that although he was a good field general, as a Commander-in-Chief he was indecisive and afraid to delegate authority. He is seen as having failed to take advantage of his victory at the Battle of Pinkie, and showed little initiative in pressing home his dominant position along the border. Equally, it is agreed that it was Somerset's military indecision and his unwillingness to redeploy his troops in 1549 that allowed the popular uprisings to get out of hand; not, as it was once maintained, his humanitarian love of the common people.

However, some historians consider that Somerset was not altogether to blame for the failure of his foreign policy. It is suggested that he had inherited an almost impossible diplomatic and military position in 1547. He was bound by Henry VIII's will to arrange a marriage between Edward VI and Mary Queen of Scots in order to safeguard the English succession. In view of the hostility created by Henry VIII's earlier campaigns against the Scots, it is considered to be inevitable that Somerset would have been forced into war with Scotland to achieve this objective. It is also suggested that, given the Franco-Scottish alliance, England's weak military position in France, and the chronic shortage of money, this was a war which could not be won.

Religious policy

The accession of Edward VI, who had been educated as a Protestant, roused the hopes of English reformers that there would be a swing towards more Lutheran, and possibly Calvinist, doctrines. Somerset's appointment as Lord Protector in 1547 established the reform party firmly in power, as intended under the terms of Henry VIII's will.

Key question
Why was Somerset cautious about introducing religious reform?

Attitudes towards religious reform

Somerset was a moderate Protestant, but although he was devout, he had no real interest in theology. He was religiously tolerant, and favoured a cautious approach towards reform. Although he is reputed to have had Calvinistic leanings, and, certainly, exchanged letters with John Calvin, there is little evidence of such influences when he was in power. The reformers were in the majority in the Privy Council.

However, among the bishops, there was no agreement. Although the majority of them fully supported the royal supremacy and the separation from Rome, they remained hopelessly divided on the issue of religious reform:

- Nine bishops led by Archbishop Thomas Cranmer and Nicholas Ridley, Bishop of Rochester, supported reform.
- Ten bishops led by Stephen Gardiner, Bishop of Winchester, and Edmund Bonner, Bishop of London, opposed change.
- Eight bishops were undecided on doctrinal issues.

With such an even balance of opinion among the bishops, Somerset and the Privy Council moved very cautiously on matters of religious reform.

The attitude towards reform outside the immediate government circle is difficult to assess:

- A majority of the ruling élites seems to have been in favour of (or at least, not opposed to) some measure of religious reform.
- In general, however, the lower clergy appear to have been opposed to religious change. This, it has been suggested, was largely because the English parish clergy were still relatively uneducated, and were anxious to maintain their traditional way of life without any complications.
- It is maintained that the same was true for the great mass of the population, who were very conservative in their outlook. Moreover, as far as they were concerned, both their popular culture, which was based on rituals and festivals associated with the farming year, and their belief in magic and witchcraft, all formed part of the ceremonies of the old Church.

Yet there were exceptions:

- In East Anglia, because of the settlement of large numbers of Protestant refugees from the continent, there was considerable support for religious reform.
- In London and the larger towns, where clergy were better educated, there were very vocal minorities demanding more rapid, and more radical, religious change.

The introduction of some Protestant doctrinal reform

In these circumstances the Privy Council decided to review the state of the Church of England, and to introduce some moderate Protestant reforms. Such a policy was opposed by the conservatives, prompted by Gardiner, who maintained that under the terms of Henry VIII's will, no religious changes could be made until Edward VI came of age at 18. In spite of Gardiner's vigorous opposition, royal commissioners were sent to visit all the bishoprics. They were instructed to compile a report by the autumn of 1547 on the state of the clergy and the doctrines and practices to be found in every diocese. At the same time, to help the spread of Protestant ideas, every parish was ordered to obtain a copy of Cranmer's Book of Homilies, and Paraphrases by Erasmus.

In July an injunction was issued to the bishops ordering them to instruct their clergy to conduct services in English, and to preach a sermon every Sunday. Furthermore, the bishops were to create libraries of Protestant literature and provide an English Bible for each parish, and to encourage the laity to read these books. Finally the bishops were told to remove all superstitious statues and images from their churches.

These modest moves towards religious reform did not satisfy the more vocal Protestant activists. The amount of anti-Catholic protest was increased by the presence of Protestant exiles who had returned from the continent after the death of Henry VIII. The problem for the Privy Council was that, while it did not wish to introduce reforms too quickly for fear of provoking a Catholic backlash, it was anxious not to prevent religious debate by taking repressive measures. As a result, the Henrician treason, heresy and censorship laws were not enforced and a vigorous debate over religion developed.

The more radical reformers launched a strong attack through a pamphlet campaign on both the Catholic Church and the bishops, who were accused of being self-seeking royal servants and not true pastors. Other pamphlets attacked the wealth of the Church, superstitious rituals, and in particular the Eucharist. However, there was no agreement among the protesters about the form of Protestant doctrine that should be adopted. With the government refusing to take any firm lead there was growing frustration, and some of the more radical protesters took matters into their own hands.

In London, East Anglia, Essex and Lincolnshire, where large numbers of Protestant refugees from the continent were settling, riots broke out. These frequently included outbreaks of iconoclasm, in which stained glass windows, statues and other superstitious images were destroyed. In some cases gold and silver candlesticks and other church plate were seized and sold, with the money being donated to the poor. Such incidents were often provoked by extreme millenarianists, who wished to see a more equal society and a redistribution of wealth to the poor. Although the Privy Council was alarmed by the violence, it refused to take any action against the demonstrators. This inaction enraged the more conservative bishops. Bishop Bonner was particularly vehement in his protests to the government, and was imprisoned for two months.

Indecision and confusion over reform

When parliament and Convocation were summoned in November 1547, the question of religious reform was freely discussed. Both assemblies were in favour of reform, and Convocation agreed to introduce clerical marriage, although this was not approved by parliament and so did not become law. Yet the Privy Council was still reluctant to make any decisive move towards religious reform. The reason for this was that the new regime still felt insecure, fearing that any major changes to doctrine might provoke even more unrest and possibly lead to the fall of the government.

The two major pieces of legislation, the Chantries Act and the Treason Act, did little to resolve the doctrinal uncertainties:

- The Chantries Act. By closing the chantries this act not only confirmed legislation already passed in 1545 but went further in its confiscation of wealth and property. Although, as in 1545, the main purpose of the Act was to raise money to continue the war with France and Scotland, the reason given was that the chantries were centres of superstition.
- The Treason Act. This act effectively repealed the Henrician treason, heresy and censorship laws. This measure only increased the freedom with which the Protestant activists could discuss and demand radical doctrinal reforms. The immediate result was a renewed spate of pamphlets demanding that the Bible should be recognised as the only true authority for religious belief. At the same time English translations of the writings of Luther and Calvin were being widely circulated.

In January 1548 the Privy Council issued a series of proclamations to try to calm the situation. However, the proclamations indicated no clear policy, and so only added to the confusion. The continued validity of Lent and feast days was defended. Justices of the Peace and churchwardens were ordered to enforce the existing doctrines of the Church of England, including transubstantiation. On the other hand, instructions were issued to speed up the removal of Catholic images from churches. Such indecision infuriated both reformers and conservatives alike. Finally, in September, the Council forbade all public preaching in the hope of stifling debate.

Positive moves towards introducing Protestant doctrine

When parliament reassembled in November 1548, Somerset and the Council were in a stronger position after the successful campaign in Scotland. For this reason they felt secure enough to take a more positive approach to religious reform. Their objective was to end the uncertainty over religious doctrine. It was hoped that the new law, known as the First Edwardian Act of Uniformity, passed in January 1549, would achieve this.

The Act officially ordered all the clergy of England and Wales to use a number of Protestant practices which had been allowed, but not enforced, during the two previous years. Holy communion (the mass), matins and evensong were to be conducted in English. The sacraments were now defined as communion, baptism, confirmation, marriage and burial. Cranmer adapted the old communion service by adding new prayers, so that the clergy and the laity could take both the sacramental bread and the wine. Permission was given once again for the clergy to marry. Many of the traditional Catholic rituals, which the Protestant reformers considered to be superstitious, disappeared. The practice of singing masses for the souls of the dead was no longer approved.

However, there was still no really clear statement on the existence, or otherwise, of purgatory. Any form of the worship of saints, although not banned, was to be discouraged, while the removal of statues, paintings and other images was encouraged. However, Cranmer's Book of Common Prayer was a mixture of Lutheran and Catholic beliefs. Fast days were still to be enforced and no change was to be made in the number of Holy Days. The new communion service followed the order of the old Latin mass, and the officiating clergy were expected to continue to wear the traditional robes and vestments. Most importantly, no change was made to the doctrine of the Eucharist, which was still defined in the Catholic terms of transubstantiation. This was a fundamental point that angered many of the more radical reformers, who continued to urge the government to adopt a more Protestant definition of the sacrament of communion.

The Privy Council hoped that these cautious measures would satisfy the majority of moderate reformers, without outraging the Catholic conservatives. Although any clergy who refused to use the new service were to be liable to fines and imprisonment, no penalties were to be imposed on the laity for non-attendance. This can be interpreted as a hope by the Privy Council that they could coerce the more recalcitrant minority among the parish clergy, while not antagonising the undecided majority among the laity.

The government decided to continue with its policy of educating the laity in Protestant ideas which it had introduced in July 1547. Bishops were instructed to carry out visitations to encourage the adoption of the new services, and to test whether parishioners could recite the Lord's Prayer and the Ten Commandments in English. The effectiveness of either the legislation, or the education programme, depended on whether the bishops and ruling élites would enforce them. There was opposition in Cornwall, Devon, Dorset and Yorkshire. However, most of the country seems to have followed the lead of the aristocracy and gentry in accepting moderate Protestantism.

Disorder and rebellion

It is difficult to judge to what extent underlying opposition to the changes in religion contributed to the rebellions of 1549 and to the fall of Somerset. Certainly, only the Western Rebellion was directly linked with religion, and even there underlying economic and social discontent played an important part in causing the uprising. To a certain extent the rebels in the west were complaining about the gentry, whom they accused of making use of the Reformation to seize church land for their own enrichment. Such views were held in other areas during the popular uprisings of 1549, but only in the West Country was direct opposition to the new Act of Uniformity the central issue.

Key question
Why did Somerset face disorder and rebellion?

The Western or Prayer Book Rebellion

The popular discontent began in Cornwall in 1549 when the Cornish people, fearing that the Act of Uniformity was going to be imposed on them, rose in rebellion and set up an armed camp at Bodmin. Because of the hostility expressed by the rebels towards landlords, only six of the more Catholic local gentry joined the uprising. However, the West Country élites were very unwilling to take any action against the rebellion on behalf of the government. The main leaders of the rebels were local clergy, and it was they who began to draw up a series of articles listing demands to stop changes in religion.

In Devon there was an independent uprising at Sampford Courtenay. By 20 June the Devon and Cornish rebels had joined forces at Crediton, and three days later they set up an armed camp at Clyst St Mary. Local negotiations broke down, and the rebels began to blockade the nearby town of Exeter with an army of 6000 men. Lord Russell, who had been sent to crush the rebellion, was hampered by a shortage of troops and a lack of local gentry support. Crucially, the rebels were led by a prominent local gentleman, Humphrey Arundell, who was a skilled tactician and an able commander. As a result it was not until August that the rebels were finally defeated.

Key date
Rebellion in the West Country: 1549

The demands of the rebels

Some of the demands put forward in the final set of articles drawn up by the rebels clearly illustrate their religious conservatism and other grievances felt in the West Country. For example, they wanted:

- to end the changes that they claimed were taking place in baptism and confirmation
- to restore the Act of Six Articles
- to restore the Latin Mass and images
- to restore old traditions like holy bread and water
- to restore the concepts of transubstantiation and purgatory

- the return of Cardinal Pole from exile and for him to have a seat on the king's ruling council.

The government clearly saw these articles as ultra-conservative demands for a return to Catholicism and they were rejected by Cranmer who was particularly enraged by such insubordination.

Assessing the Western Rebellion

Historian Philip Caramani claims that the Western Rebellion was 'the most formidable opposition to the reformation that England saw'. Historians agree that the rebels showed little knowledge of either Protestant or Catholic doctrines, but suggest that such ignorance in the West Country probably reflected similar confusion among the great mass of the population. Whether this is true or not, these demands do show that, in the West Country at least, many of the laity were still strongly attached to the familiar traditions of the old Church.

Although religion is acknowledged to be a key cause of the rebellion, some historians have drawn attention to the social and economic causes. For example, A.F. Pollard suggested that social tension lay at the heart of the rebellion and there is evidence to suggest that the rebels considered the gentry to be their enemies. Even the leader of the royal army, Lord Russell, referred to the unfair exploitation of the commons by the local gentry and nobility, whom he claimed were taxing and raising rents excessively. The rebels were particularly angry at the new sheep tax which they wanted withdrawn. However, because they failed to mention this in their list of final demands, historians tended to ignore the social and economic grievances in favour of the religious. This is no longer the case for, as Nicholas Fellows has suggested, it is possible to make a link 'between the rebels' religious grievances and their attack upon the gentry: it was after all the gentry who had gained from the Reformation'.

The Kett Rebellion 1549

Key date

Rebellion in East Anglia: 1549

East Anglia was the most densely populated and highly industrialised part of the country. Norwich was the second largest town after London, and was a major textile centre. The causes of the rebellion are symptomatic of the confused nature of lower order discontent against the economic changes. The rising was triggered by unrest over enclosures, high rents and unsympathetic local landlords like Sir John Flowerdew. Flowerdew was a lawyer who had bought up Church property in the area.

Flowerdew was also in dispute with a local yeoman, Robert Kett, over land. Kett was a tanner and small landowner who had enclosed much common land. Flowerdew tried to turn the rioters against him but Kett turned the tables by offering to act as spokesman for the rioters. In fact, Kett showed more organisational skill and decisive leadership than is usually found in the leaders of peasant risings. He quickly gathered an army of 16,000 men, set up camp for six weeks on Mousehold Heath and, in July, was able to capture Norwich. The rebellion is notable for the discipline which Kett imposed, electing a governing council and maintaining law and order. Every gentleman that the rebels could arrest was tried before Kett and his council at the Tree of Reformation.

Like the other popular uprising in the West Country, the rebellion was eventually crushed when John Dudley, Earl of Warwick (later the Duke of Northumberland), was sent to take command of the Marquis of Northampton's army of 14,000 men. Northampton had succeeded in taking Norwich but had been forced to abandon it after only a day. Unlike Northampton, Warwick was able to bring the rebels to battle at Dussindale, just outside the city, where nearly 4000 rebels and royal troops were killed. Kett was captured and eventually hanged for sedition.

The demands of the rebels
The rebels drew up a list of 29 articles covering a range of topics. For example, they wanted:

- landowners to stop enclosing common land
- rents to be reduced to the levels they were under Henry VII
- rivers to be open to all for fishing and that fishermen be allowed to keep a greater share of the profits from sea fishing
- all **bondmen** be given their freedom 'for God made everyone free with his precious blood shedding'
- corrupt local officials 'who have offended the commons' be punished 'where it has been proved by the complaints of the poor'
- incompetent priests removed from their churches, particularly those who were 'unable to preach and set forth the word of God to their parishioners'.

Bondmen
Medieval peasants who lived and worked on the lord's manor.

Key term

Assessing the Kett Rebellion
Unlike the West Country rebels who seemed to wish for religion to be returned to the good old days of Henry VIII, the Norfolk insurgents supported the Protestant religious changes. Kett encouraged Protestant ministers to preach to the rebels on Mousehold Heath and to use the new Prayer Book.

Although enclosure has, in the past, been cited as the primary cause of the rebellion in truth, it was just one among many agricultural demands made by the rebels. Indeed, apart from local incidents such as at Wymondham and Attleborough, there had been relatively few enclosures in Norfolk during the previous 50 years. Similarly, the requests that bondmen or serfs should be made free seems to be going back to past struggles, because there is no evidence that there were many unfree tenants in sixteenth-century Norfolk.

The major demands were for commons to be kept open and free for husbandmen to graze their livestock, and that rents should not be increased excessively. The Norfolk rebels appeared to yearn for the favourable economic conditions that existed under Henry VII. This does seem to support the notion that the major cause of the popular unrest in 1549 was the harsh economic conditions that prevailed in that year.

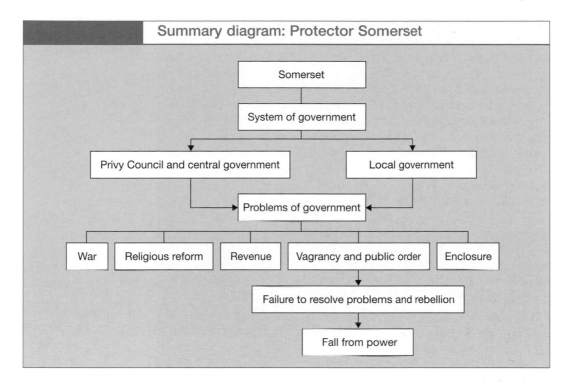

Summary diagram: Protector Somerset

```
                    Somerset
                       │
              System of government
                       │
          ┌────────────┴────────────┐
          ▼                         ▼
Privy Council and central    Local government
      government
          │                         │
          └──────► Problems of government ◄──────┘
                       │
     ┌─────┬───────────┼───────────┬─────────┐
     ▼     ▼           ▼           ▼         ▼
   War  Religious   Revenue   Vagrancy and  Enclosure
        reform                public order
                       │
        Failure to resolve problems and rebellion
                       │
                       ▼
                 Fall from power
```

2 | Lord President Northumberland

Government and administration

Dudley was as able a soldier as he was a politician. He was intelligent and well educated and although he was prone to greed and ruthlessness he was probably one of the most gifted politicians and one of the ablest rulers of his day. On the other hand, he seems not to have been a man of strong convictions or principles as may be seen from the way he used Lady Jane Grey for his own political purpose and by his apparently hasty decision to renounce Protestantism in favour of Catholicism in order to save his life when Mary swept to power in 1553.

Rise to power 1549–51

Even before his arrest it was clear that Somerset was discredited and had lost control of the political situation. Many members of the Privy Council were offended by his aloofness and his arrogance in using his own household instead of the Council to conduct business. He had undermined the confidence of the aristocracy and the gentry because of his inept handling of the popular uprisings, while his religious reforms had alienated even moderates among the conservative party.

A power struggle soon developed in which Northumberland was a leading contender. Northumberland crushed the rebel army in Norfolk on 26 August 1549 and returned to London on 14 September. This gave him a distinct advantage because, as the commander of the main army in England, he controlled the capital. Almost immediately he began to negotiate with Lords

Key questions
How effective was Northumberland's government and administration? What problems did he face?

A portrait of John Dudley, Duke of Northumberland.

Arundel and Wriothesley, leaders of the conservative party. In desperation, on 30 September, Somerset issued a proclamation ordering all troops in England to return to their duties in Scotland and France. On 5 October he issued another proclamation for a general array of loyal troops for the defence of the realm. There was no response, and Somerset removed the royal household from Hampton Court to Windsor Castle for security.

Meanwhile the Privy Council protected its own position by issuing a proclamation blaming Somerset for the rebellions. All parties were anxious to avoid civil war. On 8 October Somerset agreed to negotiate on honourable terms, and was arrested three days later. Northumberland, like Somerset, had risen to political prominence during the last years of Henry VIII's reign. He, too, had gained a good military reputation in the Scottish and French wars. He was a member of the Council named in Henry's will and was ambitious for more power.

The events of 1549 gave him his opportunity to take advantage of Somerset's political isolation. By mid-September he had emerged as the major rival for power, and had contrived to have Somerset arrested. At this point Northumberland showed his considerable ability as a politician. By pretending to be a Catholic sympathiser, he successfully conspired with the conservatives. This gave him control of the Council. However, the conservatives were secretly planning to seize power and have Northumberland arrested along with Somerset.

Simultaneously, Northumberland was plotting with the reform party, particularly Archbishop Cranmer, who had considerable influence in the royal household. With Cranmer's help he gained control over the administration of the royal household, which gave him immediate access to Edward VI. This enabled him to win the confidence of the king, and by February 1550 he was in a strong enough position to have the conservatives expelled from the Council. To secure his position he became Lord President of the Council. In April he was made General Warden of the North, which gave him military command. However, he only achieved complete power in October 1551 when he had Somerset re-arrested, and assumed the title of Duke of Northumberland. In spite of his continuing reputation for greed and ruthlessness, historians are beginning to recognise Northumberland as an ambitious, but able, politician. In marked contrast to Somerset he introduced a series of significant and lasting reforms.

Maintaining control

Northumberland had learned from Somerset's mistakes, and saw that control of the Council was the key to political power. As Lord President he was able to appoint and dismiss councillors at will, and had complete control over procedure. Able supporters of Somerset, such as Paget and William Cecil, who had been arrested, were released and allowed to return to their posts. Under their guidance the Council and its procedures were restored to the pattern established in the period 1536–47. In order to increase his authority, Northumberland enlarged the membership of the Council to 33, selecting councillors upon whose loyalty he could rely. Whenever possible he chose men of military experience, so that in the event of further rebellions, he, unlike Somerset, could be sure of immediate armed support. To make the Council more efficient and stable Northumberland created a smaller, inner committee with a fixed routine to conduct business. Seeing the danger arising from Somerset's frequent by-passing of the Privy Council, Northumberland restored it to the centre of government. For similar reasons he made less use of proclamations, preferring to use parliament to confirm legislation whenever possible.

Northumberland and the problems of government

The political difficulties facing the new government were the same as those which Somerset had failed to resolve.

Key dates

Emergence of John Dudley as the most powerful man in England: 1550

John Dudley created Duke of Northumberland and Lord President of the Council: 1551

Unfortunately for Northumberland, they had become more acute. The most pressing problems were:

- the diplomatic position
- the shortfall in revenue.

Financial problems and the shortfall in revenue

Revenue remained a serious problem. The government was bankrupt in 1549. Somerset had spent £1,356,000 on the war, and sold Crown lands to the value of £800,000. The government even had to borrow to raise the £50,000 a year needed to maintain the royal household. Ending the war drastically reduced expenditure, but a number of expedients had to be adopted to keep the government solvent. In May 1551 the coinage was debased for the last time. Although inflation rose still further, the government made a profit of £114,000 to pay immediate expenses and short-term loans. Even so, a further £243,000 had to be borrowed from continental bankers.

William Cecil, restored as Secretary of State, was put in charge of financial planning. He was assisted by Sir Thomas Gresham from the Treasury. They recommended the sale of chantry lands and church plate to start paying off loans. The London trading companies agreed to support government debts and more money was raised from the mints and Crown lands. Gresham was sent to the Netherlands with £12,000 a week to manipulate the stock market, restore the value of sterling against continental currencies and pay off loans. In March 1552 the coinage was called in and re-issued with the silver content restored to that of 1527. This helped to slow the rise in inflation and restore confidence in sterling. Strict economies were made in government spending, and Northumberland paid off the remainder of his mercenary troops. By these means most of the overseas debts were liquidated and a 'privy coffer', a contingency fund, was established.

By 1553 the financial situation had been stabilised. Even so, another £140,000 worth of Crown lands had to be sold to replace the revenue taxes, voted unwillingly by parliament, which were not collected because they were so unpopular. However, Northumberland had shown considerable political coolness and skill in resolving a serious financial crisis. Unlike Somerset, he had displayed the ability to delegate authority, and skill in selecting the right people for the task.

At the same time there was a concerted effort to improve the efficiency of the financial machinery. The most pressing need was to streamline the collection of royal revenue and to find ways of increasing government income. In 1552 a commission began to investigate the five revenue courts which carried out the work of the Exchequer. The report recommended that to avoid corruption and inefficiency the number of courts should be reduced to two – the Exchequer and the Office of Crown Lands. Alternatively all the courts should be merged into the Exchequer. It was also suggested that custom and excise rates should be revised. Although these constructive proposals had to be postponed because of Edward VI's death, they were introduced in the reign of Mary.

Economic and social problems

The government was faced by equally pressing economic and social problems, for example:

- Population, and with it inflation, was still rising. This meant that the living standards of the masses continued to decline, and that work was more difficult to find.
- By 1550 the growing instability of the Antwerp cloth market was causing widespread unemployment among textile workers in East Anglia and the West Country.
- The debasement of the coinage in 1551 raised inflation still further.
- Grain prices rose rapidly; a situation worsened by below-average harvests.
- In 1550 the country was still simmering after the recent popular uprisings and was further unsettled by the political power struggle among the privy councillors.

Consequently, the administration had to act carefully and skilfully if further serious disorder was to be avoided, for example:

- The unpopular 1547 Vagrancy Act and the sheep tax of 1548 were repealed in 1550, and this helped to dispel unrest.
- In the same year a new Treason Act was passed, which restored censorship and gave the authorities more power to enforce law and order.

Initially these measures helped to prevent the widespread popular discontent from turning into actual revolt. Northumberland benefitted from the fact that the 1549 rebellions had badly frightened the government, aristocracy and gentry, who drew closer together to avoid further disorder among the masses. At the same time, the administration introduced further measures in 1552, such as:

- It tried to improve the economic situation and relieve poverty and distress.
- The existing anti-enclosure legislation was rigorously enforced, and the unpopular enclosure commissions were withdrawn.
- The re-valuation of the coinage halted inflation and reduced prices.
- Acts were passed to protect arable farming, and to stop the charging of excessive interest on debts.
- A new poor law was passed. Although it did nothing to help the able-bodied find work, it did make it easier for the parish and town authorities to support the aged, infirm and crippled.

Again, Northumberland's administration showed a much more positive approach than that adopted by Somerset and although he did little to resolve the underlying economic problems, he did check inflation, and ease some of the worst of the social distress.

Foreign policy

The diplomatic position

By the autumn of 1549 foreign and domestic affairs had reached a critical point. The increasing Protestantism of the Church of England had alienated Charles V, and had left England in a very exposed position without a powerful continental ally. Attempts to enforce the agreed marriage between Mary Queen of Scots and Edward VI had not only failed, but had pushed Scotland into a marriage alliance with France. England was committed to a ruinously expensive war on two fronts, the cost of which was adding to the already serious problems at home. Henry II was not slow to take advantage of this situation. He declared war in August and took personal command of the siege of Boulogne. Somerset's failure to deal with all these problems led to his fall, and gave Northumberland the opportunity to seize power.

Key question
How effective was Northumberland's foreign policy?

Peace negotiations with France

The war had become increasingly unpopular with both the noble élites and the general public. High levels of taxation were undermining the economy and provoking rising hostility towards the government. For some time the Privy Council, especially Lord Paget, had been advocating peace as a means of restoring financial and economic stability. Although Northumberland was much more sympathetic to these views than Somerset had been, during the winter of 1549 he was fully occupied in gaining control of the government.

The French took advantage of this power vacuum to build up their forces around Boulogne. They were able to break English lines of communication between Boulogne and Calais, which threatened to isolate the garrison of Boulogne under the command of Lord Huntingdon. However, an English fleet decisively defeated a strong force of French galleys in a battle off the Channel Islands. This gave England control of the Channel, and meant that Boulogne could be supplied by sea. However, as the government was virtually bankrupt, Northumberland was unable to raise an army to lift the siege. Attempts to persuade Charles V to extend the treaty protecting Calais to Boulogne failed. Even so, Henry II was afraid that Charles V would intervene to help England. Northumberland was keen to end the war so that he could consolidate his own position.

Boulogne returned to France

In January 1550 a delegation led by Lord Russell was sent to France to negotiate peace. They proposed that in return for ceding Boulogne the French should pay a full ransom, and re-open negotiations about a marriage between Mary Queen of Scots and Edward VI. Henry II took full advantage of England's weak position and refused to make any concessions. Finally, Northumberland, strongly supported by Paget, persuaded the Privy Council that they had no alternative but to accept the French terms. The Treaty of Boulogne was signed on 28 March 1550.

Under the terms of the Treaty the English had to withdraw from Boulogne in return for a ransom of 400,000 crowns. At the same time they had to remove their remaining garrisons from Scotland, and agree not to renew the war unless provoked by the Scots. Finally, there was to be a perpetual defensive alliance between England and France. Boulogne was handed over to the French on 25 April, and the English garrison was sent to reinforce Calais. Although the Treaty of Boulogne removed the danger of French invasion and ended the crippling expense of the war, the potential crisis still remained.

The humiliating peace and alliance with a traditional enemy was seen as a national disgrace, and added to Northumberland's unpopularity. In spite of this, he negotiated with the French for a marriage between Edward VI and Henry II's daughter Elizabeth. It was agreed that Elizabeth would come to England when she was 12 years of age, and would have a dowry of 200,000 crowns. The alliance was ratified in December 1550 in return for English neutrality in continental wars. England's international position was still very weak, and was made worse because lack of money forced Northumberland to run down both the army and the navy. The Habsburgs remained hostile, particularly as the Church of England was beginning to swing towards more extreme Calvinist doctrines.

In many respects England had returned to the position of weakness and isolation which had resulted from the failure of Henry VIII's foreign policy in 1528. Certainly the Treaty of Boulogne marked the end of the phase of policy initiated by Henry VIII, during which the reconquest of French territories was a major goal.

Relations with the Holy Roman Empire

England's relations with the Holy Roman Empire deteriorated steadily. Apart from disliking the Anglo-French alliance, Charles V was particularly annoyed by the attempts of the English reformers to force Princess Mary to abandon her Catholic faith. A consequence of this cooling of relations was a breakdown in commercial contacts with the Netherlands, which had been protected by the *Intercursus Magnus* since 1496.

In April 1550 Charles issued an edict allowing the **Catholic Inquisition** to arrest any heretics in the Netherlands. This outraged many English merchants. Although the edict was modified to exclude foreigners, it helped to bring about the collapse of the Antwerp cloth market, as many Flemish clothworkers fled to England to avoid persecution. The situation was further complicated by disputes over piracy in the English Channel. It was not until December 1550 that Charles made any attempt to restore good trading relations, and then only from fear that England would be driven into a closer alliance with France.

Key terms

Intercursus Magnus Used to describe the protection of commercial contacts between England and the Netherlands in an agreement of 1496.

Catholic Inquisition Institution set up by the Catholic Church to search for and destroy heretics or non-conformists.

Anglo-Scottish relations

Anglo-Scottish relationships were in an equally poor state. When Northumberland withdrew the remaining English garrisons from Scotland he left the French in total control. However, the Scottish nobles and the Protestant lowlanders were becoming increasingly hostile towards the French, fearing that Scotland would become a mere province of France. The fall of Somerset had left a confused situation on the English side of the border. Lord Dacre and the Earl of Rutland at Carlisle and Berwick had no clear policy to follow. In 1550 Northumberland decided to take personal control of affairs along the border by making himself General Warden of the North, with Lord Wharton as his deputy.

To end the constant minor disputes which threatened the uneasy peace, Sir Robert Bowen was ordered to survey the border. He reported that an area 15 miles by four miles was under dispute. After strengthening Berwick and Carlisle, Northumberland returned to London, leaving Lord Dacre to negotiate a settlement of the line of the border with the Scottish wardens. Progress was very slow, and it was not until a French fleet landed supplies and troops in Scotland in February 1551 that negotiations began in earnest. Finally, in March 1552, it was agreed that the border was to be restored to the line held before Henry VIII's Scottish campaigns.

Worsening relations with the continental powers

During 1551 Northumberland maintained his policy of neutrality towards the continental powers. Charles V continued to disapprove of the increasing Protestantism of the Church of England, and considered that English foreign policy was unpredictable. It was not until March 1552, when war broke out again between Charles V and Henry II, that Anglo-Imperial relations began to improve. Northumberland resisted French pressure to join in the war against the Holy Roman Empire, and Charles V was more conciliatory over English trade with the Netherlands. Finally, by June 1552, good diplomatic relations were restored between the two countries. Then, when the French invaded Lorraine and the Netherlands, Charles V reminded England that she was bound under treaty obligations to assist the Empire if the Netherlands were attacked.

The garrison at Calais was reinforced, but England still took no active part in the war. Even so, England's relations with France deteriorated. The second half of the ransom for Boulogne remained unpaid and French privateers had begun to attack English shipping. Although England was in no position to take any military action, the French feared an Anglo-Imperial alliance and were careful to avoid open confrontation. In January, Northumberland proposed to act as mediator between France and the Empire. This action was prompted by fears over Edward VI's declining health and the illness of Charles V. The French were not interested in making peace, and in June 1553 the negotiations collapsed.

Key question
Did Northumberland
succeed in turning
England into a
Protestant country?

Religious policy

When Northumberland gained power in 1550 religious reform
became more radical. It is difficult to decide whether this suggests
that the government considered that there was no widespread
opposition to religious change, or that they thought the recent
suppression of the popular uprisings was sufficient to prevent any
further unrest. Possibly, as is thought by many historians, the
changes came about because of political in-fighting in the Privy
Council. What is certain is that by 1553 the Church of England
had become Protestant.

Doctrinal power struggle

In view of his re-conversion to Catholicism before his execution in
1553, many historians do not think it likely that Northumberland
was a genuine religious reformer. Other historians feel that his
support for such a Protestant enthusiast as John Hooper against
Cranmer and Nicholas Ridley, the newly appointed Bishop of
London, in the doctrinal dispute during the autumn of 1550 (see
page 214) does show that he was interested in religious reform.
This is a question which, without fresh evidence, is unlikely to be
resolved. Certainly the first moves towards introducing more
radical Protestantism seem to have arisen from the political
expediencies following Somerset's fall from power.

After the arrest of Somerset in October 1549 it appeared that
the conservative faction supported by Northumberland might
seize power. They planned, with the help of Charles V, to make
Princess Mary regent for the young Edward VI. However, neither
Charles V nor Mary supported the scheme which, in any case,
would not have been practical in view of Edward VI's increasing
support for Protestantism. Meanwhile, Northumberland, having
used the conservatives to strengthen his position on the Privy
Council, then switched his allegiance to the more radical
Protestant reformers. This political struggle within the Privy
Council continued when parliament met in November. Attempts
by conservatives to repeal the 1549 Act of Uniformity and
strengthen the power of the bishops were defeated. In December
parliament approved measures to speed up the removal of popish
images and old service books from the churches, and set up a
commission to revise the procedures for the ordination of priests.

By February 1550 Northumberland was firmly in control of the
Privy Council, and the conservatives were driven out of office. To
strengthen his position still further and to prevent a possible
conservative backlash, Northumberland moved against the more
conservative of the bishops. Gardiner, the most able of the pro-
Catholics, was already imprisoned in the Tower of London. In
July he was ordered by the Privy Council to agree to the doctrines
of the Church of England. He refused, and was sentenced to
stricter terms of confinement. Bishop Bonner of London, already
imprisoned by Somerset, was retried and deprived of his diocese.
He was replaced by Ridley, then Bishop of Rochester, who was an
enthusiastic reformer. During the next year active reformers were
appointed as bishops of Rochester, Chichester, Norwich, Exeter

and Durham. These changes cleared the way for more sweeping religious reforms. The Catholic laity and clergy, deprived of their main spiritual leaders, offered little opposition, although some pro-Catholic pamphlets were circulated.

A swing towards more extreme Protestantism

The first move to introduce more radical Protestantism was initiated by Ridley in London, where he ordered all altars to be removed and replaced by communion tables in line with the teachings of the Calvinists and other reformed Churches. In other dioceses the destruction of altars proceeded unevenly, and depended on the attitudes of the local ruling élites and clergy. At the same time, the Parliamentary Commission's proposals to change the form of the ordination of priests were introduced, and instructions were issued to enforce the first Act of Uniformity.

The new form of ordination, which was basically Lutheran, soon caused controversy. The major change – which empowered priests to administer the sacraments and preach the gospel instead of offering 'sacrifice and [the celebration of] mass both for the living and the dead' – satisfied moderate reformers. It removed the supposedly superstitious references to sacrifice, purgatory and prayers for the souls of the dead. However, it did not please some of the more extreme reformers, especially because it made no attempt to remove any of the 16 ceremonial vestments, such as the **mitre, cope, tippet or stole**, normally worn by bishops and priests while conducting services. These were regarded as superstitious by many of the reformed Churches, whose clergy wore plain surplices.

John Hooper, who had been invited to become Bishop of Gloucester, complained that the form of ordination was still too Catholic and started a fierce dispute with Ridley over the question of vestments. As a result he refused the offered bishopric, and in July he began a campaign of preaching against the new proposals. At first it appeared that Northumberland was sympathetic and supported Hooper, but in October he was ordered to stop preaching, and in January 1551 he was imprisoned for failing to comply. Finally he was persuaded to compromise and was made Bishop of Gloucester, where he introduced a vigorous policy of education and reform. But he complained that both laity and clergy were slow to respond.

Measures to make the Church of England fully Protestant

During 1551 Northumberland consolidated his position. This cleared the way for a major overhaul of the Church of England. Cranmer was in the process of revising his Prayer Book, to remove the many ambiguities that had caused criticism. Further action was taken against the remaining conservative bishops. Gardiner was finally deprived of the diocese of Winchester in February, and in October reformers were appointed at Worcester and Chichester. These moves ensured that there would be a majority among the bishops to support the programme of religious changes that was being prepared.

Mitre, cope, tippet or stole
Symbols of worship used in a church service.

Key term

Doctrinal changes

Parliament was assembled in January 1552 and the government embarked upon a comprehensive programme of reform. In order to strengthen the power of the Church of England to enforce doctrinal uniformity, a new Treason Act was passed. This made it an offence to question the royal supremacy or any of the articles of faith of the English Church. At the same time, uncertainties over the number of Holy Days to be recognised was ended by officially limiting them to 25.

In March the second Act of Uniformity was passed. Under the new Act it became an offence for both clergy and laity not to attend Church of England services, and offenders were to be fined and imprisoned. Cranmer's new Book of Common Prayer became the official basis for church services, and had to be used by both clergy and laity. The new prayer book was based upon the scriptures, and all traces of Catholicism and the mass had been removed. The Eucharist was clearly defined in terms of consubstantiation (see page 179) being regarded as commemorative of Christ's sacrifice or the Last Supper.

Extreme reformers did not approve of the new service because communicants were still expected to kneel, and they considered this to be idolatrous. Some historians attribute such objections to the Calvinism of Hooper and another extreme reformer, John Knox. It is also suggested that theirs was the influence behind the instructions sent to bishops to speed up the replacement of altars by communion tables, and to stop their clergy from wearing vestments when conducting services.

Further attacks on the wealth of the Church

While these measures were being introduced, the government began a further attack on Church wealth. In 1552 a survey of the temporal wealth of the bishops and all clergy with benefices worth more than £50 a year was undertaken. The resultant report estimated that these lands had a capital value of £1,087,000, and steps were taken to transfer some of this property to the Crown.

The bishopric of Durham provides a typical example of this secularisation. Bishop Tunstall of Durham was arrested in October 1552 and imprisoned in the Tower of London. It was then proposed that his diocese should be divided into two parts. Durham itself was to be allocated £1320 annually, and a new see of Newcastle was to be given an annual income of £665. This left an annual surplus of £2000 from the income of the original bishopric, which was to be expropriated to the Crown. In the event, this proposal never came into effect because of the death of Edward VI.

At the same time, commissioners had been sent out to draw up inventories and to begin the removal of all the gold and silver plate still held by parish churches, and to list any items illegally removed since 1547. The commissioners had only just begun their work of confiscation when the king died and the operation was brought to an end, but not before some churches had lost their medieval plate.

Assessment of the Edwardian Church

What is certain is that the death of Edward VI and the fall of Northumberland brought this phase of the English Reformation to an abrupt end. The Forty-two Articles which had been drawn up to list the doctrines of the new Protestant Church of England never became law. It is generally agreed that by 1553 the Edwardian Reformation had resulted in a Church of England that was thoroughly Protestant. There is less unity over whether its doctrines were basically Lutheran, or to what extent they were influenced by Zwinglian, or Calvinist ideas.

However, it is clear that, although the doctrines of the Church of England had been revolutionised, the political and administrative structure of the Church had remained unchanged. There is equal agreement that there is insufficient evidence at present to decide whether the people of England had wholeheartedly embraced the Protestant religion. Research at a local level has so far provided conflicting evidence. Although a majority of the landed élites and those in government circles seemed to favour moderate Protestantism, only a few of them did not find it possible to conform under Mary I.

Many of the lower clergy and a majority of the population seem to have been largely indifferent to the religious debate. Only in London, the counties circling London and East Anglia does there appear to have been any widespread enthusiasm for the Protestant religion. Even there, a study of the county of Essex indicates more enthusiasm among the authorities in enforcing Protestantism than among the general public in accepting it. Earlier interpretations which indicated wild enthusiasm for either Protestantism or Catholicism are now treated with caution. It is considered that Protestantism, if not widely opposed, received only lukewarm acceptance.

Lady Jane Grey and the succession crisis

By 1552 Northumberland seemed to be firmly in control. Even the rapid swing towards Calvinism in the Church of England did not appear to be provoking any serious opposition. However, his power depended upon the support of Edward VI. By the end of the year the king's health was obviously deteriorating quickly, and the problem of the succession became a central issue once again. In accordance with Henry VIII's will, Mary was to succeed if Edward died childless. Mary's strong Catholic sympathies made her unpopular with the reform party and with Edward himself. Moreover, it was feared that Mary might renounce the royal supremacy.

To prevent a return to Catholicism, and to retain power, Northumberland, with the full support of the king, planned to change the succession. As the Succession Acts of 1534 and 1536 making Mary and Elizabeth illegitimate had not been repealed, it was decided to disinherit them in favour of the Suffolk branch of the family. Frances, Duchess of Suffolk, was excluded as her age made it unlikely that she would have male heirs and her eldest daughter, Lady Jane Grey, was chosen to succeed. To secure his

Key question
Why was there a succession crisis?

Key date
Edward VI changed line of succession in favour of Lady Jane Grey: June 1553

Key dates

Northumberland's son, Guildford, married Lady Jane Grey: May 1553

Death of Edward VI, brief reign of Lady Jane Grey, and succession of Mary: July 1553

Execution of Northumberland: August 1553

own position Northumberland married his eldest son, Guildford Dudley, to Jane in May 1553.

Unfortunately for Northumberland, Edward VI died in July before the plans for the seizure of power could be completed. Jane Grey was proclaimed Queen by Northumberland and the Council in London, while Mary proclaimed herself Queen at Framlingham Castle in Suffolk. Northumberland's mistakes were twofold:

- he failed to arrest Mary and keep her in custody
- he underestimated the amount of support for Mary in the country.

On 14 July he marched into Suffolk with an army of 2000 men, but his troops deserted him. The Privy Council in London hastily changed sides and proclaimed Mary as Queen. Northumberland was arrested in Cambridge, tried, and was executed on 22 August in spite of his renunciation of Protestantism.

Assessing Lady Jane Grey and the succession crisis
The ease with which Mary upheld her right to the throne shows the growing stability of the State and the nation. Potential political crisis had been avoided because the majority of the nation supported the rule of law and rightful succession. The direct line of descent was still considered legitimate in spite of acts of parliament to the contrary. A period of dynastic weakness and minority rule had passed without the country dissolving into civil war. Two acts were passed, one in 1553 and another in 1554, to resolve the constitutional position. This legislation was designed to confirm Mary Tudor's legitimacy, and to establish the right of female monarchs to rule in England. However, no attempt was made to make Elizabeth legitimate, although she was recognised as Mary's heir in the event of her dying childless.

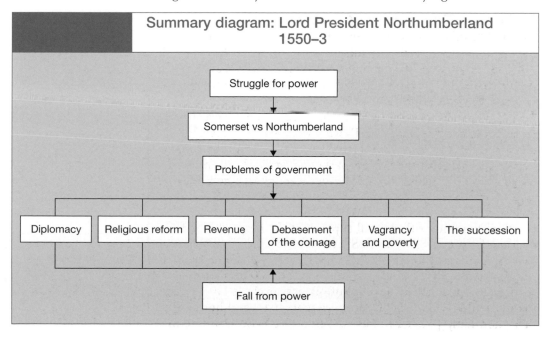

Summary diagram: Lord President Northumberland 1550–3

Struggle for power
↓
Somerset vs Northumberland
↓
Problems of government
↓
Diplomacy | Religious reform | Revenue | Debasement of the coinage | Vagrancy and poverty | The succession
↑
Fall from power

Study Guide: AS Question
In the style of OCR
Why did *both* Somerset *and* Northumberland find it difficult to govern England? (50 marks)

Exam tips

The cross-references are intended to take you straight to the material that will help you to answer the question.

Both Somerset and Northumberland had difficulty in governing England. In seeking to explain the reasons, you should point out areas of similarity where, for instance, each ruler faced the same or similar problems, but also explain why their experiences were often different in respect of the issues and outcomes. Somerset and Northumberland can be treated separately but your analysis will be stronger and less repetitive if you assess them according to particular difficulties. The main problems they faced were:

- Edward VI was a minor. Both Somerset and Northumberland exercised authority in the king's name but many questioned their legality to do so. Somerset was Edward's uncle and Lord Protector, which afforded him some justification, whereas Northumberland was only Lord President of the Council and so owed his authority to his fellow councillors (pages 191–205).
- Somerset took many policy decisions without consulting his council; instead he ruled through his own household and made extensive use of proclamations. Northumberland ruled through the council and parliament, which gave his administration greater credibility (pages 192, 193, 197–8).
- Both inherited religious issues. Somerset relaxed censorship, repealed heresy laws and supported Cranmer's Protestant reforms, which culminated in widespread criticism and rebellions in 1549; Northumberland endorsed Cranmer's more progressive reforms but suppressed any opposition more effectively (pages 202–4).
- Somerset focused on waging war against Scotland and France, which led to a rise in inflation, high taxation, debasement and acute financial problems; Northumberland implemented financial and administrative reforms and ended the wars, which minimised both military and financial problems after 1550 (pages 210–12).
- Both Somerset and Northumberland inherited severe economic and social problems. Somerset was sympathetic towards the commons' suffering and tried to tackle unlawful enclosures, engrossments and excessive sheep farming by confronting landowners; Northumberland was more pragmatic and realised that he needed the support of landed élites to maintain order and keep himself in power before he implemented reforms (pages 208–9).

Ensure that you reach a conclusion that reflects the main thrust of your argument and which prioritises your explanations.

8 Mary I: Marriage, Rebellion and Catholic Restoration 1553–8

POINTS TO CONSIDER

This chapter is designed to help you to understand the key features of the reign of Mary I. The chapter examines the political, religious and economic problems that faced the Marian regime. The fact that she was the first female monarch to rule England is also discussed. These issues are examined as four themes:

- Mary I
- Politics and government
- Wyatt's rebellion
- Catholicism restored

Key dates

1553	July	Succession of Mary I
	August	Execution of the Duke of Northumberland
		Catholic mass re-introduced
1554	January	Wyatt Rebellion
	February	Execution of Lady Jane Grey and Guildford Dudley
	July	Marriage of Mary I and Philip of Spain
	November	Cardinal Pole returned to England as papal legate England and Rome reconciled
	December	Re-introduction of the heresy laws
1555	October	Bishops Ridley and Latimer burned at the stake
1556	March	Archbishop Cranmer burned at the stake
1558		Death of Mary and Cardinal Pole

1 | Mary I

Introduction

Mary (1516–58), the daughter of Catherine of Aragon, was 37 years of age when she came to the throne. During Edward VI's reign she had resisted Protestant reform just as strongly as she had under her father. While Somerset was in power she had been allowed to follow her Catholic religion in private, and she had remained on good terms with the Protector and Edward. With the swing towards Calvinism under Northumberland, increasing pressure had been put on Mary to abandon Catholicism and to conform to the doctrines of the Church of England.

During this difficult period she had received constant support and advice from her Habsburg cousin, Emperor Charles V. It was fear of the Habsburgs that had prevented the reformers taking extreme measures against her. Mary was a proud woman, who resented the pressures put on her and was embittered by the treatment of her mother. This made her mistrust her English councillors when she became queen, and lean heavily on advice from the imperial ambassador, Simon Renard.

When Mary proclaimed herself queen on 11 July 1553, even Renard and Charles V had thought it a futile gesture. Yet when she entered London at the end of the month she was greeted with enormous enthusiasm. Political prisoners such as the Duke of Norfolk and Stephen Gardiner were released. Following the advice of Charles V, she showed leniency towards her opponents. Only Northumberland and two of his closest confederates were executed. Although some members of Northumberland's Council, like Cecil, were imprisoned, others, such as Paget, were allowed to join the new Privy Council.

As a devout Catholic, Mary was insistent that England should return to the Church of Rome. At the same time, she was convinced that national safety depended on a close alliance with the Habsburgs. Her policy rested on the achievement of these two aims. Until 1555 this strategy appeared to be prospering, but thereafter Mary's popularity steadily declined until her death in 1558.

Character and personality

The cause of this unpopularity has generally been attributed to Mary's own character. Simon Renard's assessment that she was 'good, easily influenced, inexpert in worldly matters and a novice all round' was scarcely a flattering tribute. Elizabethan propagandists were eager to depict Mary as a weak and unsuccessful pro-Spanish monarch in order to highlight the achievements of their own queen. Protestant reformers reviled her as a cruel tyrant trying to enforce Catholicism through torture and burnings. This has produced a popular picture of 'Bloody Mary' – a stubborn, arrogant, Catholic bigot, who burned Protestants and lost Calais to the French because of her infatuation for Philip of Spain.

Key question
What problems did Mary face when she became queen?

Key dates

Succession of Mary I: July 1553

Execution of the Duke of Northumberland: August 1553

Key question
What was Mary like?

A portrait of Mary Tudor painted in 1544 when she was 28 years old. Explain the significance of the date of this painting. Who might have commissioned it?

In a modified form, this has been the view of many historians, but recently there have been attempts to revise this critical appraisal. It has been pointed out that she showed skill and resolution in defeating Northumberland's attempted *coup d'état*. Mary has been criticised for indecision in the negotiations over the restoration of Catholicism to England and her marriage to Philip of Spain. This, it has been suggested, was in fact masterly political inactivity and pretended weakness, designed to win greater concessions from the Papacy and the Habsburgs, similar tactics to those that her sister Elizabeth used so successfully.

Indeed, it is suggested that Mary had the broad support of the majority of the people until 1555. The problem was, it is suggested, not the weakness of Mary's character and policies, but her failure to produce an heir to consolidate her position. This, the outbreak of war with France and the declining economic position, was the real cause of Mary's growing unpopularity. On the basis of the existing evidence it is difficult to assess Mary's true character, and the present consensus of opinion lies somewhere between the two extremes.

Profile: Stephen Gardiner c.1483–1555

c.1483	–	Born
1520	–	Educated at Cambridge University and became a doctor of civil law
1521	–	Became a doctor of canon law. Appointed tutor to Duke of Norfolk's son
1524	–	Appointed secretary to Lord Chancellor Wolsey, Henry VIII's chief minister (1524–9)
1530–4	–	Principal Secretary to Henry VIII
1532	–	Appointed bishop of Winchester
1535–8	–	Ambassador to France
1538	–	Led resistance to Thomas Cromwell's changes in religion. Fell out of favour with the king
1539	–	Promoted Act of Six Articles
1540	–	Took part in destruction of Cromwell. With the Duke of Norfolk led Conservative faction at Court
1542–7	–	One of Henry VIII's leading ministers
1548	–	Forced out of government and imprisoned in the Tower of London for opposing Somerset
1551	–	Stripped of his title as Bishop of Winchester
1553	–	Restored to all his offices and titles by Mary who appointed him Lord Chancellor. Led the Catholic counter-reformation and promoted conservative legislation in parliament
1554	–	Married Mary and Philip of Spain
1555	–	Died

Gardiner was a talented government minister, and respected thinker and theologian. Although he supported Henry VIII's divorce and break from Rome, he opposed any major changes in religion. He was an able leader of the conservative faction at Court which brought about the downfall of Cromwell. His opposition of Somerset in the last years of Henry VIII's reign ensured his downfall after the king's death. Although Somerset was prepared to work with Gardiner the two could not agree on the religious direction the Edwardian government should take. His downfall was the inevitable result of his refusal to compromise. In spite of his strong Catholic beliefs, he tried to save the leaders of the reformist party, Cranmer and Northumberland, from execution. The accession of Mary rescued his career and although he had supported the break with Rome in 1534 he was willing to restore the Pope as Head of the Church in 1554. He served out the remainder of his life as a trusted adviser to the Crown.

Key question
What was the Spanish marriage so important to Mary?

Key date
Marriage of Mary I and Philip of Spain: July 1554

Spanish marriage

Mary's political inexperience and stubbornness is shown in the first major issue of the reign – the royal marriage. The Privy Council was divided on the matter. There were two realistic candidates for Mary's hand:

- Edward Courtenay, Earl of Devon, who was favoured by Gardiner
- Philip of Spain, who was supported by Paget.

Courtenay was a descendant of the Plantagenet kings and such a marriage would have strengthened the Tudor dynasty, but Mary favoured a closer link with the Habsburgs through Philip. It was not until 27 October that Mary raised the matter in Council, and then only to announce that she was going to marry Philip. This disconcerted Gardiner, who was blamed by Mary for the petition from the House of Commons in November, asking her to marry within the realm. Mary disregarded all opposition to her plans.

On 7 December a marriage treaty, drafted by Mary, Paget, Gardiner and Renard, was presented to the Council. It was ratified at the beginning of January 1554. Mary had achieved her objective of forming a closer alliance with the Habsburgs. The terms of the treaty were very favourable to England. Philip was to have no regal power in England, no foreign appointments were to be made to the Privy Council, and England was not to be involved in, or pay towards the cost of any of Philip's wars. If the marriage was childless, the succession was to pass to Elizabeth.

In spite of these safeguards Mary's popularity began to ebb, as many people still thought that England would be drawn into Philip's wars and become a mere province of the Habsburg Empire.

By the end of January 1554, anti-Spanish feelings led to rebellion. The rebellion was led by Sir James Croft, Sir Peter Carew and Sir Thomas Wyatt. These men had all held important offices at Court under both Henry VIII and Edward VI. Although they had supported Mary's accession, they feared that the growing Spanish influence would endanger their own careers.

2 | Politics and Government

Government

Key question
How effective was the system of government under Mary?

The system of central and local government remained fundamentally unchanged during Mary's reign. The Privy Council continued to be the centre of the administration. One of the main criticisms of Mary's Privy Council has been that it was too large to conduct business effectively. Certainly, at times the membership did reach 43. In addition it has been claimed that the Council contained too many members who had no real political ability and who lacked administrative experience. The reason for this was that in the first few weeks of her reign Mary was forced to choose councillors from her own household, and from among leading Catholic noblemen who had supported her. By October several moderate members of Northumberland's Council had been sworn in as councillors, although they were never fully in the queen's confidence. However, they supplied a nucleus of political ability and administrative experience previously lacking. Apart from this making the Council too large, it has been suggested that it caused strong rivalry between the Catholics, led by the Chancellor, Gardiner, and the moderates, led by Paget.

However, it is now thought that, although there was disagreement, these two very able politicians co-operated closely to restore effective government. In any case, affairs of state were soon largely handled by an 'inner council' consisting of those experienced councillors who had reformed the Privy Council under Northumberland. Much of the original criticism of the Privy Council came from Renard, who was jealous of the queen's English advisers and wished to maintain his own influence with Mary. The main problem was that Mary did not appear to exert any leadership, or show any real confidence in her Council. Frequently she did not consult the Privy Council until she had already decided matters of policy in consultation with Renard.

Previously it has been maintained that parliament was strongly opposed to Mary's policies. This view has been modified by recent research. There seems to be little evidence that Mary controlled the House of Commons by packing it with Catholic supporters through rigged elections, and she had strong support from the higher clergy in the House of Lords, especially after the imprisonment and execution of Cranmer, Ridley and Latimer. Apart from the dislike of the Spanish marriage, both Houses seem to have co-operated with the administration throughout Mary's reign. As was the case in the Privy Council, there were lively debates and criticism of policy, but these were generally constructive. Like previous parliaments, the main interest of the members centred on local affairs and the protection of property rights.

Financial reforms

The Marian administration was still faced by the financial problems that Northumberland had been trying to solve. To make matters worse, Mary had given away more Crown lands in order to re-establish some monastic foundations. Consequently, it was important both to find new sources of government revenue and to increase the income from existing ones. To achieve this the Privy Council largely adopted the proposals put forward by the commissions in 1552.

In 1554 drastic changes were made to the revenue courts:

- The Exchequer was restored as the main financial department. It took over the work of the Court of First Fruits and Tenths, which had dealt with clerical taxation, and the Court of Augmentations, which had administered income from monastic and chantry lands.
- The Court of Wards, which collected feudal taxation, and the Duchy of Lancaster, administering lands belonging to the monarch as Duke of Lancaster, retained their independence.

Key question
What financial problems faced Mary and how did she deal with them?

- It was planned to remove the large number of debased coins in circulation and to restore the full silver content of the coinage, but Mary's death meant that the scheme was not put into effect until 1560.
- The 1552 proposal to revise the custom rates, which had remained unchanged since 1507, was implemented. In 1558 a new Book of Rates was issued, which increased custom revenue from £29,000 to £85,000 a year.
- In 1555 a full survey of all Crown lands was carried out. As a result rents and entry fines, a payment made by new tenants before they could take over the property, were raised in 1557.

Mary died before these measures had any real effect, and it was Elizabeth I who benefited from the increased revenue brought about by these reforms.

Key question
Why was the economy in crisis during Mary's reign?

The economy

During Mary's reign the general economic situation grew even worse, with a series of very bad harvests and epidemics of sweating sickness, bubonic plague and influenza. Towns were particularly badly hit, with high mortality rates and severe food shortages. The government's reaction was to continue the policy, started under Henry VIII, of restricting the movement of textile and other industries from the towns to the countryside. This, it was hoped, would prevent an increase in urban unemployment and reduce the number of vagrants seeking work. This, however, was short-sighted because what was really needed was an increase in the amount and variety of industries in both town and country, which would provide jobs for the growing number of unemployed.

To achieve this the government needed to encourage the search for new overseas markets to replace the trade lost with the decline of the Antwerp market. In 1551 English ships had begun to trade along the north African coast, and between 1553 and 1554 Sir Hugh Willoughby was trying to find a north-east passage to the Far East. However, until after 1558 successive English governments were too anxious to avoid offending Spain and Portugal to encourage overseas enterprise. It was not until the reign of Elizabeth I that any real progress was made in this direction.

Key question
How has Mary's reign been assessed by historians?

Assessment of Mary's reign

Philip II's visit to England early in 1557, and his success in drawing the country into his war against France, marked the final stage in Mary's growing unpopularity. The last two years of her reign saw rising anti-Spanish feelings, mounting opposition to religious persecution, and discontent with the adverse economic conditions. The war with France and the loss of Calais, England's last continental possession, united the country against the ailing queen. The enthusiasm which marked her death in November 1558 and the succession of Elizabeth to the throne was even greater than that which had greeted Mary's overthrow of Northumberland five years earlier.

Yet, despite its apparent failings, her reign was not one of complete sterility. Important reforms had been made and constitutional monarchy and the State machinery remained intact. Although the loss of Calais was seen as a national disaster, it can be interpreted as the crucial moment when England turned its attention away from fruitless continental conquest towards opportunities in the New World. Indeed, some historians would go as far as to claim that Mary's failure was her childlessness and her relatively early death, rather than her policies.

3 | Wyatt's Rebellion

Key question
Why was the Wyatt Rebellion so dangerous to Mary and her government?

Wyatt Rebellion: January 1554

Key date

Sir Thomas Wyatt was a member of a wealthy and well-connected gentry family from Kent. He succeeded to the family estates on the death of his father, also called Sir Thomas, in 1542. Sir Thomas Wyatt senior had been a courtier and diplomat, and his son was expected to follow suit. He became friendly with the influential Henry Howard, Earl of Surrey, who acted as his patron. Wyatt fought in France under Surrey in 1543–44 and in 1545 he was promoted to the English council governing English-controlled Boulogne. Unfortunately for Wyatt, his career suffered a setback in 1546 when Surrey fell into disfavour with Henry VIII and was later executed. As a committed Protestant Wyatt found favour with the Edwardian regime which he defended in 1549 when riots broke out in Kent. He was trusted by Northumberland who appointed him to represent the English government in negotiations with the French in 1550.

Wyatt served the Edwardian regime loyally but he declared his support for Mary when Jane Grey was proclaimed queen. Wyatt's initial support for Mary soon evaporated when he heard of the Spanish marriage. As an MP he became involved in the opposition to the proposed marriage in parliament but his hopes of persuading the queen to reject the marriage failed.

Conspiracy and rebellion
By the end of January 1554, anti-Spanish feelings led to rebellion. Unlike the rebellions of 1549 this was a political conspiracy among the élites, and there was little popular support. The rebellion was led by Sir James Croft, Sir Peter Carew and Sir Thomas Wyatt. They feared that the growing Spanish influence at Court would endanger their own careers. The conspirators planned to marry Elizabeth to Edward Courtenay, Earl of Devon, who Mary had rejected as an unsuitable match.

Simultaneous rebellions in the West Country (Carew), the Welsh borderland (Croft), the Midlands (Suffolk, father of Lady Jane Grey) and Kent (Wyatt) were to be supported by a French fleet. The plan failed because the inept Courtenay disclosed the scheme to his patron, Gardiner, before the conspirators were ready. In any case, Carew, Croft and the Duke of Suffolk bungled the uprisings. Wyatt succeeded in raising 3000 men in Kent, and this caused real fear in the government because the rebels were so close to London, the capital. The situation was made worse because a number of royal troops sent to crush the revolt under the command of the aged Duke of Norfolk deserted to the rebels. Realising the danger, the Privy Council desperately tried to raise fresh forces to protect London.

An over-cautious Wyatt failed to press home his advantage and although he led his motley troops with some dash his delay in marching on London gave Mary the time she needed to see to the capital's defence. In refusing to flee her capital Mary's courage impressed those whom she called on to support her regime and by the time Wyatt arrived at the gates of the city the revolt was doomed to fail. Repulsed at London Bridge and the Tower, Wyatt crossed the Thames at Kingston, but found Ludgate closed and his troops began deserting in droves.

Key date

Execution of Lady Jane Grey and Guildford Dudley: February 1554

Wyatt surrendered and the revolt was crushed. Paget suggested leniency for the rebels for fear of provoking further revolts. Fewer than a hundred executions took place among the commons and most were pardoned. As for the rebel élite, apart from Wyatt and Suffolk, only Jane Grey and her husband Guildford Dudley were executed. Croft was tried and imprisoned but he was pardoned and released after nine months in the Tower. Carew fled to France but returned in 1556 on promise of a pardon. Both Elizabeth and Courtenay were interrogated and imprisoned but were later released.

The Wyatt Rebellion came as close as any to overthrowing the monarchy. According to historian Paul Thomas:

> Mary's new regime was pushing its luck, not so much with a policy of Catholic restoration, as with the Spanish marriage and the provocation of those members of the Court élite who either felt excluded or feared imminent exclusion.

Frustrated and increasingly desperate, men like Wyatt felt compelled to act in a way that had only two possible outcomes – failure would result in his own death while success would almost inevitably lead to the death of the monarch. In the opinion of Diarmaid MacCulloch, the fact that the Wyatt Rebellion failed demonstrates 'the bankruptcy of rebellion as a way of solving' political crises.

4 | Catholicism Restored

The religious situation in 1553

Key question
Why did Mary restore Catholicism and what problems did this cause?

In 1553 no one in England doubted that Mary, after her 20 years of resistance to the royal supremacy for the sake of her religion, would restore Roman Catholicism. There is good evidence to suggest that it was just as much Edward VI's wish to preserve Protestantism, as Northumberland's personal ambition, that led to the attempt to exclude Mary from the throne. Mary and her Catholic supporters saw the failure of the scheme as a miracle, and she was determined to restore England to the authority of

Rome as quickly as possible. What Mary failed to realise was that her initial popularity sprang not from a desire for a return to the Roman Catholic Church, but from a dislike of Northumberland, and respect for the legitimate succession.

Her main supporters in England and abroad urged caution. Both Charles V and Pope Julius III warned her not to risk her throne by acting too rashly. Cardinal Reginald Pole, appointed as papal legate to restore England to the authority of Rome, stayed in the Netherlands for a year before coming to England. Whether this was because Charles V refused to allow the Cardinal to leave until the planned marriage between Philip and Mary had come to fruition, or whether it reflected Pole's natural caution about returning to his native land and a possibly hostile reception, is difficult to decide. Even Gardiner, Mary's most trusted English adviser, who had consistently resisted reform, was unenthusiastic about returning to papal authority.

Mary singularly failed to realise the political implications of restoring Roman Catholicism to England. A return to papal authority would mean an end to the royal supremacy, which was strongly supported by the ruling and landed élites. Even the most ardent of the leading conservatives had been firm in their allegiance to the Crown and the Tudor State. It is agreed that the major causes of Mary's widespread unpopularity by the end of her reign, apart from the religious persecution, were the return to papal authority and the Spanish marriage. Most of the population regarded this as interference by foreigners and an affront to English nationalism.

The restoration of Anglo-Catholicism

However, in 1553 there was no doubt about Mary's popularity and the élites rallied to her support. The aristocracy and gentry were initially prepared to conform to Mary's religious views, and the bulk of the population followed their example. But some 800 strongly committed Protestant gentry, clergy and members of the middle orders left the country and spent the remainder of the reign on the continent. Such an escape was less easy for the lower orders, and most of the 274 Protestant activists executed during Mary's reign came from this group. At the beginning of the reign even the most zealous of the urban radicals were not prepared to go against the mainstream of public opinion, and waited to see what would happen. Certainly, when Mary, using the royal prerogative, suspended the second Act of Uniformity and restored the mass, there was no public outcry.

This lack of religious opposition was apparent when parliament met in October 1553. Admittedly, the arrest and imprisonment of Cranmer, Hooper and Ridley, along with other leading Protestant bishops, removed the major source of opposition in the House of Lords. After a lively, but not hostile debate, the first step towards removing all traces of Protestantism from the Church of England was achieved with the passing of the first Statute of Repeal. This Act swept away all the religious legislation approved by parliament during the reign of Edward VI, and the doctrine of

Catholic mass re-introduced: August 1553

Key date

the Church of England was restored to what it had been in 1547 under the Act of the Six Articles.

Although Mary had succeeded in re-establishing the Anglo-Catholicism of her father, her advisers had managed to persuade her into some caution. There had been no attempt to question the royal supremacy, or to discuss the issue of the Church lands which had been sold to the laity. Both these issues were likely to provoke a more heated debate.

Opposition to Mary's proposed marriage to Philip II of Spain and the consequent rebellion meant that further religious legislation was postponed until the spring of 1554. Gardiner, anxious to regain royal favour after his opposition to Mary's marriage, tried to quicken the pace at which Protestantism was removed by persuading parliament to pass a bill to re-introduce the heresy laws. He was successfully opposed by Paget, who feared that such a measure might provoke further disorder.

Thwarted in this direction, Gardiner proceeded to turn his attention to Protestant clergy. The Bishops of Gloucester, Hereford, Lincoln, Rochester and the Archbishop of York were deprived of their bishoprics, and were replaced by committed Catholics. In March 1554 the bishops were instructed to enforce all the religious legislation of the last year of Henry VIII's reign. Apart from ensuring a return to 'the old order of the Church, in the Latin tongue', these injunctions demanded that all married clergy should give up their wives and families, or lose their livings. The authorities largely complied with these instructions, and some 800 parish clergy were so deprived. Although some fled abroad, the majority were found employment elsewhere in the country.

Return to the Church of Rome

Cardinal Pole finally arrived in England in November 1554, and this marked the next decisive stage in the restoration of Roman Catholicism. Parliament met in the same month and passed the second Statute of Repeal. This Act ended the royal supremacy, and returned England to papal authority by repealing all the religious legislation of the reign of Henry VIII back to the time of the break with Rome. However, to achieve this Mary had to come to a compromise with the landed élites. Careful provision was made in the Act to protect the property rights of all those who had bought Church land since 1536. This demonstrates that Mary had to recognise the authority of parliament over matters of religion. It meant that she had to forgo her plans for a full-scale restoration of the monasteries. Instead she had to be content with merely returning the monastic lands, worth £60,000 a year, still held by the Crown.

Religious persecution

At the same time, parliament approved the restoration of the old heresy laws. This marked the beginning of religious persecution. The first Protestant was burned at the stake for heresy on 4 February 1555, and Hooper suffered a similar fate five days

Key dates

Cardinal Pole returned to England as papal legate; England and Rome reconciled: November 1554

Re-introduction of the heresy laws: December 1554

Key question
Why did Mary follow a policy of religious persecution?

later in his own city of Gloucester. In October Ridley and Hugh Latimer, the former Bishop of Worcester, were likewise executed at Oxford, where they were followed by Cranmer in March 1556. The death of Gardiner in November 1555 had removed a trusted and restraining influence, and thereafter the regime became more repressive. Although Gardiner had started the persecution on the grounds that some executions would frighten the Protestant extremists into submission, he was too astute a politician to fail to see that the policy was not working. Far from cowing the Protestants, he realised that the executions were hardening the opposition to Mary and encouraging the colonies of English exiles on the continent. He counselled caution, but his advice was ignored.

After his death, Mary, and Pole, who had been made Archbishop of Canterbury in December 1555, felt that it was their sacred duty to stamp out heresy, and stepped up the level of persecution. It is now estimated that the 274 religious executions carried out during the last three years of Mary's reign exceeded the number recorded in any Catholic country on the continent over the same period, even though it was much less than in some other periods. This modifies the claim by some historians that the Marian regime was more moderate than those on the continent.

Key dates

Bishops Ridley and Latimer burned at the stake: October 1555

Archbishop Cranmer burned at the stake: March 1556

Popular reactions against religious persecution

Gardiner's unheeded warnings were soon justified, and Mary's popularity waned rapidly. There was widespread revulsion in the south-east of England at the persecution, and to many people Catholicism became firmly linked with dislike of Rome and Spain. Many local authorities either ignored, or tried to avoid enforcing, the unpopular legislation. The number of people fleeing abroad increased, reinforcing the groups of English exiles living in centres of Lutheranism and Calvinism on the continent. They became the nucleus of an active and well-informed opposition, which began to flood England with anti-Catholic books and pamphlets. The effectiveness of this campaign is shown in the proclamations issued by the Privy Council in 1558, ordering the death penalty by martial law for anyone found with heretical or seditious literature. If before 1555 the English people were generally undecided about religion, the Marian repression succeeded in creating a core of highly committed English Protestants.

Attempted measures to consolidate the Marian Church

Although Pole actively tried to eradicate Protestantism, his first priority appears to have been to restore stability after 20 years of religious turmoil. It is widely considered that, in view of his lack of administrative experience and ability, such a formal and legalistic approach was a mistake. Ecclesiastical revenues had been so denuded that there were insufficient resources available to reorganise the Marian Church effectively. Indeed, a great part of

Pole's three years in office was spent in the virtually hopeless task of trying to restore the Church of England's financial position.

Pole's attempts to reorganise and reconcile the Church of England to Rome were not helped by the death of Pope Julius III in 1555. The new Pope, Paul IV, disliked Pole and hated the Spanish Habsburgs. He stripped Pole of his title of Legate and ordered him to return to Rome. Pole refused to comply, and continued his work in England as Archbishop of Canterbury, but the Papacy would not recognise his authority. This further hindered his work because he could not appoint bishops, and by 1558 seven sees were vacant. Such quarrels, and the blatant papal intervention in English affairs, did little to convince anyone except the most zealous Catholics of the wisdom of returning to the authority of Rome.

Certainly, such events did not help the government in its task of winning the hearts and minds of English men and women to the Roman Catholic faith. Pole's hopes that, while he struggled with his administrative tasks, the re-establishment of the old religion would lead to wholehearted acceptance of Roman Catholicism were not to be realised. Pole was fully in favour of the educational programme which was being adopted on the continent. He appointed capable and active bishops, all of whom subsequently refused to serve in the Elizabethan Protestant Church of England.

In 1555 the Westminster synod approved the passing of the Twelve Decrees that included the establishment of seminaries in every diocese for the training of priests, but shortage of money limited the programme to a single creation at York. This meant that the majority of the parish clergy remained too uneducated, and lacking in evangelical zeal, for the new laws to have any immediate impact on the laity. Mary's death in November 1558 came too soon for Catholic reform to have had any lasting effect. That is not to say that if Mary had lived longer, Catholicism would not have gained wider support than the significant minority, who clung to their faith after the establishment of the Elizabethan Church.

Key date
Death of Mary and Cardinal Pole: 1558

Assessment of the Church of England in 1558

Key question
What was the state of the English Church at the end of Mary's reign?

To assess the state of religion in England in 1558 is just as difficult as it is to measure the advance of Protestantism by 1553. It is almost impossible to decide to what extent the bulk of the population had any particular leanings towards either the Protestant or the Catholic faiths. While it is easy to trace the changing pattern of official doctrine in the Church of England through the acts and statutes passed in parliament, it is a much greater problem to determine what the general public thought about religion. At present the consensus among historians is that the ruling élites accepted the principle of the royal supremacy, and were prepared to conform to whichever form of religion was favoured by the monarch.

Although the lower orders are generally considered to have had a conservative affection for the traditional forms of worship, it is thought they were prepared to follow the lead of the local élites. Whether the religious legislation passed in parliament was put into effect very much depended on the attitudes of the local élites, and to a lesser extent those of the parish authorities.

In general it appears that by 1558 the majority of people in England were still undecided about religion. Among the élites there was strong support for the royal supremacy, but they were willing to follow the religion of the legitimate monarch. The mass of the population do not appear to have had strong formalised convictions, and in most cases they were prepared to follow the lead of their social superiors. Although there were small minorities of committed Protestants and Catholics, neither religion seems to have had a strong hold in England when Mary I died. When Elizabeth I came to the throne the country was willing to return to a form of moderate Protestantism. However, during her reign deeper religious divisions began to appear, and the unity of the Church of England ended.

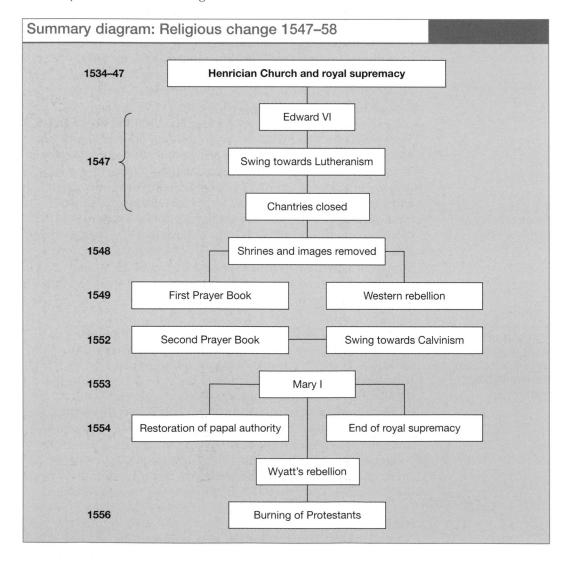

Summary diagram: Religious change 1547–58

1534–47	Henrician Church and royal supremacy
	Edward VI
1547	Swing towards Lutheranism
	Chantries closed
1548	Shrines and images removed
1549	First Prayer Book — Western rebellion
1552	Second Prayer Book — Swing towards Calvinism
1553	Mary I
1554	Restoration of papal authority — End of royal supremacy
	Wyatt's rebellion
1556	Burning of Protestants

Study Guide: AS Question

In the style of OCR

Assess the problems that faced Mary I in restoring Catholicism to England. (50 marks)

Exam tips

The cross-references are intended to take you straight to the material that will help you to answer the question.

It is tempting to list the problems that stood in the way of Mary returning England to the Catholic faith but the highest marks will be awarded to those who assess them. This means that you must evaluate each problem in respect of its nature, extent and consequence for Mary's government before arriving at a judgement on the most serious problem. You are likely to consider the following:

- The unpopularity of Mary's desire to restore the Papacy and parliament's concern that the Papacy might try to re-assert its authority in England and overrule the royal supremacy and statute law (pages 227–8).
- England in 1553 was attached to Protestantism to a far greater degree than either Mary or her principal advisers recognised (page 228).
- Mary's strategy of persuasion followed by the imposition of heresy laws and death by burning did not work and led to an increase in martyrdom (pages 229–30).
- Limited government finances meant that it was very difficult to restore chantries and monasteries or to make clerical livings more attractive, and the new owners of Church property were unwilling to surrender their deeds without compensation (pages 228–9).
- There was a limited number of competent clerics ready to fill positions vacated by priests expelled after 1554; many priests would rather give up their livings than lose their wives and mistresses (page 228).
- Mary's decision to appoint Cardinal Pole as her Archbishop of Canterbury was unwise as he had been in exile for 20 years and failed to understand the importance of working with the gentry if Catholicism was to be effectively restored (pages 230–1). Although some of his ideas were sound, most of the Twelve Decrees of 1555 were not implemented in Mary's lifetime.
- Pope Paul IV opposed Pole and hindered his reforms whenever possible (page 231).
- Mary feared that her sister, Elizabeth, would reverse most of the religious reforms when she came to power, and in her haste to bring about a speedy Catholic reformation, many of Mary's policies and methods proved counter-productive (pages 231–2).

Further reading

A.G. Dickens, *The English Reformation* (Batsford, 1964 – second edition 1989).

E. Duffy, *The Stripping of the Altars* (OUP, 1992).

G.R. Elton, *The Tudor Revolution in Government* (Methuen, 1953).

G.R. Elton, *England Under the Tudors* (Methuen, 1955).

John Guy, *Tudor England* (OUP, 1988).

Peter Gwyn, *The King's Cardinal: The Rise and Fall of Thomas Wolsey* (Barrie & Jenkins, 1990).

C. Haig, *English Reformations* (OUP, 1993).

E.W. Ives, *Anne Boleyn* (Blackwell, 1986).

D.M. Loades, *The Mid-Tudor Crisis, 1545–65* (Macmillan, 1992).

Diarmaid MacCulloch (ed.), *The Reign of Henry VIII: Politics, Policy and Party* (Macmillan, 1995).

D. MacCulloch, *Thomas Cranmer* (Yale, 1996).

R. Marius, *Thomas More* (Dent, 1984).

Rosemary O'Day, *The Debate on the English Reformation* (Methuen, 1986).

Richard Rex, *Henry VIII and the English Reformation* (Macmillan, 1993).

J.J. Scarisbrick, *Henry VIII* (Methuen, 1968).

J.J. Scarisbrick, *The Reformation and the English People* (Blackwell, 1984).

David Starkey, *The Reign of Henry VIII: Personalities & Politics* (George Philip, 1985).

R. Williams, *The Later Tudors: England, 1547–1603* (OUP, 1995).

Joyce Youings, *The Dissolution of the Monasteries* (Allen & Unwin, 1971).

Glossary

Annates   Money equivalent to about one-third of their annual income paid to the Pope by all new holders of senior posts within the Church in England and Wales.

Bondmen   Medieval peasants who lived and worked on the lord's manor.

Catholic Inquisition   Institution set up by the Catholic Church to search for and destroy heretics or non-conformists.

Charlatans   False or untrustworthy people who pretend to be what they are not.

Chattels   Possessions.

Conformist   Someone who follows the rules of the State.

Constitutional historians   Historians who study political and governmental structures and a nation's laws.

Consubstantiation   Belief that the wine and bread taken at communion represent the blood and body of Christ.

Convocation   Church equivalent of parliament where clerics meet in two houses – upper house of senior clerics, etc. – to discuss and transact Church affairs.

De facto   Existing in fact, whether legal or not.

Dei gratia   By the will of God.

Dictator   Non-democratic rule of a country by a single person or party.

Dogma   Doctrine or set belief proclaimed as true by the State Church.

Expeditionary force   An army sent to fight in another country.

Fleet Prison   A prison in London used by the Crown to imprison criminal gentry and nobles.

Heresy   Refusal to conform to the State religion.

Humanists   Scholars who question the belief systems of the Church and who embrace free-thinking, culture and education.

Iberian kingdoms   Portugal and Spain, which occupy the Iberian peninsula.

Intercursus Magnus   Used to describe the protection of commercial contacts between England and the Netherlands in an agreement of 1496.

King Arthur and the Knights of the Round Table   The Arthurian legends would have been very popular at the time.

Legatine powers   Having the powers of the Pope.

Legatus a latere   A position normally awarded for a specific purpose so that a representative with full papal powers could be present at a decision-making occasion far distant from Rome.

Litigants   People who take their disputes to court.

Lucre   Another term for money.

Machiavellian   Cleverly deceitful and unscrupulous. Named after an Italian political writer and thinker.

Macro-political level   Term used to explain the bigger picture such as in this instance the actions of the monarch and of parliament.

Micro-religious level   Used to explain the smaller picture such as in this instance the beliefs and practices of ordinary people.

Mitre, cope, tippet or stole   Symbols of worship used in a church service.

Non-residence   Parish priests who did not live in their parish.

Norman Conquest   Conquest of England after 1066 by Duke William of Normandy.

Objectivity   Focusing on an issue without bias.

Pale   Irish territory (including Dublin) settled by the English. It was the centre of English power in Ireland.

Pluralism   Term applied to priests who served more than one parish.

Praemunire   A legal provision, arising from three fourteenth-century laws, which forbade clerics to take any action that cut across the powers of the Crown – especially recognising any external authority without the monarch's explicit permission.

Primogeniture   English legal term to describe the right of the eldest male child to inherit land.

Purgatory   In Catholic belief, occupies the middle ground between heaven and hell.

Quartermaster-general   The person responsible for feeding, arming and generally supplying the army.

Renaissance man   Someone open to new ideas in politics, culture and education.

'Revisionist'   Historians who revise earlier historical opinions or interpretations.

Royal prerogative   Certain rights and privileges enjoyed by the monarch such as making war, negotiating peace treaties, calling and closing parliament.

Sack of Rome   Attack on and looting of Rome by Habsburg troops.

Sectarian controversy   The conflict and differences of opinion between Catholic and Protestant historians in the way they interpret changes in the Church.

Schism   Literally meaning break, but used by historians to describe England's break with the Pope in Rome.

Star Chamber and Chancery   Royal courts.

Statute law   Acts or laws passed by parliament.

Valois–Habsburg   Names of the French (Valois) and Austrian (Habsburg) royal families.

Vicegerent   Cromwell became the king's deputy in Church affairs.

Index